TRAVEL WRITING

TRAVEL WRITING

L. PEAT O'NEIL

WRITER'S DIGEST BOOKS
CINCINNATI, OHIO

Other fine Writer's Digest Books are available from your local bookstore or direct from the publisher.

Visit our Web site at www.writersdigest.com for information on more resources for writers.

04   03   02   01   00   5   4   3   2   1

Library of Congress has catalogued hard copy edition as follows:

O'Neil, L. Peat (Louisa Peat).
     Travel writing : a guide to research, writing, and selling / by L. Peat O'Neil.
       p.   cm.
     Includes bibliographic references (p. 217-223) and index.
     ISBN 0-89879-671-7 (pob)
     1. Travel—Authorship. I. Title.
G151.054   1995
808'.06691—dc20   95-34121
                                                       CIP

ISBN 1-58297-000-9 (pbk: alk. paper)

Edited by Jack Heffron and Roseanne Biederman
Interior and cover design by Sandy Conopeotis Kent

This book is dedicated to all who preserve and care
for Earth, the traveler's home.

ACKNOWLEDGMENTS

Along the path traveled to complete this book, I received advice and encouragement from friends, colleagues and kin. I would like to particularly note the guidance of Jim Yenckel, travel writer for *The Washington Post*, who early on in my freelancing, helped me understand the structure of travel articles and whose writing continues to inform and inspire. Rosemary Brown, Sandra O. Martin and Marge Benjamin Warren, valiant readers of manuscript drafts, made useful suggestions without deflating my enthusiasm. Finally, were it not for my mother and father's wisdom and foresight in providing me the latitude to travel alone at an early age, I might never have become the traveler I am. To them and the entire cast of characters who helped me along the way—sincere thanks.

ABOUT THE AUTHOR

Louisa Watson Peat O'Neil, an artist and writer, is on the staff of *The Washington Post*. She writes for many publications, teaches writing and travels the rest of the time.

TABLE OF CONTENTS

• Taking a Draft Version to Completion • Structural
Gimmicks • Writing the Long Draft

CHAPTER FIVE
Style and Tone

• Crafting Stories With Style • The Writer's Voice and
Point of View • Identifying Boring Writing • Self-
Editing • Finding the Right Word • Connecting With
the Reader • Letting the Reader Discover • Styles to
Avoid

CHAPTER SIX
Fact Checking and
Research Resources

• Get Organized! • Building a Rolodex of Travel
Information Sources • Pre-Trip Research • During the
Trip • Why Check Facts? • Using Facts • Timeliness
of Facts • Honesty and Facts: Recording Facts in Your
Journal • Generalizations and Facts • Facts and
Writing Style • Responsibilities of a Travel Writer
• Time and Truth

CHAPTER SEVEN
Travel Photos

• When Are Photos Required? • Taking Photos for
Travel Stories • Other Sources of Travel Photos • What
Can Go Wrong • Legal Issues • Storing Photos • The
Mechanics of Submitting Photos • Hints for Travel
Photographers

INTRODUCTION

This book is for travelers and writers. Whether you plan to publish articles about your travels or improve the descriptive power of your letters home, this book will help you.

While the focus is on creating travel articles for publication, anyone with an urge to travel will find in these pages fresh approaches to the art of traveling. A traveler using the ideas expressed in this book will hone skills for appreciating detail and uncovering unusual experiences. The writer intent on producing travel articles will receive guidance on how to record impressions and create a stylish personal account of a journey.

Novice travel journalists as well as published writers can use these techniques for turning journal entries into travel articles. People who want to expand their love of travel into a travel writing career will find advice for getting started and writing exercises for building skills. Writers from other disciplines who are interested in exploring the travel genre will learn how to keep a travel journal and construct travel articles that will sell. People who haven't decided that writing travel articles for publication is their goal will find helpful advice about what it takes to be a travel writer.

WHY THIS BOOK?

I learned to write by keeping a journal. The notebooks I have filled during thirty years of journal writing cover twelve linear feet in a bookcase. Many of the notebooks were written while I was on a journey, and those pages became the nucleus of travel articles which have been published in newspapers and magazines. There are also many stories in those journal pages that are waiting to be transformed into print.

Over the years, I've shared journal writing techniques with many people during workshops. A question often arose during those journal writer's workshops: How can diary and journal entries be published? While talk soared around the international success of diarists such as Anaïs Nin, I had to interject a note of realism. Most of us aren't recording the intimate details of lives that the general public wants to read about; our diaries are for and about ourselves. However, readers are clamoring for well-written travel narratives, and if a good diarist were to travel and write about unusual experiences and personal impressions, then perhaps the diary would be useful. The workshop participants understood the point and soon I found myself leading workshops about journals and travel writing. The workshops led to this book.

HOW I BEGAN

My travel career began when my younger sister and I rode the Greyhound by ourselves from Canada to Washington, D.C., after a summer vacation with our cousins on Lake Ontario. I was eight. I'd been on many car and train trips before that with my parents, but this was my coming out as a responsible traveler. By thirteen I'd decided to go to Europe and worked an array of jobs to save money for the trip. The money came in coins from typing for my teachers and dollars from baby-sitting and ironing shirts for neighbors. I learned that I could always make money for travel, just by working harder and saving. Prices may have gone up, but motivation is a more significant factor than cash in achieving travel goals.

In June 1966, at age sixteen, I flew alone to Luxembourg on Icelandic Air with $300 in traveler's checks, a notebook, and a return ticket for the student ship, M.S. *Aurelia*. Three months later, after a summer of adventure, hitchhiking, hosteling and homestays with friends of my parents, I had two full notebooks and an expanded vision of the world and my role in life. I've been traveling ever since, writing in notebooks, sketching what catches my eye, and in the process, making friends all over the globe. Writing travel articles, based on excerpts from my journals, was a logical next step. I wanted to share my stimulating personal journeys with readers. And I had high-minded ideas as well. Travel writing provides a way to communicate what I have learned by keeping my eyes wide open, noticing, questioning and listening as I move through the world. If others could understand the world better by reading what I had experienced, perhaps human unity would be improved. Writing clearly and simply was part of the plan. The Zen master Shunryu Suzuki comments on communication in *Zen Mind, Beginner's Mind*, "Without any intentional, fancy way of adjusting yourself, to express yourself as you are is the most important thing."

The thirst for travel exerts a powerful force in my life. I believe that a journey can be an art form and be instrumental in personal growth. An appreciation for the subtle aspects of travel propels my urge to write travel articles and to encourage others to share their experiences with readers. I want to share the beauty I've seen so that others will experience the world at richer levels of sensual perception. I hope that other travelers will take up the pen, or keyboard, and express what they see and feel on the road. Perhaps those who have been keeping detailed notebooks about their wanderings will venture to share their experiences with the assistance of this book.

WHAT ARE TRAVEL ARTICLES?

Travel articles are essentially about a place, and that includes the people, landscape, weather, flora and fauna. The history, politics, culture and folklore are also part of the travel story. It is a genre that offers wide latitude for communication. Some travel stories are personal essays, adding the dimension of the writer's inner life. Humor is allowed, and indeed prized, in travel articles. Service-oriented travel articles are dedicated to providing the reader with useful information. Stories about the poignancy and similarity of the human experience can be told against a travel backdrop. With such a rich tapestry of descriptive possibility in each travel story, a writer can really stretch.

That's what appealed to me—the opportunity to elegantly communicate my travel experiences, help other people, continue to travel the world, and perhaps even generate some income from my travels. And, it would be fun!

THE LITERARY TRADITION OF TRAVEL WRITING

Beyond the basics of informative, service-oriented travel writing, lies the literature of travel. If you've delved into travel literature at all, you know the feeling of being carried away to distant places on the prose horse of a confident writer. For a paragraph, perhaps a chapter, we are transported. This is the work of a seasoned travel writer; to transcend, to break the barrier of print and time, to bring the reader to the place described.

Absorbing writing need not be rare. With careful honing of descriptive skills, ruthless paring of cliché, and cultivation of words that communicate sensual awareness, a serious and dedicated wordsmith can create travel articles that stand out from the mainstream.

Some of the most vigorous contemporary prose appears in the travel genre. Think of Jan Morris, Peter Matthiessen, Norman Lewis, Alex Shoumatoff. And a few decades back, Patrick Leigh

Fermor, Somerset Maugham, Rose Macaulay, Freya Stark, Rebecca West. Don't overlook Samuel Clemens, Robert Louis Stevenson, Flora Tristan, Fanny Trollope. These and so many other thoughtful writers probed the elements and spirit of place. They explored their reasons for going to a place and reactions to that place.

Admirable writing is simple writing, using the enduring wealth of the English language in original ways. When prose is elegantly written, the words are fluid so that the reader steps into the writer's shoes and uses the writer's eyes. This is the goal for a travel writer then, to bring the reader close, so close that the writer disappears. Readers may finish the piece feeling like the experience described actually happened to them.

Clearly this is an art. Though writers may have little in common with their most devoted readers, prose connects and dissolves boundaries. There is an element in the skilled travel writer that evokes the everyman or woman, putting the reader at ease. The unspoken thought—-I've felt that, I've seen that—comes to the reader's mind.

Truly evocative writing flows from the writer's ability to open the inner self, to dig in and explore what the senses reveal. Setting down personal impressions can be a risky, vulnerable activity. But confident writers are willing to be held accountable for their perceptions. Bravura writing requires confidence born of experience. A writer's self-confidence endows the prose with a quality irresistible to the reader.

The world is wide open, waiting for you. No one owns the rights to writing about a place. Though Paul Theroux may have had a lot to say about riding trains the length of South America, he doesn't have the last word on that experience. Time changes everything, and each person's informed sensibility builds a different narrative. D.H. Lawrence probed the hinterland of Sardinia, weaving an ethnographic portrait from his perspective that has yet to be challenged. But it could be. The field is broad, and there are unlimited ways of viewing it. Anyone can write herself into the landscape of a beloved place. Personal ideas and experience distinguish one piece of writing from another. When writers put their whole selves on paper, giving of inner experience, the reader is truly rewarded. Go then, and celebrate of the art of travel in your writing.

ARE YOU A TRAVEL WRITER?

Does this sound like you? You want to be a travel writer because you enjoy life and seek pleasant experiences. There is work, to be sure, but the net experience is entertaining, stimulating, elevating. Travel writers aren't investigative reporters. Your antennae are up, you write the truth, but your focus is on the act of travel and what you discover while traveling. You can overlook some of the tough parts. You are responsible for being accurate and to travel and write within a set of standards that respects all the world's living creatures and the environment they need for survival. The bottom line is to have a good time—your idea of a good time—without adversely affecting the world in which you travel.

Despite the ambivalent hero in Anne Tyler's *The Accidental Tourist*—a novel about a travel writer who hates traveling—the fact of the matter is, you really do need to enjoy traveling; the process, the going, not just the destination. An appreciation for the act of traveling is integral to writing about it. Attitude influences writing, and if a writer isn't happy about traveling, the feeling will color the text. An ill-disposed traveler may place too many expectations on the destination, ignore experiences and the transformation that occurs during transport, and lack an understanding of how the place is reached in space and time. A true traveler strives to know more about the process of traveling than just the abrupt change wrought by a jet landing in a new location. This is not to say that jet travel should be ignored, but that we writers be aware that our minds may still be in Omaha while our bodies land in Okinawa. Perhaps we should focus on the travel process to the extent of communicating how near or far a place is in terms of attitude and atmosphere as well as literal distance.

Consider whether you like to travel or whether you are passionate about travel. Cultivate an appreciation for all aspects of travel; this love will ease the difficulties that will surely arise. How do you see yourself as you travel—as an ambassador, a missionary, a student, an observer? Has travel changed you? Do you expect travel to change you? Perhaps you are yearning to travel, but need an excuse, like travel writing, to get you started. There are no right or wrong reasons if the purpose you shape comes from your heart and you are dedicated to it. While reading this book, you may design a plan to travel and write, but it may take three years to save enough money to pay for the trip, as it took me when I was a novice traveler. Don't give up your dream if your plans are stalled. Stick with your idea.

The first step on the road to travel writing is a personal contract. Make the decision that you are going to be a professional travel writer. You enjoy traveling, of course, and you'll certainly have to like writing. If you don't have a yen to hit the high road and a knack for writing, planning to be a travel writer might not be right for you. But read on; there are plenty of suggestions useful for travelers who intend only to write a summary of their journey for family and friends. Included are tips on how to keenly see what you merely observe, where to meet people, and how to find the heart of a place when you are just a visitor. To really travel, you'll need purpose— interests that focus your journeys. Or, be willing to surrender to the flow of travel itself, making the trip a meditation on life. Whether you decide to write about your travel experiences or not, this book should help you think about the process of travel, the catalytic role of the traveler in the world, and the impact of travel on your own psyche.

A love of human connection and a thirst for knowledge sends you out on the four winds and seven seas. Enthusiasm drives you to gather experience and record the details of daily life. Yes, you must be enthralled by curious sights, surprised by other cultures, eager to meet people, taste exotic food, smell raw and refined odors, feel the elements on your face. At times, you'll be bored, frustrated, angry and lonely. You'll make mistakes, but you'll also forge friendships around the country and around the globe. People will ask "Where's your next trip?" instead of "How are you?" Do you mind? Not at all; you wouldn't trade the traveling life for anything. Resolve to have stimulating experiences, be deeply interested in the place you visit and do no damage. Leave a smile as your footprints.

Time management is important for a travel writer, and chances are, you'll be continuing in a job, so the travel will have to fit into your working life. If you have family responsibilities, you'll need a supportive partner and helpful relatives. You'll need ready cash. Beginners rarely are invited to join free familiarization tours—also known as fams—and until you have some published clips, you'll pick up the tab. Indeed, unless you land a staff job on a magazine or newspaper, you'll pay at least some expenses throughout your career, since many publications don't accept articles that result from free trips sponsored by either the airlines or tourist information offices.

THE TRAVELER'S JOURNAL

The human voice, rich with emotion and curiosity, has enduring appeal. Travel journals reporting the observations of wanderers centuries ago, such as Michel de Montaigne, for example, or Marco Polo, are still read avidly today. Some places those travelers visited have changed drastically, yet we are still curious about what they saw and how they achieved their destinations. We are even more enthralled by the telling of the story, the unfolding of the process of traveling. The writer's voice, above all, creates suspense, humor, consternation, satisfaction, wonder. As we turn the pages, we hang on the expression of the emotions. Do you have that voice? Are you able to tell a story about a place you know? Does your writing express intensity of feeling? Are you in tune with your senses, able to report what you smell, see, hear and touch?

You can practice travel writing skills while still at home. A travel writer who lives in a place that people want to visit or read about can stay at home and compose wonderful stories. Writers who live in Paris or San Francisco or Hawaii can feed stories to editors from their home computers. The rest of us actually have to pack and go. Even if you think your hometown isn't worth writing about, try the exercises in this book and learn how to write with a keen eye. You'll soon develop the nose for the original story that makes an aspiring travel writer a published writer.

USING THIS BOOK

This book is organized to help you get started toward achieving your dream of traveling artfully and writing about your experiences. Writing, marketing and other exercises follow the relevant chapters.

Start by reading the overview of the types of travel articles in chapter one. A working knowledge of the vocabulary of freelance travel writing will help you understand the rest of the book. For more information about editorial terms, take a look at the glossary in the Appendix.

Chapter two discusses how a travel writer's trip unfolds. That all-important tool, the travel journal, is discussed in chapter three. Then comes the nuts and bolts of constructing a travel article, shown in chapters four, five and six. Photography lessons for travel writers are covered in chapter seven. Advice and exercises for getting started in travel writing by developing visual and reporting skills while in your hometown are included in several of those chapters.

Check out the path for marketing your travel stories in chapter eight. Strong promotional and marketing skills will make a part-time effort grow, but have no illusions that you'll be supporting yourself as a travel writer, unless you are already successful in a related field of writing. The business end of being a professional travel writer will be covered in chapter nine.

Finally, the Appendix includes resources for the travel writer and a glossary of editorial terms.

Chapter One

GETTING STARTED

I n every discipline there are standards and rules. Although travel writing can be whimsical and personal, there are certain conventions which provide structure. These categories or types of travel articles help the writer stay on topic and give cues to the reader about the content of an article. When a writer composes a travel article that demonstrates a knowledge of the currently accepted types within the travel writing spectrum, he or she signals to an editor a level of professionalism and familiarity with the travel genre.

UNDERSTANDING THE CONVENTIONS OF TRAVEL WRITING

Knowing the various types of travel articles will serve you during both the writing and marketing phases of producing publishable travel articles. Once you've decided what kind of travel article you are working on, then you can narrow the focus and select the right details and anecdotes to tell the story. Let's say you've decided to write a travel article about a weekend excursion to a new state park. You want the piece to have an outdoor recreation focus. The colorful details you will use to engage the reader will be different from the scenes you would show if you were writing about the same excursion to the same park but with a family travel story focus. In the outdoor recreation story, you'd narrate your experiences doing one or more sports activities in the park and include factual information about options for sports enthusiasts who will be reading your piece. In the family travel story, you would tell the experience from your perspective as a family member and how the park facilities met or did not meet the needs or expectations of children, elderly relatives, visiting kin and yourself.

To help you understand the varieties of travel articles, this chapter contains explanations of several types of travel articles. They are guidelines, not carved in stone. As you become more familiar with the travel writing genre, you'll notice that many travel stories overlap several categories. Nor is the list comprehensive, because writing is always growing and changing. Travel writing evolves as its practitioners broaden their experience and hone their skills. Now that you've decided to become part of the travel writing community, you are joining that process. As you read this book and learn about the rudiments of constructing travel pieces and become conversant with the conventions of the trade, you also have the opportunity to improve the genre, to offer readers fresh perspectives, and perhaps even invent new types of travel articles. A note of caution: Inexperienced writers often use the explanation that they are inventing unusual formats or using different language as their unique way of telling stories to excuse writing that is really only random jottings or just plain bad. I'd suggest holding off on reinventing the genre until you have at least enjoyed some success using its current forms.

While you read my descriptions of the types of travel articles, make your own evaluations of travel articles. Let the descriptions become part of your thinking process so that the next time you read a travel article, you can identify its type. If you have written an unpublished travel article, try to pigeonhole it in one of the categories. Think about ways it could be changed to fit into one type or another. In a way this chapter is a list of objectives that you will direct your writing toward. When you know what you are striving to fit, the going becomes much easier.

Reading this chapter should stimulate your marketing sense, too. Knowing the categories of travel articles will make conversations with editors or query letters flow more smoothly. When editorial guidelines state that the publication wants family-oriented destination articles, regional weekend getaways, and humorous first-person essays, you will know what is expected. Should you need to call the publication to clarify the length or deadline, it will enhance your presentation and self-esteem if you really understand the differences. Staying tuned, as you write, to the conventions of specific articles will improve your writing skill because you have predefined parameters for a given story that encourage you to stay on point.

Each type of travel article has loosely defined conventions of style and tone as well. A first step to developing the writing skills to shift styles and tones to match the publication is to understand the types of articles that come under the rather large heading of travel writing. As you read travel articles, be sensitive to which category the piece matches and notice the type of language and voice used by the writer. You'll see that within the travel article there is a particular way of getting the reader's attention and presenting the material, known as the style and tone of the writing. As you read, you'll hear the individual character and personality in the writer's voice. You may even start to picture the face behind this voice and in your imagination develop other aspects of the person's life. This focus on the writer's voice may last only for the duration of your reading, but during that time, that voice becomes real to you. Analyze whether the voice is appropriate to the content of that type of travel piece. In your own writing, you'll be striving to achieve a distinct voice appropriate to the material you are sharing with readers. Thus, the travel writer who wants to publish an article in a hunting magazine will use language and diction that resonates with readers who are rod and gun enthusiasts. The travel article destined for a country living magazine will have a completely different tone. We'll discuss this, the structure, style, voice and pace of the article, in later chapters.

Accepting the utility of knowing the types of travel articles, each with its own set of rules, was the first lesson I learned about travel writing. I asked the travel editor at *The Washington Post* how I could learn to write travel articles. At the time, I had worked on my university's daily newspaper, sold a few freelance pieces, and successfully completed several business writing assignments. About to embark on a year's travel in Europe and North Africa, I had the idea that travel writing would suit my penchant for travel. The editor's advice was to study other travel articles, well-crafted pieces in the best newspapers I could find. I took the advice seriously and devoured the travel sections of the *New York Times, Boston Globe, Los Angeles Times* and *Miami Herald* as well as smaller papers like the *Baltimore Sun, Minneapolis Star Tribune, Christian Science Monitor* and *St. Petersburg Times.* Casting farther afield, to England, I read travel articles in the *Manchester Guardian,* the *Independent,* and the *Times of London.* Since I'm from Washington, D.C., I also read *The Washington Post.*

After analyzing paragraph by paragraph what happened in quite a few newspaper travel articles, I noted whether a piece was told in first or third person, whether it was a personal experience essay or an objective description of a specific place, or a collection of short informational paragraphs about a related topic without a narrative. I crammed as if for an exam and internalized the analytical information that explained the skeleton of the travel story. I figured the words would flow much easier if I knew where I was headed in my writing.

From newspaper travel articles, I branched out and studied magazine travel articles. I analyzed structure, pace and the writer's voice. If an article pleased me, I searched through the article to see how the writer piqued my interest. The travel articles I couldn't finish because the writing couldn't sustain my interest were nonetheless instructive. I went back and marked the point where my attention stumbled and tried to determine why the writing lagged. Of course, I also continued to read travel books and articles for pleasure, but analyzing articles to see their structure and type became second nature.

Not long ago, I had a discussion with a student who wanted to break into travel writing as a way of financing a postgraduation adventure in Central Asia. She was bright, literate, a competent writer of term papers and the occasional published letter to the editor. She thought travel writing would be easy, like a long letter home. Actually, the letter home model is a good one, because practiced correspondents generally have an eye for amusing detail, and letters tend to have a natural voice. I asked her which type of travel article she planned to write. Surprised, she responded she didn't think it mattered. She would just write about what happened to her. My answer was, "OK, that's fine, but why should a travel editor want to publish what happened to you? What is so special about your experiences?" Perhaps I was too hard on her, but I persisted: "Is your writing so brilliant that you can afford to ignore the traditional structures of the genre? Since all you've written is college papers, aren't you concerned your story might sound like a senior thesis? How do you know what makes a travel article? Will you be able to make the story relevant and appealing to older people, to honeymooners, parents traveling with their children, handicapped travelers? And why approach an editor with only one story, the overdone and obvious one—'what happened to me on my vacation.'" Immediately, she understood my point—that a travel writer who wants to earn money can't afford to write a self-indulgent, rambling "my story." It won't sell.

You can still write it "your way," but placing the story within the framework of the traditional types of travel articles garners more interest from editors. They will recognize what you are attempting to cover in the article and be able to consider your topic in light of their editorial needs. At least while you are developing a portfolio of published pieces, write within the rules. Then, with an established byline, with total familiarity with the conventions of travel articles, you can bend and break these rules.

Reading travel literature will heighten your sense of what is worth writing about. When you read evocative writing about travel you align yourself with a remarkable assembly of people—true travel writers. Just think, you are going to join that group! Or at least try. Dip into the animated pages of the well-known travel authors—Freya Stark, Peter Fleming, Robert Byron, Kate Simon, Paul Theroux, Jan Morris—and you'll find that their pieces are more than personal experience essays. Necessary information is carried within the prose seamlessly, so that the reader learns many of the practical facts through the author's personal descriptions. Their writing is of a piece, knit together, finished. Their experience permits them the luxury of digression, dialogue, reminiscence, musing.

You'll probably want to begin collecting travel magazines and the travel sections of newspapers. Ask friends and colleagues to share their magazines with you. Use the periodicals department of the local public library. Scout for out-of-date travel magazines at yard sales, used bookstores and flea markets. Read them to develop your sensitivity to fine writing and to flat writing.

TYPES OF TRAVEL ARTICLES

I've heard writers criticize travel writing because it is written to a formula. True, novices need to practice travel writing within the structure in order to have the skills to break out of it. Like figure skaters, beginning writers must do their "school figures," retracing time and time again the same structure. Writers vary the subject and choice of words, but writing to fit the rules, to cover the expected content without letting the structure overpower the writing, does take skill. Mystery novels, romances and thrillers have their own patterns. After lots of practice, a writer internalizes the structure, and the story follows the outline expected by readers.

The various types of travel articles include: destination, side trip, roundup, special interest, holiday or historical peg, outdoors/recreation, personal essay and news peg. Now you'll read a brief description of each type of travel article, along with story ideas for each type. There's also a discussion of humorous travel stories, food and travel articles and travel advice articles. Don't forget to try some of the writing exercises.

Destination

Destination articles are designed to hook readers' interest and send them to a travel agent. Taking the broad view, hitting all the worthwhile tourist spots, a writer working on a destination piece pays attention to telling an attractive story with useful facts.

The writer's presence is muted, but perceivable. Usually, some of the piece is written in the first person. The writer confides why the trip was undertaken, so the reader can identify the purpose. For example, an opening like "My companion and I decided to explore Bethlehem this Christmas. Pennsylvania is somewhat closer than Israel," explains why the writer is going to this place and even does so with a dose of humor. In such a destination piece, the writer would narrate what was found and experienced in Bethlehem, Pennsylvania, occasionally using the writer's voice, the mighty I, but attempting to convey most of the information in narrative form. The story should help readers decide whether they

---

EXERCISE 1

What is your favorite destination? Why? Explain the appeal of the place. Where have you returned time and time again? The reasons might be: climate, history, land- or seascape, architecture, food, or some other quality or special characteristic. Try to write specific statements. "Nice people, pretty scenery, friendly atmosphere" are bland generalizations and inadequate for saleable travel articles. To help you get started, write: I see _____ , I hear _____ , I smell _____ , I walk _____ and fill in the blanks with specific adjectives and nouns or prepositional phrases and finish the sentences.

want to go to this place. What does the place offer in terms of landmarks, charm, beauty, history, entertainment? Is the destination interesting?

Typically, destination articles focus on specific places along heavily traveled tourist routes, like Florida, California, Hawaii, New England, New York City, Europe, the Caribbean. But articles about destinations farther afield such as the Yukon, Tasmania, Chile or Kenya are just as worthy. In fact, travel editors need articles that describe new travel destinations.

EXERCISE 2

Using the starting phrases below, continue writing descriptive sentences about your own experiences. The sentences do not need to relate to each other or be about the same place, although they could if you so choose. If you can't think of a personal travel experience to fit the opening, imagine a scene. Try to use active verbs and avoid pronouns. These sentences could each be the beginning of a paragraph if you want to continue your thoughts. Coax out the details of that special travel destination you know so well. You could even write about your own neighborhood!

The streets _____

Stately trees shade _____

Buildings constructed of _____

Light fills _____

The backdrop of sunset _____

Night noises _____

Entering the _____

A guide in period costume _____

History tells us _____

The people here _____

Stone monuments _____

Did you notice that the second set of exercises does not use the pronoun "I" to open the sentences? Practicing narrative descriptive writing where you, the writer, are invisible, is an important part of developing your skill as a raconteur of travel observations.

In analyzing popular destination pieces, let's focus on Florida. Newspaper travel sections routinely devote a section to travel in Florida. Magazines feature Florida regularly as a family destination, an outdoor paradise, a cultural center, a honeymoon destination. Consider this question: Why is Florida such a popular destination? It can't always be the weather because from May to October, Florida is hell's vestibule. There must be something else attracting so many visitors. The Disney expo-parks near Orlando? The space shuttle launching complex at Cape Canaveral? The Everglades alligators and palm trees? Fast paced Miami? The climate has a lot to do with Florida's winter popularity, but I think the real reason is the state's diversity brought by its huge and growing population. Florida has been home to various cultures for centuries, and the involvement of residents with the land makes it a diverting, intriguing travel destination. Your job, as a travel writer, is to discover a *unique* place in Florida and find something *new* to say about Florida, a fresh approach to a multi-faceted place.

Special Interest

The special interest travel article deals with specific activities as they relate to travel: food, shopping, accommodations, sports, gardens, art, antiques—any topic set in a specific location. The purpose of the piece is to inform readers how they can learn more about their hobbies or personal interests or pursue them while on vacation. The railroad buff, doll collector, vintage car restorer, orchid grower and many more all have magazines devoted to their hobbies. Usually people who are passionate about a leisure time pursuit are eager to learn more about it. A travel article focused on these interests should find a berth in its respective magazine.

Writers of special interest articles need to have grounding in the subject—credibility suffers if a writer discusses golf courses and has never played the links. There, you see, I could be making a golfing gaffe by writing "played the links." Be wary of using specialized phrases like "walked the links" or "putted on the green" or "played the holes," unless you know the subject. Perhaps, with tenacious research, you could write a credible piece with only a passing acquaintance of the subject, but I'll bet the article would sound stiff and lack the personal touch. One way to write a special interest piece if you aren't versed in the topic is to take the novice's point of view. For example, the lead might go: "I don't know a thing about golf; so how did I come to be swatting balls across the clipped green grass of St. Andrews?"

EXERCISE 1

Make a list of your own special recreational interests, hobbies, areas of expertise. If you subscribe to newsletters or magazines related to these interests, study them. Are there any travel stories? Next to each special interest on your list, write down a possible travel article related to it. Be creative: Special interests can be so familiar that we don't think of them as special. Do you have a pet? Do you make crafts or knit? Tend a garden? Do you play a sport or follow sports teams regularly? There are travel stories in all these activities.

Journey

Different from destination pieces, journey articles emphasize the way you get there. Scenic drives, vintage railroad, tramp steamer, bicycle, courier flight, footpath—the story focus is on the mode of travel. Think of times past when the going was good, the grand age of travel when steamships were standard, airplane seats were comfortable, attentive service the norm. The journey travel article attempts to recreate that mood, to unfold a story as the journey progresses, so that the destination is less important to the story focus than the means of travel.

Some advice will creep into the piece, but the romance of the journey is the main attraction, the focus of the prose and description. History will likely figure in several paragraphs, and there is always room for humor.

Articles about particular types of transportation are important to armchair travelers who are fascinated by trains, planes, boats, etc., and may never actually travel. The writer's impressions and feelings serve as the reader-writer bonding point. Travel articles that focus on the journey are also attractive to the general traveling public who do use these articles for specific trip planning. So the journey type article needs a strong personal narrative story line and useful facts.

Perhaps you are a devoted railway rider and yearn to take a

cross-country train trip. In this era of air travel, long-distance rail travel is somewhat unusual. Such a story would discuss the history of long-distance rail travel in the United States, the amenities past and present, the scenery along the way, and perhaps include comments or anecdotes from railway employees and other riders. Narrative about points of interest along the journey and thumbnail sketches of people encountered make the journey come alive. The start and finish are briefly discussed; ultimately, in this piece, the spotlight will focus on the act of travel. Shall we call this imaginary piece "Riding the Rails: Sea to Shining Sea"?

EXERCISE 1

What is your favorite mode of transportation and why? List some journeys that appeal to you. For example: the drive along the Big Sur coastal area in California, a ride on the Amtrak auto-train from Virginia to Florida, a paddle-wheel boat cruise on the Mississippi.

EXERCISE 2

List a few memorable journeys you've taken when the transportation, the getting there, was more important than the arrival. Write a pretend postcard to a friend and inject life into your words about the experience.

The Roundup

No, it's not a preview of rodeos or a story about dude ranches. In the roundup travel article, the writer collects information on a half dozen or so different places with a common thread drawing them together. A paragraph or two introduces the theme which binds the elements together. Ideally, the lead sets the tone and hints at two or three of the individual items.

Some newspaper travel sections publish roundups of brief stories by many travel writers about bad journeys. The roundups have overall titles like "Holidays from Hell," "Turkey Trips," "Vicious Vacations." Other publications publish travel vignettes with a romantic theme around Valentine's Day. Bear this in mind if you have a story about a rotten travel experience or a travel anecdote steeped in romance. When you make marketing inquiries, ask about contributing to the annual roundup features.

Here are a few topics for a roundup article: Great palaces and churches in Rome which are open to the public all day. (Most important Roman buildings close for two or three hours at midday, a source of anguish to visitors who are short on time and long to pursue culture. An article that offered midday opportunities for cultural experiences would be useful to travelers.); modestly priced family restaurants (not fast-food stores) in New York City that are open on Sunday; how the lunar (Chinese) New Year is celebrated around the world; a dozen romantic weekend getaways; Seattle microbreweries that offer tastings; free museums in London.

Consider these roundup titles with potential for humor: "Where to Get a Bad Meal in Paris"; "See the Treasures of the British Museum in Twenty Minutes"; "Festivals to Avoid"; "Jogging Paths Where You Won't Get Mugged."

EXERCISE 1

Using your own interests and experiences gleaned either in your hometown or during trips, jot down a dozen roundup story ideas. Then flip through your collection of magazines and travel sections and note the subjects of roundup stories. Evaluate your list of roundup ideas: Are they original? Why would an editor want to use them?

Historical or Holiday Peg

Tied to an anniversary, holiday or historical event, the holiday peg story depends on a date. But beware, many editors ignore holidays—President's Day, Arbor Day, Thanksgiving, etc.— because they see it as a hackneyed method of structuring a travel section. Other editors follow the predictable cycle and accept holiday peg stories as soon as they can get them. For the writer, this means approaching an editor with a holiday story idea months in advance. In fact, a few months after the event is a good time to pitch a story for the following year. Such a conversation might go something like this: "I read your President's Day travel feature on 'Ford's Theater and the House Where Abe Lincoln Died.' For next

President's Day, would you be interested in a travel story about tracing Lincoln's life in Springfield, Illinois? I had in mind a 'Footsteps of the Future President' type of piece."

Periodic events such as the Olympics, World Cup, World Expos, and the annual naming of the European City of Culture are natural pegs for travel stories. Major travel magnets such as these will draw lots of tourists, and travel editors know to provide a range of stories to satisfy this market. Many publications assign their staff writers to handle travel stories in conjunction with news-related coverage. If the staff writers are swamped with work, however, the freelancer may have an opportunity. So, even if you are turned down early because a staff writer may be doing travel stories related to the major event, try again closer to the event if the editor has expressed an interest in your work. If the editor has flatly rejected your ideas and your previously published work, don't annoy the editor by reapproaching. Try another publication. Research will pay off here. You need to know where these events will be held for the next several years so that you can sell stories and side trip pieces pegged to the events and destination. Visit a reference library and consult books that forecast annual events and list future Expo sites or Olympic Games locations.

The holiday peg story can overlap the other types of travel

EXERCISE 1

Write down six holiday-pegged or event-keyed story ideas. Writing "Winter Olympic Games, Mother's Day, Christmas, July Fourth" is not sufficiently specific. Create complex story ideas that focus on the holiday in unusual ways. For example, consider this idea for July Fourth: a story about touring a factory that makes American flags or fireworks. For Mother's Day, examine how another country or ethnic culture honors mothers. At Christmastime, brave the Alaska cold and write about travel just a sleigh ride away from the North Pole. Before Winter Games season, write a travel piece about winter sports at Mt. Olympia in Washington State or Mt. Olympus in Greece, or some other mountain named "Olympia." Another idea would feature travel to former Olympic stadiums that are still in use.

stories. Think of a New Year's holiday food and travel story or an outdoor recreation story focused on Thanksgiving. Indeed, it's possible to write travel stories focused on an important world cultural or recreational event in every category summarized in this chapter.

Side Trip/Getaway

The name clues you in: a side trip from a major destination. The side trip or weekend getaway story spins off the well-traveled route, revealing a new facet of a popular attraction, or a nearby destination for a weekend escape. Smart travel writers know that today's travelers are adding a day trip or weekend excursion to business trips. And residents of large urban centers are traveling on the weekend to accessible recreation spots that offer respite from the weekday grind. Side trip articles related to perennial travel favorites—European capitals; California, Florida and New England; the Caribbean, and, increasingly, cities on the Pacific Rim—enable an editor to create a travel section with several stories on aspects of the region. Getaway and side trip articles serve the leisure and business traveler who is pressed for time as well as the traveler who has the urge to explore. Usually, side trip and getaway excursions are written to cover a day or a weekend. Details about transportation, museum opening hours, nearby hotels and inns are very important to include in the side bar. These travelers don't want to find out the attraction they have planned to see is closed for the day.

Here are a few samples of getaway or side trip stories: "Historic Plantations Near the Nation's Capital"; "Brittany: Hours From Paris, Centuries Away"; "Escape Los Angeles on Breezy Catalina Island."

EXERCISE 1

Write down three major destinations that you are familiar with. They might include your hometown or a nearby city and other places where you have lived or traveled to often. For each destination, write down six side trip story ideas. Break open new boundaries! Think of where to take children, where elderly people might be comfortable, where your nephew the computer hacker would visit, where the poor art student, the wealthy executive with only two hours of free time or the sports fan would want to go.

Outdoors/Recreation

The outdoors and recreational travel article is much like a special interest story except it takes place outdoors. It resembles a destination piece and could be a side trip, except it takes place outdoors. It is also like a roundup, a holiday peg or a food story, but again, it is set outdoors. You got it—outdoors. The outdoor travel story overlaps the other categories in terms of structure but usually involves physical challenge and an element of adventure.

The market for travel stories about outdoor activities is growing and covers all demographic groups. Guided biking adventures, water and mountain sports, recreation for handicapped people, family sports, retirement camping, eco-tourism, luxury walking tours, the list goes on. If there is one area to pay attention to in addition to family travel or food and travel, it is outdoor travel, soft adventure and sport related travel. Soft adventure usually refers to a packaged adventure tour involving physical activity—hiking, mountain bike riding, horseback riding, rafting—and led by an experienced guide. A travel writer with an interest in an outdoor activity can specialize and corner a niche. Paragliding, rock climbing, biking, surfing, scuba diving, sea-kayaking, walking, hunting, fishing, bird watching—whatever athletic challenge you choose to write about, the criteria are that you know the terminology, do it yourself at least once, and that it be outdoors.

The great thing about being a travel writer is that even if you have never done an activity before, you can try it out at an interesting location and write about the experience! Readers will understand; they are often first-timers, too. Your going out in advance and writing about how to tackle a new outdoor activity helps them take that long awaited bicycle tour in France, that first scuba plunge in the Cayman Islands, that first family camping trip in the Great Smoky Mountains in Tennessee.

One final note: Over the past few years, "eco-tourism" has entered the outdoor travel lexicon. The concept of eco-tourism or sustainable tourism embraces a range of principles which include leaving minimal impact on natural areas, supporting indigenous businesses and travel services, participating in local conservation or cultural efforts, learning about the people, and finding ways to share experiences with them. In practice, many tour operators label travel products "eco-tours" which aren't. Before using the phrase, a travel writer should become familiar with the principles that guide responsible tourism.

EXERCISE 1

What is your favorite sport or outdoor activity? Envision this activity in connection with travel. What story emerges?

Right Now: News Peg

Two sobering aspects of the modern world, civil conflict and terrorism, usually mean that if a place is in the news, it should be avoided. So it's no surprise that travel editors, knowing that people don't spend their vacations in a war zone, rarely print travel articles about areas in conflict. Writers, on the other hand, seem to flock to troubled areas in search of award-winning stories about refugees and the fortitude of human character. I'll bet some of those writers are stashing away notes for travel pieces they'll write in the future. I guess they figure that just because a place is torn up and terrorized doesn't mean a travel story won't sell; they just need to wait a few years. Change is inevitable. Consider Vietnam, barren and bombed, a pawn of raging political forces. Once a battlefield, it has been reopened to tourism and commerce.

Getting there first when a country does resume normalcy will enhance a travel piece. Writers who pioneered contemporary writing about the Eastern European countries after democratization created a rewarding niche for themselves. When peace accords flourished in the Middle East, savvy travel writers were booking flights to Syria, Jordan and Lebanon, fascinating countries long off the tourist route. An ability to read the news with an eye for forthcoming political and economic changes is a handy skill for a travel writer. The writer doesn't have to be a fortune-teller, just an attentive observer of the world scene. Which country is angling to trade with whom? Are hostilities between political factions shifting from combat to the peace table? Where are infrastructure investments flowing?

The journalism aspect of this kind of story means that the writer will have to be diligent about balanced sources. If the tourist board of a nation-state just emerging from a war/racial disturbance/health crisis waxes long that all is well, send in the visitors, then a writer should also talk to people who don't have a vested interest in the resumption of the tourist trade. Of course, one's own observations and experiences in the newly opened area, go the longest way to telling a vibrant travel story.

EXERCISE 1

Quick, what countries are in combat? Were they tourist destinations before the current troubles? Or, bring the focus close to home: Are there tourist destinations in the U.S. that have fallen out of favor because of crime, environmental disasters, or infrastructure problems? Which areas, recently engaged in war, civil unrest or environmental problems, have become accessible to visitors again? Can you envision these sample titles in print? "Down a Lazy River—Rafting the Mekong," "Traces of Ancient Greece in Libya: A Tour of the Mediterranean Coast," "Dubrovnik: Rebuilt and Reborn."

Humorous

Like a stand-up comic, the writer of a humorous travel article uses personal experiences for the story line. Inevitably, the butt of the joke will be the writer. We all know that elements of humor depend on the audience and the skill of the storyteller. The anecdote that sends one person into gales of laughter might not amuse the next time it is told. What sparks the reading public's funny bone changes over time, but there are some universal witticisms— misadventure, simple human error, things or people that are out of place. We tend to see humor in a situation when a person's response, actions or words are inappropriate but still achieve a satisfactory outcome—the inadvertent success of a befuddled adult, a child's unintended wise phrases, animal behavior that seems almost human, contrasts in body types.

The humorous travel article might be about a single event or a collection of lighthearted incidents. For example, a humorous article about a writer's penchant for mispronouncing foreign words might be titled "Speaking Only the English, Yes?" and explain why the writer never uses other languages after botching so many. A story about misadventures related to faulty map-reading could be called "Lost With a Map" and discuss the wonderful places that were seen only because of misreading a map at the outset.

Readers will either recognize their own foibles and create an identity bond or look at the writer's mistakes and learn what not to do; perhaps they'll even feel a tad smug at the hapless writer's errors.

Confronting prejudices and misunderstandings can be funny, if we the writers are willing to be honest and humble about our mistakes and illuminate the larger issues through humor. A funny story could be constructed from encounters with people in other lands and how they view the United States or a particular American pastime or region.

Humorous pieces with a light touch are always welcome on an editor's desk. Strive for the giggle; avoid clichés. The same old joke isn't really funny.

Before the spell-check and proofread, the piece should be scrutinized for offensive language and bigotry: sexual, racial, economic or cultural. We all have our blind spots, and what might seem funny to one person may well outrage another. Maintain standards of good taste in your writing; editors tend to stay on the conservative side.

EXERCISE 1

Consider the times when you laughed at your mistakes. Are any of them related to travel? Have friends told you odd and amusing stories from their travels? For example, did you ever mispronounce a city name and receive wrong information? I know someone with a French accent who wanted to go to Dulles, an airport near Washington, D.C., but the reservations clerk quoted flights to Dallas, Texas. Jot down a few sentences about those occasions.

Travel Advice

Topics such as saving money, packing lightly, staying healthy, shopping in crafts markets, international business etiquette, overcoming language barriers, travel tips for wheelchair users, what to do if your rental car is broken into, the best computer equipment for working while on the road and dozens like them form the basis for travel advice articles. You can research these pieces in the library, add a few quotes from interviews with appropriate experts, salt well with your personal anecdotes and, voilà, you have a travel advice story ready to sell. Well, not quite. You'd better be sure that the experts really are qualified, that the library sources are up to date, and that your anecdotes are startlingly unique. A travel advice piece about lost luggage, for example, had better be funny or useful, because the theme has been "done to death," as editors say.

Look for anecdotes and quotes to communicate the scene. Another traveler's observations can shift the focus from yourself and still convey the information or ambience. Don't take anything for granted. Lessons you learn in your travels can become the nucleus for articles. Your chagrin becomes the genesis of a story. Experiences like running out of gas, missing train connections, or being fined for having the wrong metro ticket are part of real travel. The trip where nothing goes wrong isn't a learning experience.

Travel advice pieces can usually be resold to different markets, especially outside of the traditional travel publications. For example, an advice piece on "sandwich generation travel"—families who travel with children and their grandparents—could be pitched to magazines for parents, senior citizen's publications, and the general travel market.

EXERCISE 1

List a few travel-related topics on which you could offer advice. Perhaps you have personal experience with business travel in a foreign country, taking a pet on a long flight, buying and shipping antiques home during a vacation, or some other topic of general interest to travelers. Then, list a few travel advice topics that you would like to know more about. Nothing drives the research like a personal interest in the topic!

Food and Travel

With appetites for travel and fine dining skyrocketing, articles covering both make strong contenders in today's travel writing market. The food-related article is evergreen because interest in food is timeless. Stories that explore the cultural traditions attached to eating, cooking and celebrating with food always interest editors and readers.

Lucky the travel writer who goes to a region knowing about prized local ingredients or with an introduction to the local bread baker. This writer already has a path to follow, contacts to call. But it's also possible to start with no information; just follow your nose. The right aroma will lead you to an innovative kitchen and the chef who just might share the names of a local olive oil press, chili pepper grower or wine cellar. Ask questions that stimulate more detailed stories.

Without breaking the guidelines of polite behavior, make gentle inquiries of waiters, chefs and even other diners. I've often smiled at people at other tables and asked if they are enjoying their meals or how they heard about this restaurant. Such an approach depends on the degree of formality at the restaurant, of course, and the willingness of the other people to respond to a careful, polite inquiry. During meals a writer can certainly taste a table companion's meal, with permission, of course. Ask for recipes if the opportunity arises. Note the chef's name and where he or she trained and has worked before.

If you plan to write about food, better learn the basics of cooking. Experience will equip you to tell a good meal from a bad one and pinpoint where in the preparation the chef went wrong. Read *Larousse Gastronomique*, the massive French encyclopedia of food, and Brillat-Savarin's "The Physiology of Taste." No one can ever know everything about food, nor cease to learn more. Constantly evolving, the world of food offers great opportunity for travel writers.

Story ideas or sample titles for timely food oriented travel articles include: "The Wild Rice Capital of America," "Hawaii's Coffee Plantations," "Organic Wineries in Sonoma County," "Where Chefs Eat in New York City."

EXERCISE 1

Remember the best meal you ate? Where was it and what made the meal special? Did you wonder where the ingredients came from? Focus first on the taste, texture, combination of sauces, spices and ingredients, then the arrangement of the food on the plate. Don't forget to mention the quality of service, restaurant decor and general ambience.

Personal Experience Essay

Classic travel writing that endures as literature usually is a personal essay. Told in the first person, the personal travel essay is the one article that only you can write. Even if the travel subject has been examined hundreds of times, your sensibility applied to the topic makes it unique. Your perceptions and experiences told against the backdrop of life experience are the meat of the essay.

Far and away the most difficult to write, this type of travel story demands supple facility with the flow of words and an ability to use comparisons, allusions, metaphors and irony with skill. The writer draws on all experience, rather than impressions rooted solely in the location under discussion to produce a personal experience essay. Skilled essay writers usually have something to say beyond simple description. A strong point of view forms the track along which all the descriptive elements ride.

A personal experience travel essay is a collection of personal truths about events experienced in a place or during a journey. It is not meant as a psychological investigation of your inner motives and reactions, although touches of personal insight are useful and help the reader find a human connection. One of the strongest appeals of a personal experience essay lies in that identification with the writer, the sense that yes, the reader could have had the same experiences, felt the same way. How you care about the things that happen to you needs to be expressed in the essay; your opinion matters.

The travel essay is not a series of diary entries about what happened. You don't want to be like that eager student who thought that travel writing was just stringing together all her experiences during a particular trip.

For example, in a personal experience travel essay, you may be revisiting alone a romantic island where you once spent an idyllic week with a close personal friend. You'll notice differences—perhaps the rosy-colored lens through which you saw everything during your previous visit has faded, or maybe the quiet one-hammock beach is now enclosed by private haciendas or high-rise hotels. Whatever you notice will be affected by time and your feelings. There is an edge between soppy personal reminiscences and clever, self-aware comparisons that have broad appeal. Guess which one sells to editors?

In travel articles that explore personal experiences, readers won't be able to check whether or not the set of anecdotes really happened. So, it is important to create a level of believability. If the experiences were so surprising and fabulous that the story begins to read like fiction, it may be wise to explain. A litany of nasty complaints isn't quite believable either. Ideal writing strives for balance.

The mark of a deft personal experience travel article, and thus a publishable one, is in the selection of details, the authority of the voice, the elegance of the prose. You may want to postpone an attempt at writing a personal travel essay until you have successfully handled more basic travel writing assignments. Much depends on your goals. If you want to publish your travel writing, stick to the other types of travel articles which are discussed in this chapter and work toward writing personal essays after your writing facility has matured. If you just want to write, there is no harm in striving to write the most difficult type of travel piece from the start. However, as with bodybuilding, or learning any complex skill, steadily increasing the difficulty as you progress has a more enduring effect.

As part of the self-education process, read travel essays collected in books, or articles in magazines, and note what kinds of details are included to illustrate the writer's experiences. Develop your own appreciation for the passing scene by practicing active looking and listening.

Chapter Two

HOW A TRAVEL WRITER TRAVELS

A ll the world's a potential travel story, but how to choose? Dedicated travelers won't have any trouble selecting their next destination; the "list" is probably longer than one lifetime will permit. Personal desire is the best motivator for visiting and writing about a place. After all, if you want to be there, you've a better chance of communicating experiences to an audience. A lackluster travel story comes from a writer's boredom. Care about the places you choose to write about.

Do you have that list of places you want to visit? If you haven't done so, take a few minutes to jot down ten destinations or journeys that you truly want to experience within the next three years. Don't think about the cost, child care arrangements, your day job or financial commitments. Just let your imagination run wild and scan the world map for your special trips. Write down why you want to visit these places, what influenced you to select them. Perhaps you've read a book that inspired you, or a figure from the history of that region has personal significance. Search your memory back to childhood for places that have overwhelming personal meaning that you want to visit and write about.

This list is your dream sheet. It helps focus your travel plans, research and marketing. You can always add to it, but I don't think erasing dream trips makes sense. The list is a reminder for you as a travel writer: It represents the travel segment of your goal. Later, in the marketing chapter, we'll cover another goal of travel writers: achieving publication.

SPOTTING TRAVEL TRENDS

Before you select a destination, consider what will make your story unique and how it will fit with current trends and focuses in travel.

If you just read a travel article in a national magazine about New Orleans and noticed another one about Cajun cooking, and you see an airline advertisement promoting New Orleans in a newspaper and you know the Super Bowl is going to be held there soon, then you have spotted a rather predictable travel marketing focus based on the annual football event.

Let's say you flip through a women's magazine at the dentist's office and the travel article is about walking tours in California. A couple of days later, you see the same subject done in a fitness magazine. There's a spot on the evening news about walking for health and the Sunday travel section reports on walking tours for senior citizens. Get it? The travel trend here is walking vacations.

How do you get on the front end of the information curve for travel trends? Realizing that walking vacations are hot after you've seen two or three articles means that you aren't going to be able to sell the story to those publications. And likely, lots of other publications have already assigned stories on related aspects of walking vacations. You are picking up the trend after it has begun. To be on the cutting edge, talk to travel agents, tour promoters, discount travel club organizers, and others in the travel industry. Ask where their clients are going, what kinds of tours are selling.

Destinations become trendy for seemingly frivolous reasons, but there are ways of discovering what will be hot, and when. A travel writer can be sensitive to trends in other industries—fashion, food, entertainment, personal fitness—and the task of figuring out where travelers are going (and what they want to read about) becomes easy. Leisure travel is a discretionary expense, so it tends to feed off other lifestyle industries. Has a movie that features a place been released (like *Notting Hill* or *Seven Years in Tibet*) or released (*Gone With the Wind*)? The movies may sway people to visit London, Tibet or Atlanta. They'll want to read about those places, and you'll have a timely hook for selling to an editor.

When southwestern cuisine hit the expense account palates in Los Angeles and New York a few years back, travel articles about New Mexico and Arizona cropped up in national magazines. The Save the Whales effort fostered a wave of whale watching cruises and, of course, travel articles about spout gazing.

But the biggest influence in the process of selecting a destination should be your personal preference. That's why you have the travel dream list to consult.

Judgment should color the decision of where to travel. Visiting the international trouble spots doesn't make good marketing sense. Besides the inherent danger, there is the fact that travel editors aren't interested in stories from places that are falling apart politically. Putting yourself in the line of fire in order to research a travel story is just plain stupid. If you've just gone to a place where unrest is brewing, consider reworking the story with a news angle and approach a news editor. Travel editors are reluctant to commit space to stories about places people are afraid to visit or can't get to easily.

Stay up with the news and think of events in terms of both business and leisure travel. After you read a news story, ask yourself: Will people be encouraged to travel here because of this event or will they stay away? If they stay away, where will they go instead of this place? What place is similar to the troubled area and can handle the influx of tourists?

Seasonal timeliness is crucial. Plan travel destinations to coordinate with your marketing schedule. Know how far in advance an editor lines up seasonal stories. Summer travel is planned by consumers three to six months in advance; editors try to get the jump on consumer interest and purchase stories up to six months in advance of running them. Of course there are exceptions, but a lead of time of six to nine months is not unusual for weekly travel sections and magazines.

PREPARING TO GO

A trip to the library or your own reference shelf is a must. I photocopy pages from guidebooks for the cities or areas I'll be visiting. Rather than tote around heavy guidebooks, I use these pages as my basic on-site information. City maps from guidebooks are particularly useful, as well as plans or charts related to the interiors of museums and churches, archeological sites, etc. Not all countries provide guide materials in English. Consult chapter six on facts for more information on pre-trip research and preparation.

Take the time to call the tourist office or visitor's bureau of the destination country or city. Many countries sponsor tourist offices in New York or Los Angeles. Countries without tourist bureaus funnel inquiries through the commercial counselor of the embassy or consulate. Within the United States and Canada, each state and province and many cities have tourist bureaus that will provide brochures, maps and information. I recommend leaving most of the material at home, ready for the writing phase.

DEVELOPING LOCAL CONTACTS

A sure way to gain a true picture of a place is to meet a family and share a meal with them. While this might seem impossible if you have no friends in the place you will be visiting, there are ways to network to find contacts.

Where do you get contacts if you don't have international friends? Many countries have "Meet-the-People" programs whereby visitors are matched to native residents of similar age, education and professional status. The hosts invite the visitor to share a meal or tea, depending on the culture. Basic personal information is exchanged before the meeting. The smart visitor has photos of family and hometown to show the hosts.

Before you depart, call or write one of the exchange programs such as Servas and seek the name of a family who would be interested in inviting a visitor to dinner. British Commonwealth nations and many European, Asian and South American countries run programs that match visitors with families and individuals. Contact the appropriate national tourist board for specifics on each nation's Meet-the-People program.

Another way to develop local contacts before you embark is to find the counterpart to your club, hobby, religious, school, professional association or other affiliation. Do this even if you are traveling within the United States. People who live in the place you are writing about will almost always know more than you do. Developing contacts at the destination is also possible, but it is much easier to arrange meetings in advance. Everybody has commitments these days and your hosts may not have time for you if they don't know you are coming. Sports and hobbies have international associations, so you could make contact with a resident overseas who shares your interests and could provide valuable information about the local scene. The sister cities program may yield a foreign contact if your hometown or a nearby city participates. Check with the chamber of commerce or city government public relations department for information on sister cities.

Ask work colleagues if they know anyone where you are planning to go. Perhaps they can set up appointments for you. Make the phone call prior to your trip or just after you arrive so that there will be time to arrange a convenient meeting time. If you are invited somewhere for a meal, always bring a small gift to your host or hostess.

When the list of local contacts seems like too much to handle, simply phone people during your stay and don't try to arrange a meeting. You discharge any perceived social obligation by making the call and chatting about the mutual friend and what you've been doing during your visit. Since you are gathering information, ask for suggestions during the conversation, particularly on shopping areas or restaurants.

PACKING PRACTICUM

How you pack and what you pack will affect the quality of your travel experience. Here are some of the things I've learned in over thirty years of travel.

When I set out on my first solo trip in 1966, I used an extra large size suitcase, a copious zippered tote bag, and a purse with a shoulder strap. Inside were clothes for three months of experiences ranging from hiking to attending the ballet at the Salzburg Festival. I had toiletries, books, a travel iron, a jar of peanut butter, and many pairs of shoes. I was only sixteen and didn't yet know that you could find everything you need in Europe. Well, maybe not the peanut butter, at least back then.

Twenty-three years later in 1989, I knew better. It's difficult to be a travel writer and a pack horse. During a two-month jaunt through Asia that would cover both northern and tropical latitudes, I carried only an expandable shoulder bag and a small soft backpack. When I left the cold countries, I mailed the down vest and heavy knits home, continuing with lightweight slacks, two skirts, a white blouse that doubles as a jacket, several T-shirts, a cotton knit suit, and a Gore-Tex rain jacket. As I progressed in the journey and acquired books, filled notebooks and painted pictures, I mailed items home.

Choosing Luggage

Travel experiences will hone your packing technique. The first step in the process is to find a bag or combination of two small bags that fit your body. The only thing worse than carrying a heavy bag is toting several heavy bags that can't be handled easily by one person. Just try to run for that airplane gate or that bus or train with a cumbersome suitcase slamming against your leg. Where did you plan on stowing all that luggage as you squeezed on the ferry or in the last place in the jitney that runs from the train depot to your hotel?

The piece of luggage that you settle on should be sturdy, with zippers or latches that don't separate when you stuff the bag, handles that don't cut your palms or drag on your shoulder. I prefer lightweight nylon luggage and have more than a dozen different travel bags for various purposes. I'm loathe to surrender valuable weight to the bag itself. The choice of color and material is individual, but waterproof nylon canvas is durable and resists dirt. May I suggest that if you take more than one bag, that they not match and have a few road scratches on the surfaces. Wherever you go, you'll want to blend into the crowd, and an expensive suitcase or matched set of luggage screams "tourist target."

For me, carrying a purse or briefcase is difficult to manage safely when traveling. I stash cash and valuable papers in my shoes and money belt. Everything else is stowed in my shoulder bag. Since I rarely surrender the bag, all that I need is close at hand. If the bag is checked somewhere, I just remove the irreplaceables (camera, documents, notebook, etc.) and put them in a fanny pack or light daypack which stays inside the other bag until needed.

Along with the shoulder bag, the most versatile choice for carrying clothes would be a small sports duffel bag in a subdued color like khaki or black or a small suitcase. Bright colors are fine for identifying luggage, if you prefer them, but dark quiet colors don't show scuffs and will serve you in a wide variety of travel milieu. Your one or two bags should be small enough to fit in the overhead luggage rack or under an airplane seat. While you may have to check luggage from time to time, real travel freedom is never waiting at the baggage carousel. Garment bags are the standard for many American business travelers, but they are awkward to carry for any distance, and as your travel takes you to the antipodes, you'll be flying on aircraft that may lack compartments for stowing them. With two modest-sized bags, one slung over the shoulder, you should be able to walk with one hand free. By switching the bags from one side to the other, you can avoid muscle fatigue and stiffness. By using just these two bags, you can keep track of them and what's inside them—papers and business items in one, clothes in the other. Where you cram your souvenirs is up to you!

What to Take

When you're satisfied with the bags and have checked that all the zippers, latches and straps are in working order, it's time to think about what to take along. Define the activities and climate and make a list of what you think you'll need. During the days before departure, accumulate the items in one place. Then cut the pile down. Consider whether any of these clothes or accessories can be bought at the destination. Don't take anything you can't afford to lose.

A selection of knit tops and easy-care slacks or skirts are the nucleus of a traveler's wardrobe. Knits weather the perils of packing; so do some silk garments and many synthetic fibers if you can stand them. Cotton and linen wrinkle, but some clothes are intended to be worn rumpled. If the clothing is coordinated so all the pieces go with each other, adding a few distinctive accessories—scarves, an unusual shirt, a belt or bright tie—you can stretch the basics into more outfits. On a long trip, the clothing should tolerate hand washing. For those who have business meetings and will be dressing formally, take a clothes steamer (rather than a travel iron) and, if appropriate, an international voltage and plug adapter. (A steamer is a small appliance weighing under one pound which smooths wrinkles with puffs of hot steam. All of these travel accessories are available through travel goods mail order companies—see Appendix—or specialty retail stores.) Test drive all outfits before packing. Do the clothes stay wrinkle free? Are they easy to clean? Are the colors neutral?

Roll or fold the clothes to fit the bag. Use tissue paper in the creases as the clothes are folded. Dressy garments can be further protected inside plastic bags. Put underwear in large resealable plastic bags. Stuff socks into shoes and put each shoe into a plastic bag. Heaviest items go on the bottom; work up to the lightest-weight garments. Keep a change of clothes and nighttime essentials with you on the aircraft. Try to travel light and use one bag, the bag you take in the cabin.

Use sample size toiletries or buy everything on arrival at the destination. It makes no sense to carry a twelve-ounce tube of toothpaste on a one-week trip. Take one book unless you are going to a remote non-English speaking area. Handy items to have along include duct tape, large safety pins, nylon cord and extra plastic bags.

Dressing the Part

Consider the purpose of your trip and the destination. If you are staying at the Savoy or the Ritz Hotel in London, you probably could show up with your clothes in a paper bag and be greeted with aplomb. The most elegant places usually aren't pretentious, but in the range of hotels between youth hostels and five-star hotels with unflappable desk clerks there are places where you may feel uncomfortable if your luggage and clothing look out of place. Ragged jeans may be fashionable in Seattle, but not in Singapore.

A word or two about dress. May I suggest that we writers do nothing to further the regrettable reputation that North Americans have for wearing gym clothes and sneakers for all occasions? This may mean dressing differently than you normally would, upgrading from a sweater to a jacket, jeans to slacks or skirt. It might also mean leaving the cocktail dress and sleek high heeled pumps at home. Dressing too elaborately is just as unsettling as wearing athletic clothes everywhere. Being mindful of dress customs in other cultures is part of the travel writer's pre-trip research. Don't forget that dress codes vary by region and city here in the United States, too.

As a writer, you're not expected to dress upscale every day and evening, but I'd recommend having one ensemble for chic evenings, just in case there's an invitation from the ambassador or the concierge locates a ticket for the sold-out opera performance at Milan's LaScala. You're a working professional; that means being able to meet anyone at anytime. "Dress the part" is an apt motto.

PERSONAL COMFORTS

When I travel, certain amenities are always with me. A bottle of water, high-protein snacks, fruit, a Swiss army knife, a small pillow, earplugs and an eye cover go in my carry-on bag. I used to travel with a cassette tape player and earphones, but I've decided that the space is better employed for an extra book. A hooded sweatshirt completes the overnight flight kit. The hood blocks light and sound while providing warmth around my neck. After a neat brandy or scotch, sleep comes at the usual hour and I manage to snooze, if not slumber deeply, the entire trip.

Keep in mind that you can place advance orders for vegetarian and kosher meals on most airlines. Sometimes the special meals are passed out before the general food service. I supplement meals offered by airlines with my own fruit and snacks because I don't like processed food. If you have special dietary needs, provision yourself for the journey. If you've ever traveled on foreign trains, you know that it's the custom to carry a bag of food, bottles of water or wine, fruit and bread. While you don't have to carry a load of groceries along on a flight, being self-sufficient gives you an edge on circumstances.

The stresses of travel, jet lag and long hours on the road will cut into your sleeping routine. If you skip time zones, your natural circadian rhythms of sleeping and wakefulness will be altered. Circadian rhythms are twenty-four-hour cycles of body temperature, hormone and plasma levels and other biological factors. Sunlight affects your body clock; try to spend several hours in daylight as soon as possible after you arrive at your destination. If there are breaks in your travel, use every opportunity to be out of doors in daylight.

Sleep is your friend and will sustain you during difficult times. You don't want to leave home without it. Try to start out on your journey well rested and alert. Whether you drive or fly, take the train or bus, you'll be taxing your reserves of patience and equanimity just by being away from home. With enough sleep you should be able to handle whatever comes up. I find that when my body is deprived of sleep, I'm crabby and unable to focus my attention on the business at hand.

Adjusting your body to the new time zone can be started prior to departure by changing your sleep and waking times to fit the destination. Reset your watch to the new time zone as soon as you enter the aircraft. Health professionals recommend avoiding stimulants like alcohol, coffee, cola and tea before bedtime, but I use a shot of cognac to put me out. Drink lots of water, not carbonated soft drinks which can aggravate the digestive system.

Get out in the daylight on your first day at the destination. The first thing I do after arriving and settling into the hotel room or with my hosts is take a walk. Whenever I'm trapped at airports because of delays, layovers, or waiting for connecting flights, I head outdoors. Even a stroll around the parking lot provides the needed jolt of daylight. And just because the sky is overcast doesn't mean the sun isn't doing its work. Exposure to daylight is the main factor in adjusting your circadian rhythms to the new time zone.

If you have sleeptime and waking rituals that you can maintain while traveling overnight away from home, they will help you feel comfortable. Ask the hotel to reserve a quiet room, specify non-smoking if you don't smoke, arrange for two wake-up calls in case you miss one. Bring family pictures, a favorite small pillow or a coffee mug to make the temporary environment seem more familiar. Stretching and exercise will improve your physical well being. If you can, pamper yourself the first couple of days; head to bed when you are tired and sleep until you awaken naturally.

THE TRIP BEGINS

Your bags are packed. The airport limo is on its way. Guidebooks and notebook are in your carry-on bag. Passport, tickets and funds are securely stashed. Does your heart beat a little faster knowing you are about to embark on a thrilling adventure with exotic cities, curious sights, stunning sunsets? Or have you traveled so much that you take it in stride, just one more stamp on the passport? I hope your passion for travel hasn't faded, no matter how often you've set out. Let yourself revel in the anticipation. That's part of the appeal of travel. Prime your curiosity; the adventure is about to begin.

Oh, but wait; there's more. You're also embarking on a double life—seeing for readers and for yourself. The path you are starting involves some effort, alertness and finely attuned perception of the passing scene. You are traveling as a travel writer! Too often the lure of perceived glamour of travel writing obscures the real work involved. Of course, gathering information in the field is more fun than passing the day at a desk. The skills are the same, whether practiced on the road or at the library study carrel: research, organization, self-discipline, attention to detail and follow-up.

You'll find few travel writers who describe their work as easy, relaxing or non-stop fun. Dash your illusions of a pampered lifestyle in luxury hotels and the first-class section. At least at the beginning of your career. The average travel writer preparing a story for a regional travel magazine drives to a motel, tours the destination and snaps pictures, all the while asking questions and writing down information. That night, our freelance writer transcribes the notes and types a first draft, falling into a fitful sleep on an unfamiliar bed. Next day, more of the same or hurry home to finish the piece for an impatient editor. OK, I admit it, that's an extreme worst-case scenario, but novice writers should be aware that the process of seeing the world as a travel writer is more demanding than traveling for personal pleasure. Rarely is it glamorous.

THE TRAVEL WRITER'S DAY

Vacation trip or travel writer's trip? Though a vacation can be structured to permit research for travel articles, working travel writers aren't vacationing—which means to leave or vacate the usual routine. We are involved and working on the job. Our travel is our usual routine. So a travel writer's workday should run pretty much like a day at the office, except that it is in the field. Rise early, breakfast well, move into work mode, and leave time for a coffee break. After lunch, which will probably include a brief interview with the chef or restaurant manager, the travel writer again opens the notebook and pursues experiences. Perhaps there will be an interview or scheduled tour. Mindful of when museums and monuments are open, the writer has compiled a personal checklist of specific landmarks to visit and when. Most important, though, will be time allowed for serendipity and discovery.

Let me share with you a story about serendipity and travel. In 1991, I planned a six-week journey to New Zealand and mentioned to Chip Crews, an editor at the *Post*, where I was headed. He exclaimed that he would be in the same part of the world, on a three-week trip to Australia and New Zealand. We laughed that it would be remarkable if we met, considering that neither of us knew the other's itinerary and considerable distances would be covered. I had no idea where I would be on a given day since I make plans as a trip unfolds. I wagered him that we would meet, so great is my confidence in the serendipity factor in travel. Well into my trip, I was walking down a street in Queenstown, New Zealand, looking for a beer and dinner. Lo and behold, there was my friend Chip heading toward me. He'd just arrived in Queenstown, and I had been hiking all day on a nearby mountain. The window of opportunity for us to meet was under six hours and we did! What's the lesson? Trust the forces of nature. Be alert, pay attention to your surroundings, and use your eyes all the time. You might see someone you know!

On that same trip, I sat beside a businessman on an inter-island flight. Glancing at his reading material, I noticed a newsletter about meat exports. Prior to departure, an editor had asked me to research and write a story about trade. Did I miss this opportunity to meet a potential source for the article? Of course not. I introduced myself, apologized for reading over his shoulder, and we launched into a friendly discussion of New Zealand's meat exports, which he managed for the government. A few weeks later, I interviewed him for the story on trade. Paying attention pays off!

Cultivate an appreciation for chance by intentionally getting lost on foot—during daylight in a nearby city that you do not know. Stay lost for a while, noticing where you go, what you see and how you feel as you proceed. Look around, not so much for an exit to the experience of being lost, but to intensify your perceptions of place. The reason you get lost is that your mind will be more alert once you know you are not on familiar ground. If you can suspend for the moment the need to find your way out, your internal antennae will be called upon. Any chance to exercise your dormant powers of perception will serve you in your quest to see and describe new places and experiences.

Now don't get the impression that travel writing can be left entirely to chance. Nor is a trip to research an article all work. There has to be some time for reflection and absorption. After all, with so many stimulating experiences happening to you and so much fresh information coming in, your mind needs some stretch time to consider what has been seen. And you wouldn't have embarked on the travel writer route if you didn't expect to mix work and pleasure to some extent. Just keep the professional commitment in mind.

TIME FOR REFLECTION AND LEARNING TO NOTICE

When I need time to reflect on what I've seen, to process incoming information, I take a long walk without my notebook and let thoughts flow. If anything really important comes to mind, I can write it down when I get back to my hotel room. The idea is to release myself from the pressures of having to notice and write. Usually, a couple of hours "off duty" provides a fresh start. Ironically, some of my most interesting travel encounters have happened while I was just wandering without a particular objective. Trust that you'll find enough material to write about, so that you can take time away from your plans and just be.

As Shunryu Suzuki writes in *Zen Mind, Beginner's Mind*, "When you do something, if you fix your mind on the activity with some confidence, the quality of your state of mind is the activity itself.

When you are concentrated on the quality of your being, you are prepared for the activity." Make time to focus on yourself and how you are feeling as a traveler, then inspiration and activity will emerge. Concentrate on sensing yourself in the place where you are, noticing all that is going on around you. Put your energy into your senses, so that your eyes, ears, nose, skin and mouth take in all the ambient information. Prepare yourself to be an attentive observer and you will be doing the activity itself.

This technique works particularly well if you are trying to write travel articles about a place you know well. And in the beginning of your career, you will probably be writing travel stories for local and regional publications. Roam around your hometown and discover what you never knew was there. Fully participating in your immediate environment will open a whole new spectrum of experiences. After your walk, write down what you saw; teach yourself how to be a full-time observer. Don't let your rambling thoughts, memories and associations dominate your perceptions. Pay attention to all that you can see, hear, smell, feel on your skin or taste. For the moment, don't rank what you see as important or not important; just notice and record in your mind and then in the journal. That familiar street will never be the same again if you are really engaged in the present.

Honing a quality of alertness will serve you in many ways. You'll learn to sense difficulty and potential danger; you'll learn how to ask the questions that will get you the information you need when you need it; you'll spot the extraordinary; you'll be ready when opportunity manifests; you'll be living in the now. Learning how to be present is fundamental for travel writing.

Train yourself to notice in a fresh, thorough way by pretending you are a spy or a visiting stranger, or some other role that encourages you to really look at what your eyes register, from the orange candy wrapper on the street to the constantly burning bulb in the streetlamp to the single pink rose blooming in January in an untended garden and so on around and up and over and down the street. Develop a sense of curiosity by making up stories about what you see. What questions would you ask and of whom? Use your home ground to train your sense perception. Then go ahead and visit places farther away, finding ever more challenging places. Make a list of all the places you want to visit and write about.

ORGANIZING TRAVEL TIME

All of us confront the challenge of organizing time and how to find time for the projects we want to do. When you are traveling, much of your time seems to be wasted en route. Don't fret; use long train journeys, flights and even drives to work on manuscript drafts or catch up with your travel journal entries. Focus your thoughts on the work and the miles fly by. I carry printouts of stories along on all journeys or, if I am driving, I have a tape recorder ready to capture ideas. Whether you are a naturally organized person or not, I recommend learning how to use your time effectively by reading one of the many time management books or taking a course in personal efficiency. If you expect to take all those marvelous trips and write about them, you'll have to plan ahead and be organized.

Budgeting time for various targeted research forays will depend on the proposed articles. Let's say you've decided to write about a winter getaway destination—a ski resort in the western part of the state or a Caribbean island—and plan to produce three travel stories for either destination. One story might be an overall roundup of destinations for the solo vacationer, either ski oriented or beach oriented. Another story might focus on family travel options with the ski focus: how to keep the kids amused while you hit the trails or an evaluation of children's ski classes offered at resorts. Using a warm island destination, the second story would explore family outings on the island or talk about whether baby-sitters are available at each island resort hotel. A third article might fill a special interest niche, like Caribbean gardens or food or, for the other topic, après-ski dining options; outdoor adventure such as windsurfing and snorkeling or snowboarding and skating; or shopping—crafts, market bargains and duty-free luxury goods in the Caribbean or crafts and ski accessories at the winter sports resort.

Of these three potential stories, the one that will require the most time is probably the outdoor action adventure; the windsurfing/snorkeling or snowboarding/skating piece. If you're writing it from a novice point of view, you'll have to attend the classes offered for tourists, interview other participants and teachers, and go out and windsurf, snorkel, snowboard or skate. At least for a day. Even if you have mastered the techniques of a sport already, you'll want to explore several locations geared to the skilled sports enthusiast and that kind of research takes time. Figure out which pursuit will take the most time and make arrangements to do it first.

For the family story, you'll either have to bring your own along or pay close attention to what other families are doing. Develop a list of questions that cover family needs: Does the restaurant have high chairs? Are baby-sitters available at the hotel? Is the swimming pool, ski slope or toboggan run supervised? Where are the entertainment attractions for youngsters, and how much are children's tickets?

The shopping story is what I call a "blend in." Research for the story is done along with everything else. Information can be gathered during visits to shops, museum gift boutiques, markets. Ask local contacts where to find quality goods and where residents browse for bargains. Data on prices and store hours is easy to gather on site, although post-trip research by phone and fax may be an alternative. Information about duty-free shopping, export and import taxes, customs forms, certificates to export works of art and the like are useful to readers.

BE INTERESTED IN THE TOPIC

Many different stories can be constructed from one visit to a particular destination. The only limiting factors are lack of research material and personal stamina. It's downright difficult to write a story back home without sufficient data. As for stamina, I think the easiest way to maintain morale on the job is to invest a high level of personal interest in the project, wherever you go. Keep focused on the task and have some reason for the trip beyond just going to write about it. Investigate a hobby, visit a school, seek out a local artisan, find the farm where vegetables are grown, watch a favorite sport—the topic matters less than the fact that it gives you, the travel writer, a focus. Experienced travel writers tackle several interests and are exploring new ones to keep their curiosity levels elevated.

The dedicated novice travel writer might be more successful choosing an avocation or hobby as a focal point. If you play an instrument, for example, seek out local musicians or instrument makers or composers as a starting point for your travel article. Visit the local concert hall or jazz lounge. When writers like their subjects, enthusiasm comes across to the reader. By the way, knowledge and enthusiasm also go a long way to convincing an editor that your article is unique. When you get to the point of marketing your story, the interest that shines in your voice and on paper makes your story more attractive than a well-researched but flat piece of writing. Travel for its own sake is fine, but the writer who pursues a private passion while traveling brings more to the story.

ONCE YOU'RE THERE

Look around, check out the neighborhood near the hotel or home where you are staying, study the map, and plan efficient ways of visiting significant landmarks or monuments. Coordinate outdoor tours with the weather. Is it raining in the morning? You might have to postpone the walk in the park and head for the nearest museum, library, church or shopping area. Of course, with appropriate garments (boots, umbrella, rain hat, rain pants and coat) you need not let rain change your plans. Indeed, experiencing the mood of a locale in all kinds of weather is the way to really understand the place. How local people react to the weather is also part of the research.

If there is a concierge at the hotel, introduce yourself. Or make certain the desk manager knows of your interests. Special invitations and tours won't be offered if no one knows what you are doing. On the other hand, be discreet about how you describe your project, lest you be inundated with information. Perhaps you are reviewing the hotel; you may not want your true purpose known at all, as the management may lavish special treatment designed to impress. Maintain your own agenda, but be sensitive to interesting alternatives that may arise.

For example, in Malucca, one of the earliest British settlements in Malaysia, I stayed at the youth hostel. The couple managing the Malucca hostel were engaging, energetic and outgoing. Making the most of their situation, they ran tours on the side and invited the half dozen or so travelers in residence to visit a rubber plantation. A small fee would cover gasoline and lunch. Two of the hostel guests, a lawyer and a teacher from the United States, passed on the tour, saying they didn't want to pay the $15 fee, which they considered too expensive. I found that attitude difficult to understand. Two Swiss students and I accompanied our host. It turned out that this side trip was both interesting and rewarding. I came away with a saleable story and photos about how rubber is harvested and cured. I think the two American visitors just didn't have sufficient curiosity about the region they were visiting. When we returned and described the day's adventures, they complained that they wished they had gone along. Curiosity is standard equipment for the travel writer, and indulging it our pleasure and profit.

On another occasion, I was staying near Carthage in Tunisia and noticed a crowd of people bustling inside a community recreation center, setting up a platform for a band. I asked a bystander what was happening. He said that his relatives would be celebrating a wedding there in the evening and promptly invited my companion and me. And we went, discovering a noisy and joyful scene rich with colorful costume, wailing music and singing, spinning dancers and tables crowded with delicacies. Everyone drank fruit juice, cola or tea. The bride sat on a throne-like chair at one end of the stage, robed and heavily veiled, with elaborately dressed women standing all around her. The groom watched the celebrations from a chair on the other side of the stage. He wore a dark suit and was surrounded by male relatives and friends. We didn't stay until the end, but we heard the music nearly all night long.

Just think, if I hadn't satisfied my curiosity by asking what was going on when I first noticed the preparations, we'd never have been invited to the wedding party and instead, probably would have been annoyed by the all-night revelry. As it happened, I wished the couple well around midnight and caught up on sleep the following night.

When your first day as a travel writer has ended and it's time to rest, reflect on all the fascinating sights and encounters that you've experienced during the day. Take time to record your impressions in your journal. The sun's long transit is over and tomorrow promises a world of adventure and opportunity.

What to Look For

Finding local culture and activities once you get to your destination isn't difficult if you think in terms of equivalent sites in your own town. Where do people congregate: around markets and shopping areas, in cafes and restaurants, central squares and parks, schools and places of worship, at laundries and bakeries, bars and city hall? In rural areas, the center of town might be a crossroads where the bus stops or the mail is delivered. Find out where people eat breakfast, and join the crowd.

Develop a feel for local society by watching what happens among the people. Are women huddled at one fountain and the men around another? Do children play freely or do they stay right by their parents? Are all ages and genders and economic groups present in the public areas? Do you see beggars or musicians busking in the streets? Are you the only obvious visitor?

Test your observations with a reliable source, a personal or professional contact who can verify where the various economic and ethnic groups live, work and play. Find out where the rough part of town is and where the wealthy people dine and shop.

How to Find Out What's Happening

Open your eyes and look carefully. Listen. Posters, flyers, local newspapers and radio all may lead to festivals, celebrations, concerts, dances, theater and parades. Ask people what's happening, where they go to have fun, eat, dance or gamble. Even in the smallest of villages, there will be a store, a cafe bar or a church where people congregate to share food, stories and entertainment. As a travel writer, you want to participate in all aspects of daily life, to give a human face to the places you write about.

Practice this kind of research while you are still at home. Instead of skimming over the events listings in the local paper, consider which ones might lead to a travel article. The Civil War reenactment, the sheep dog trials at the historic farm, the annual St. Lucia's Day candle lighting and events like these could make interesting travel stories. Look for posters and banners announcing dances or sports events in your hometown to train your eyes to notice what often fades into the background. Teach yourself to pluck out the details, look for what seems out of place, different or in contrast. Scan a street scene and then let your eyes pan slowly. Memorize what you see in a mental video camera so that you can replay what you've seen if you want to, understanding, of course, that memory is always a kind of fiction and is never absolutely exact.

Approaching Strangers

In many parts of the world, the news is passed by word of mouth. Hesitate to ask, and you might miss the story. Bars and cafes are informal community centers in many places. We're not talking about the glittery coffee shop or dim cocktail lounge at the American-style hotel, but the local taverna or tea shop where people— usually men—huddle like conspirators and talk about politics, their kids, the crops and the weather. Perhaps all the village women congregate at the laundry or market. Ask about local meeting spots. In North America, the local meeting place might be a fast-food restaurant, or, even more likely, a diner or cafe in smaller towns. Cashiers and service staff at truck stops usually know what is happening in the region. Poke through the thrift shop or the hardware store or get a haircut at the local barber. Use every encounter to absorb information.

Of all the places I've traveled, the United States is statistically the most dangerous. Yet, most of us know that except in the stress-primed urban blender, chances are slight that we'll catch a stray bullet or be attacked by a mugger or rapist. Travel through small towns and rural areas, and the likelihood of trouble decreases even more. Succumbing to fear can ruin a trip. Know your limits and strengths; if you are frightened of going out alone, travel with a friend or change your fear by learning self-defense techniques. Let the hotel desk clerk know you are going out and when you are likely to return.

Take on protective coloration by dressing like the local people. If the women wear pants or long skirts and tunics and scarves over their heads in public, you might consider doing the same or a close approximation. Do the men wear shorts and tank tops or are they all in trousers and long-sleeved shirts even in hot weather? You may think that in the age of the global village and CNN that how you dress makes no difference; however, I make these suggestions based on conversations with people I've met around the world. Wearing clothes that somewhat resemble the garments of the local population is visual evidence that you have noticed how they dress and respect them. How you look then becomes part of the unspoken dialogue and if your garments seem familiar, this gives you leverage, and, I believe, a degree of protection.

There are no set rules on how to start conversations with strangers. Here are my guidelines: Watch the group dynamics, find a physical opening if there is a group, make eye contact, smile, say a word or two of greeting and then state your question. Ask for advice or information. Don't rush. While this is an interruption and you may feel that you shouldn't take their time, most people like to help. If you speak too rapidly, you may not be understood, or may be perceived as being aggressive. Try to keep your emotions in check; don't be intimidated and don't get angry or loud if no one responds immediately or helps you. There may be reasons for their lack of communication. In the hundreds of times I've asked people for help in dozens of countries, I can't think of but a few instances when I was rudely treated. Some failures come with the territory.

Tough as it may be at first, the ability to approach strangers anywhere in the world is not just a useful skill for a travel writer, it could be a survival skill. The more often you practice asking questions, the better you will handle situations. Develop the habit of asking a complete range of questions about whatever information you seek. Sometimes people don't volunteer the one answer you need. There will be false starts, you may be rebuffed, scolded or laughed at. You may ask the wrong person and have to try several times to get the information you need. People may give you an answer that is partially right but mostly wrong, because they want to give you some kind of answer. In some places, you'll need to ask the same question of several people and make a guess as to which one is right. Soon, though, you'll find that you have developed an innate sense for who knows what is going on and how to approach them with easy grace.

It's been my experience that most of the world's people have good intentions. They aren't "out to get you." Try to cultivate an attitude of neutrality and acceptance rather than suspicion and hesitation. In my travels abroad and in North America, I just don't find the French rude or the Mexicans cheats or southerners slow or any of the other lame cultural and ethnic stereotypes promoted in movies and television situation comedies. Am I just lucky that over the years I've met wonderful people and built friendships in many states, provinces and countries? Some of the friendships started when I asked directions. I've crossed North America by land nearly a dozen times and have received singular hospitality here, too. Perhaps the way we are treated is the way we approach others.

Finding a Story

In the international arena, the same kinds of sources—posters, radio and television programs, local newspapers—will yield potential material for your travel story. Language might present a hurdle, but if you have a pocket dictionary or some familiarity with the language, you ought to be able to figure out the specifics. Stymied by a poster? Ask someone on the street or at a nearby shop to interpret. Use simple English words and modulate your tone.

When I was exploring Spain and Portugal during a leisurely two-month driving tour in 1985, my willingness to ask questions paid off. I remember we crossed the border into Portugal and found a grand commotion in the streets of a town called Elvas. What was going on, I wondered. This town is just a border outpost, yet the streets are crowded and the public spaces bristle with energy. There were even other tourists. We explored and discovered a huge carnival and fairground. Cowboys in leather chaps milled around. Bronze-skinned men hoisted tents and tacked strings of lights between poles. Pink posters stapled to telephone poles showed a bull's head and some large Roman numbers. After a conversation with an older Portuguese couple who appeared to be permanently settled into their campsite with TV, lawn chairs and a full-size kitchen stove, I pieced together the story. The town was famous for its bull festival and farm fair. It wasn't too widely known to foreign tourists, but people from all over the Iberian Peninsula flocked to this fiesta. When I checked the guidebooks later, all mentioned the bullfights and this May festival. We just happened on it.

Another serendipitous travel find occurred while I was with an adventure group trip in the Russian Far East. Overhearing one of the guides discussing a native festival that he planned to attend after the tour was over, I asked for more information. The festival would be held in a remote village way off the beaten track, which in that part of the world—Siberia—means truly inaccessible. A group of young villagers and a few dedicated old-timers who remembered the tribe's rituals that had faltered during the Soviet era would be celebrating the Alkhalalalaj harvest festival of the nomadic Koriak tribes of eastern Siberia. Cultural anthropologists from Germany and the United States would participate and record this revival of a traditional celebration long dormant during the Soviet Communist regime. And, sure, I could tag along if I paid my own way and didn't cause any difficulties. Who could resist such a unique opportunity?

Using Guidebooks

Choose the top tourist attractions selected from guidebooks, brochures and booklets from tourist boards, information from friends or colleagues or your personal knowledge. Evaluate these popular venues with a keen eye. Is the climb up the Statue of Liberty really worth suffering the stuffy heat inside? Are the lines painfully long, as I found at the Taj Mahal, and will you need to find an alternative entry that you'll share with your readers? Is the museum or monument so overrun with visitors that you can't see anything, as often happens at Washington, D.C.'s Air and Space Museum? Most important, are you visiting these places because you think you should or because you are really interested?

To taste the flavor of a place, put yourself in a variety of situations. While you will start with a focus on your own interests, you'll also have to explore sites of interest to a wider audience. You may love sports events and detest formal gardens, but your readers may want to know about both. While you shouldn't attempt to create a story about a topic in which you have feeble interest, check out other activities that will be mentioned in your travel articles.

Look beyond the guidebooks and read literature and history for other story ideas and landmarks to include in travel articles. In chapter six, there is a discussion of what to read before a trip to stimulate your curiosity.

Traveling Incognito

There will be times when a travel writer wants a protective identity. Objective reporting is easier when the hotel or restaurant staff are not aware they are serving a travel writer. If you don't reveal what you are writing in your notebook, or for whom, you maintain neutrality. Once the word is out that you are a travel writer, special services may ensue. Nice for you, but those perks are not likely to be forthcoming for other guests. Table service may be swift and gracious for you, curt or disinterested for your readers. If asked, you can honestly say you are keeping a travel journal and leave it at that. Privacy and invisibility allow the writer to ask questions and probe.

On a junket, which is a free trip offered to travel writers and editors or other people working in the travel industry, it is difficult, if not impossible to maintain a low profile. In the eyes of the travel promoters, the writers are on the job day and night. Before accepting free group promotional tours, ask yourself: Is this the kind of trip I want? Find out if you are going to be able to pursue your travel pleasure and develop real stories, or if you will be herded around and have to rely on what is dished out.

For me, the answer is clear. I've never had a great time on a junket. Problems beyond my control dampened the experience or the dynamics of the group itself dominated the daily scene. While going on a junket occasionally is a good way to network and meet editors, traveling on your own itinerary and following personal interest propels the best journeys and makes the richest travel writing. There's more discussion of press junkets and other free travel in chapter nine.

Finding the Out-of-the-Way Story

Sometimes travel writers just have to rely on instinct. Practiced voyagers have a sixth sense about direction, nosing out hidden corners of a city, discovering a remarkable restaurant, happening upon the organist at the cathedral, visiting the beach as the triathlon begins, approaching the proper stranger who just happens to speak English and teach at the university. Instinct develops after years of practice. If you don't have much travel experience, better stick to the tried and proven, testing yourself slowly with small forays off the beaten track. We're not talking about taking life-threatening risks into the outback; just explore places where there are no historic monuments, no famous churches. As with any set of skills, making mistakes will broaden experience and ripen instinct. Let serendipity happen. As one editor at *The Washington Post* said to me recently when we discussed regional travel, every travel story has been done already; we just have to experience it differently and tell it better.

Here are some suggestions for sniffing out unusual stories. Pay attention to what is happening around you. Can you trace that distant sound of music? Are musicians practicing for a party? Why are all the drivers blowing their car horns and waving flags out the window? What do the posters on every lamppost say? Is that crowd at the edge of town gathered for a circus, a crafts festival or a cattle auction? What do the banners on the statues say? Why are all the museums closed on a certain day? Do police stop cars routinely or is there a problem? Why are the streets deserted?

Set out on bicycle or foot to the dusty, forgotten places off the beaten track for the story that no one else will find. Change your mode of transportation: if the place you are exploring is near a body of water, rent a boat or ask a fisherman to take you for a tour. Go to the train or bus station if you arrived by plane or car and take a short excursion to a nearby village. If you're in a city, find out all the ways people arrive. Pause for a moment at a rail or bus station or metro and notice whether they are carrying briefcases, shopping bundles or books—perhaps there is a special market nearby not marked on the map or in your guidebook. Your readers will need this information in the travel article. Hang out at the college or university. Read bulletin boards and strike up conversations with students. If you are in another country, people may be pleased to practice English. If you are in North America, explore the youth beat at clubs and colleges. Be sure to spend time in ethnic neighborhoods, which are often the most vibrant in urban culture.

By the way, you should know that youth hostels are for travelers of all ages, and though I enjoy the amenities of elegant hotels, people staying at hostels off the beaten track can be infinitely more approachable and always interesting. I've gotten great travel tips from people staying at hostels. Even writers who aren't researching a budget travel slant will profit from the occasional hostel stay to broaden travel knowledge.

Go behind the scenes. Arrange a backstage tour at the theater. Tour a museum with a guide or a volunteer docent who can talk about how exhibits are planned and the provenance of the collection. Ask to meet an artist or crafts person. Talk to gardeners, museum guards, waiters; they may have been working there for decades and have stories to tell. Find out where the sports teams practice; can visitors watch?

Visit a monastery, the principal cemetery, an archeological dig, an old hospital, or the local historical society. If you find someone to talk to on site, so much the better. If not, take notes and pictures; look up the history of the place later on. Sometimes, you'll just learn some interesting facts about an old building which won't find a place in your article, but more often than not, you'll discover new material for travel articles.

Look into people's daily lives. Attend a religious service or a trial. Visit the local library. Ask a school principal if you can tour a school. Go to the market at dawn when the farmers are arriving and the restaurant staffs are buying. Talk to a seamstress and a cab driver and ask where they eat lunch. Then go there. Why poke your nose into all these aspects of a place when all you plan to do is write about your visit to the museum, the civic monument, the trendy chic restaurant and the fishing wharf? Because just about every travel story has been done already; you have to find a fresh angle, a new twist that sets your story apart. A different perspective and an unusual voice are what a travel editor seeks.

Read the local newspapers. Even if they are in a language you don't understand, a picture might spark your curiosity or you can ask someone to translate for you. While visiting Hilo, Hawaii, I picked up a copy of the free local paper and scoured the listings for events that might be fun for me, my friend and her eleven-year-old son. Tall order. Few preteens share the same interests as their mother and her friends. Regrettably, we had to pass up the evening's jazz and theater offerings, but a costume parade celebrating Mardi Gras was scheduled at dusk. We never would have known about it without checking the local rag.

Stay-at-Home Travel Writing

Not all travel stories take the writer far away. In fact, a logical beginning for a travel writer is to write about places close to home. However, the local places you know and love may be known and loved by others and thoroughly covered in travel articles. Finding a unique story close to home is a useful assignment for a novice to get started. Your job is to seek subjects for travel articles, if not in the town where you live, then in a nearby city, the state or provincial capital or within the region.

Most of us care about our home ground. The trick, of course, is to select familiar subjects nearby that will interest readers and haven't been "done to death." Market research is the key. All through this book, I discuss how you figure out what editors and readers want, but as I've stated many times, your own interests should drive your travel. To get yourself started, thumb through small local papers, newspaper travel sections and all the nearby regional and state or city magazines. Take notes on the types of articles you see. Many of these regional periodicals carry sections on recreation and leisure and regularly include travel stories. Check to see if they are written by staff members or by freelance contributors.

Special interest magazines are also fertile ground for a novice freelancer with a travel article written close to home. Your residence becomes a type of credential—who better than a local person would know the best aspects of travel in the region? The unique qualities of a place close to home may not be immediately clear to an inexperienced writer. Someone may live in the heart of a dynamic city and not be able to think of story ideas that haven't been done already. But even in suburban towns and rural counties, there are stories galore for writers who have investigated the market and plumbed their memories.

For example, one of my dearest childhood memories is going to the public library. On first blush, I can't think of any reason why a visitor would care about my neighborhood library. Or can I? Two of the libraries in the local county system were housed in charming old bungalows. One has been declared a historic landmark and is devoted exclusively to children's literature. Children's reading and storytelling programs are held there. The other was torn down, the one I used to visit as a child. Aha! The story unfolds. My personal memory and public interest do intersect. Visitors from out of town might well be curious about the children's library in a house that has been named a historic site. Families might want to attend the story hours for children. My travel article could start with my memories, then explain the historical background of the library to expand understanding of why this library is significant.

During research, I might learn that there are other significant buildings in that neighborhood that can be linked with this library to broaden the story. The point is that a travel article lurks behind the simplest personal memories.

EXERCISE 1
Find a travel article idea close to home.

Here are the kinds of questions to ask yourself: Is there a nearby college campus with historic buildings? Does the community have a park featuring a nature center or wildlife preserve? Have any famous people lived in the area—writers, artists, performers, political notables? Are their former homes open to visitors? Perhaps there is a nearby shopping district for local crafts or antiques. What is the history of that statue in front of the civic center? Why are all the Italian restaurants in a certain neighborhood? What is it about the river that attracts all the kayakers in spring? Why is the art gallery named after a certain family?

EXERCISE 2

There's no point in trying to write about a place if you don't have a feeling for it—some reaction or opinion or observation. Probe your suitcase of memory and pull out the names of local places that have personal significance. Jot down a word or two saying why. Now put yourself in the shoes of a visitor: What about the place would interest a stranger, a person with no history invested in the location? Find points where your reasons for caring about the place and a visitor's interest will intersect. That is the place to begin the story.

EXERCISE 3

What creature comforts do you need when you are away from home? List a dozen (or more) aspects of daily life that you consider important. For example: daily hot showers, three sit-down meals a day, air conditioning, reading in bed before sleep, freshly brewed coffee, etc.

Now, refer to your list and think about how deeply you would be troubled if you had to forego any of these habits or comforts. Make a list that reflects the absolute minimum of comfort that you could handle away from home. Have you ever experienced travel without those comforts? How did you react?

EXERCISE 4

Make a packing list for a five-day trip to a tropical island. Imagine that you will be sightseeing in cities and the country-side, taking pictures to illustrate your article, learning a new sport, going to restaurants and nightclubs, shopping for crafts, sunbathing on the beach. You know the temperature is stable and warm, but the nights are cool. Do you have more than twelve individual garments on the list (not counting under-wear)? Can you edit the list to nine pieces or fewer? Hint: Think double-duty for each item you put on the list.

Chapter Three

THE TRAVEL JOURNAL

Whether it's called a diary, log, notebook or journal, the written record of immediate impressions is the travel writer's most valuable tool. The travel journal will hold written notes on your general observations and specific experiences of places and people. While at first it may be difficult to train yourself to write down what you see, in time the process will become natural. You will turn to your travel journal to report what you've experienced as you would confide in a trusted friend. I can't imagine taking a journey without a notebook to log my thoughts and sensations. Reporting the day's events to my journal helps me relive them.

THE IMPORTANCE OF KEEPING A JOURNAL

The reason you'll be keeping a travel journal is to have a vast supply of information about what happened during your travels. The entries will be fresh if you report them on site right after they happen or a few hours later. Using these descriptions that pulse with the energy of the moment, you'll later be crafting travel articles. The more you write down, the better your travel articles will be—not because you'll use every entry you record in your journal, but because you'll hone your writing and observation skills in the process of creating a travel journal.

Into the travel journal, you'll jot down the colors, sounds and smells you encounter. You'll write word sketches of people and scenes. There may be a sign you'll want to copy verbatim, or a menu item that will help you recall a particular meal. At this, the notebook stage, your writer's eye is like a magpie collecting elements that shine, cramming the journal pages with description. Just as an artist always has sketch pad close at hand, the travel writer needs the journal to record intriguing scenes, descriptions of people, perhaps even drawings.

The word "journal" comes from the French word "jour," or day. The travel journal is a record of each day's events, experiences, highlights, observations. You may decide to write several times during the day or sum up your experiences at the end of the day. The goal is to fill pages with bold description and sensual detail. When you read your travel journal entries, you should be able to follow your path again, seeing the glorious (or depressing) scenes that met your eyes, hearing the cacophony, smelling the aromas. Your journal is private, not for publication, so write freely without constraint or self-editing. Grammar, vocabulary and sentence structure are secondary considerations at this point in the writing process.

While there is a place in the travel journal for the introspection and analysis of feelings and their meaning that is typical of traditional diary keeping, the travel notebook goes further. In the wanderer's diary, the writer sets down details of incidents great and small that paint a panorama of a place which will be the "main character" in the travel article. A writer planning to craft a juicy profile of a person requires interview material from diverse sources to capture the essence of a personality. Similarly, the travel writer collects more material than is really needed, to have a wide range of descriptive anecdotes and colorful scenes to draw from during the intense writing phase after the trip is over. While a diarist writing at home may not notice the physical details of the passing scene or consider the routines of daily life worthy of comment, the travel diarist must engage the senses and write until the well of each day's impressions is dry.

The travel notebook will serve in many ways: for noting train or bus schedules, entry hours and fees, addresses of new friends, books recommended by other travelers. When I am uncertain about the local language, I ask a bilingual friend or hotel staff member to write in my notebook the address where I am going and where I am staying in the native language. When I was traveling in China, for example, this system was indispensable. I would show the addresses written in my notebook to a cab driver or passerby for help with directions.

There will be times when whole conversations are conducted through pictographs. Traveling in rural Indonesia where I found few

English speakers, I recall drawing pictures of buses, boats, food and other necessities in my notebook. Later, when I wrote travel articles, these oddities reminded me of half-forgotten incidents.

What Kind of Notebook?

Should you take a laptop computer along on your journeys to record travel notes? I do if I'm interviewing people and need exact quotes, but even a lightweight computer can be a drudge to carry, an annoyance at security checks and a magnet for grit and thieves. One aspiring travel writer circled the globe using an electronic organizer to E-mail messages to friends which became a rough draft. My ideal unit would be paperback book size with a full keyboard, all the communications goodies and a battery the weight of a pearl earring. Meanwhile, we can all rely on paper notebooks small enough so you won't be tempted to leave it behind when you prowl around gathering material and large enough so you can really stretch out and write. I use hardcover bound artists' sketchbooks with heavyweight unlined paper. Try several options before you settle on the notebook that works best for you.

Put your name and address and phone number inside the cover; this unique notebook is valuable. I remember when a respected writer at *The Washington Post* lost his personal journal in unfortunate circumstances. Luckily, his name and phone number were in the book and it was returned. Storing your travel journal in a reclosable plastic bag protects it from rain. Use inexpensive pens with waterproof ink. The best notes in the world aren't much good if you can't read them, so take the time to write clearly. When interviewing someone, pay attention to accuracy and use quotation marks around verbatim statements. Print the person's name and a contact phone number or address next to their remarks in your notebook, so you can contact them again if needed.

WRITING THE TRAVEL JOURNAL ENTRY

Some people write as they go, noting incidents as they happen. Other writers, and I fall into this group, absorb the scene for an hour or so, then pause and write what they've seen or felt. The intervals of observation vary, of course. At a festival of indigenous peoples I attended in Kovran, a hamlet on the Sea of Okhotsk in the Russian Far East, I wrote an impression every few minutes, then stopped writing to give my full attention to the dances and drumming. I resumed writing again after the performances ended. The process continued: watch for a while, then pause and report. On the few occasions when I've tried to write down every incident as it happens, I suspect the true experience was lost. Visual memory faded quickly because I wasn't fully there, concentrating on the moment.

Each person is different in processing experiences and information. I favor a Zen approach—experience the moment and develop a strong visual memory. I think we remember best what we experience deeply. For me, writing continuously while trying to capture events I'm experiencing results in a diluted impression. Perhaps the key is to be alert to interludes when notes can be taken without losing full attention to the unfolding scene.

On the other hand, I've been with other travel writers on press junkets while they diligently recorded the facts as a guide delivered them. When they sit down at the computer or typewriter, those writers have concrete information for story construction. But do they have experiences to share? Facts can be obtained afterward, on site or in the library. Experiences can't be fully re-created. I'd rather try to concentrate on what was happening while it was happening, then meet one-to-one with a guide or museum caretaker after a tour and ask questions that arose during my visit.

While I'd like to think that every fact can be recovered through research, the truth is some questions can only be answered on site. This poses a dilemma. How can you simultaneously concentrate on the passing scene, formulate questions to be asked later, and write down your impressions and factual data?

Experience comes but once, while you're in it. Focus on the present, develop a prodigious memory and try to write down what is happening. Some information can be researched later, but the intimate, first-hand details you seek are best obtained on site. You may create a personal notation system for flagging questions as they arise so that you can get answers before you leave the site.

This is the way I do it. On guided tours, or any situation where I'm taking notes from spoken information, I listen attentively, jotting notes about what I notice and what I hear. I record the highlights that interest me or seem so generally significant that they would be necessary in any travel article about the place. I figure what appeals to me will be sufficient to craft an article. If I have a question, I draw a box around the note then try to get an answer immediately. Sometimes that isn't possible, but when I do subsequently maneuver into a conversation with a guide or curator, the box around the note reminds me that I had a question. My memory is sharp enough that I can remember what the question was within a short time frame, but if I wait until I'm back home at my desk, there's the frustrating possibility that I will have no idea what I wanted to ask. Whenever possible, seek answers to your questions on site, at once.

One drawback of tours organized for travel writers is the constant refrain of irrelevant facts dripping like a leaky faucet in the background. Participants dutifully scribble notes, filling their reporter's books with data that they'll never use in an article because it is just too dull. Or maybe they do use avalanches of facts in their stories, which may be why they remain unpublished. Some people fill tape after tape with statistics about per capita income, crop yields, demographics of tourists, and the number of hotel rooms. And all that bland information that the tourist bureau deems important will then have to be transcribed, just in case a really titillating fact sneaked into the lecture. Where is the unique travel experience? How can an interesting story be told using only facts? Might as well rewrite a page from the tourism promoter's press kit or cull data from guidebooks and construct an article that reads like a high school term paper.

You will develop a personal sense of what experiences to record in the travel journal. At first, you will probably write more material than you need. As you write in the journal, keep in mind the purpose of your trip, your interest, or the quest that has sent you forth.

For example, here is an entry from the travel journal I kept during an off-season trip to Italy. I didn't have an assignment from a publication, but I was deeply interested in the Etruscan culture and knew that editors have a perennial need for absorbing stories about European destinations. Tuscany is hardly an undiscovered area, so I knew a saleable story needed to have a personal twist. Dry historical detail on the remains of Etruscan civilization would weigh down my story. A travel story larded with history is a sure-fire no-sale. To make the story contemporary and gripping, I planned to focus on atmosphere and my unique experiences.

The journal entries concentrated on what I saw, what I heard and smelled. My writing also records the tangents of my imagination, an important ingredient in travel writing with a history theme, where the writer's musing, mixed with fact gives the article buoyancy and dimension in the present.

> Inside the large tomb {Tomba dei Vasigreci 6 b.c.} at Ceveteri—round on outside, cut into compartments inside. Did they preserve the dead bodies or let dust become them. Worms and slugs—could they penetrate these tombs or did the bodies lie as if asleep until plundered for their jewels. Roman wealth as grave robbers. Did the Etruscans come here while alive to get the feel of the tomb? And I, stepping up into the light have veils of rebirth shaken from my shoulders like the cobwebs on the tomb ceiling covered my eyes. . . . You can hear birds outside and in the ones by the road that aren't part of the pay-to-see section. Cars are heard and vibrations from airplanes too. This tufa rock carries vibration well.
>
> Inside another there are also three smaller chambers with beds and in the large room, chairs on either side of the entrance, facing the rooms of the dead. Everything feels slightly tilted so the head parts of the dead rooms are visible to the people in the chair. I can see four places inside the rooms at once, plus the 4 couches outside.

Enclosed in brackets, the fact written in the first line was added after the journal entry, culled from a guidebook and noted in the margin later that day. The writing is rough and often I slip from the active voice, but in the journal, the task isn't necessarily to craft faultless prose, but to capture the mood, the telling gesture or evocative detail. In final form the story hung on my fascination with tombs and gravesites and ran on Halloween. This diary entry mutated into the following paragraphs in the story which appeared in the *St. Petersburg Times*, October 31, 1993:

> Inside one tomb I sat in the stone chairs that are on each side of the doorway. From that position, one could see the carved stone beds provided for the dead.
>
> The notables were laid out in full regalia on these stone couches, whole families together in the large rooms. Weapons, jewels and household goods for the afterworld were distributed among them, but these items have been removed for museum display or plundered for the international antiquities commerce.

I peeked inside another tomb, cut in a rock wall and with its neighbors, resembling a row of townhouses, each with its own oblong door. Inside, there were three small rooms with niches for stone beds. Oddly, though one would think the sound wouldn't carry through the stone city, inside certain tombs I could hear chirping birds, cars and airplanes. . . .

Ultimately, my visit to the necropolis at Cerveteri created more questions than answers for me. Why are some of the tombs round on the outside and divided into square compartments inside? I wondered if the Etruscans preserved the dead bodies or let dust overcome them. Were the tombs sealed as the Egyptians did? Their funeral rituals—equipping the dead with household goods for the afterlife—somewhat resemble the Etruscans.

Did Etruscan families come here and visit their dead, sitting on the chairs at the entrances, becoming familiar with the tomb they would later occupy?

Much of the finished article follows the text in the journal. What I recorded from sense perception found a place in the final piece. Passive voice became active voice; "cars are heard" became "I could hear." The questions raised during my visit remained questions in the article, designed to provoke curiosity in readers. When people who read this piece visit the Etruscan tombs, perhaps they too will wonder as I did. Even if a reader never visits this archeological site, the story entertains and may even spur further research.

Other parts of the article were captured by recall. I brainstormed, looked at photos taken that day and racked my mind for visual memories that could be brought forth to words from that visit to the necropolis. Reading over my travel journal, I found entries about the weather, fruit trees in bloom, a chill wind, the isolation of the archeological site. During the trip, I read D.H. Lawrence's book about visiting the same site, and referred to his observations in my article.

I could have written more in my travel journal that day, but the visit was so overwhelming that my mind was filled and I needed some time to process the experience. That evening, I talked about the tombs with a friend who lives in Rome and has been to Cerveteri many times. I jotted down some comments from our discussion and further thoughts and questions raised by our conversation.

The travel journal then, becomes more than an on-the-site report. My journal material about Cerveteri included quirky personal questions raised by the visit, dialogue with myself, fragments of conversation with guards and other knowledgeable people, research notes taken from signs and guidebooks, titles of books to consult. Perfecting the recall method of visualizing the place and oneself in that landscape takes mental discipline. Try to record as much as possible in the travel journal while you are on site and concentrate on refining your powers of description.

What happens when the travel notebook is thin, the entries sparse and cryptic, composed mostly of isolated facts? You'll be in trouble when you sit down at the computer or typewriter and find bare bones notes in your journal. I learned this after a visit to Terme de Saturnia, a spa in Tuscany. I was so busy enjoying the heated pool and the herbal facials that I neglected my journal. When an editor called me looking for a travel piece for a winter issue of her publication, I had to scramble to construct a story from my Saturnia notes that were fat with facts, but lean on description and experiences. For structure, I chose an upbeat format of ten lessons for spa life explained through capsulized experiences. Compare the brief journal entries with paragraphs in the published article:

> A.M.—table flatware. classic and white dishes. 17th & 18th c. portraits. armoires. old oil paintings. white walls. breakfast in robes or exercise togs. street clothes to leave. castle in village of Saturnia on hill mist rising from pool. A few energetic bathers paddle in the turquoise water. Italian celebrities. Romans. Swiss. U.S.—Beverly Sassoon, Wim Winders. nobility.

Those notes became:

> Next morning, I dressed casually for breakfast, but everyone else was tucked into terry robes and slippers. Talk about overdressed; I was the only person in the room with shoes on. Lesson two: Despite the silverplate, napkins, and 17th century paintings on the walls, comfortable informality is the rule at Saturnia. . . . You probably won't recognize the Italian celebrities who swing up from Rome and this isn't the kind of place you'll ever see Howard Stern. Saturnia protects its

celebrity guests and won't reveal who has been there recently. Anyway, the Vidal Sassoons and Tony Bennetts of the world look mighty different swimming in steam with no stage makeup. Those look-alike robes and baggy exercise togs provide anonymity for a reason. Lesson three: If you see celebrities, ignore them.

A few intrepid souls paddled through the winter chill in the warm turquoise water. After breakfast, I joined them, happily soaking . . . until I looked at my hands and the silver rings I wear. They were blackened and tarnished by the sulphur. Lesson four: Don't wear jewelry in the water.

Washington International, *Jan.-Feb.*, 1994.

A few brief words in the journal formed the foundation for three paragraphs. One sentence in the journal— "A few energetic bathers paddle in the turquoise water"—found its way nearly intact into the paragraph about wearing my silver jewelry in the sulphurous water.

I remembered that the cryptic entry "Italian celebrities. Romans. Swiss. U.S.—Beverly Sassoon, Wim Winders, nobility" derived from the assistant manager's comments about famous people who had visited the spa (she steadfastly protected the privacy of current guests). Howard Stern's name was added because he was prominent in the news at the time this article went to press. Since it was written for an American audience, I added Tony Bennett because he is well known, without saying he had actually been there.

The diary entry about the gym classes:

Jones Pizzetti—trainer—aqua gymnastic—gentle gym workout. Classes are designed to take it with you—recreate the feeling. Water: sulphur property calms. Training: autogenesis calming. Massage. In gym, doesn't count out beats. everyone finds own rhythm. video to use at home but only people who've been there really may use successfully. spiritual, inner peace and harmony.

The published paragraph went like this:

As if I weren't already relaxed enough, I signed up for a relaxation instruction session led by Jones, a marvelously preserved former Olympic ski champion. During relaxation meditation, I learned that everybody has their own movement pace, so none of that tedious counting out exercise beats. Everyone find own rhythm, cooed Jones. I was striving for spiritual peace and inner harmony, rather than to define muscles or erase love handles. A couple of participants fell asleep. Jones said that was the optimum response and showed true relaxation. Class ended with a long lesson in self-hypnosis. . . ."

Fortunately, I remembered Jones's appearance, and his Olympic history had come up in a conversation which I recalled. Better note taking would have included a description of his tanned face, salt-and-pepper hair and astonishingly trim sixty-something body artfully clad in a silky track suit. During the exercise and autogenesis class I was very attentive and still remember the details four years later. Summoning the class scene to mind after the fact was not a problem for me, but other writers might not have focused so clearly and retained that sequence. My notes could have been more color-ful and specific, helping me during the writing phase. However, the notebook served its purpose, stimulating my memory and providing enough minutiae to stitch a story together.

For every page of notes I did use, there were three or four pages of phrases and jottings that didn't fit in the story. Facts abounded: the chemical composition of the water, the relative percentages of visitors who come for stress or cosmetic treatments, the kinds of questions on the stress assessment questionnaire, the number of kitchen staff, the manufacturer of the hydrotherapy massage ma-chines. I had reported pages of facts that I suspected couldn't be found elsewhere or were written only in Italian. I knew that certain information had to be gathered on site, and so the notebook is largely devoted to the mechanics of spa life at Saturnia. This partic-ular travel notebook is weak in personal observation. The reason I didn't feel I had to write down my experiences is that I was so fully focused on each day's events that I have a fairly accurate memory-video in my head. Events unfolded in a contained environment and my attention was completely attuned to the process, so I con-centrated on getting down facts that would be hard to obtain later.

FROM JOURNAL ENTRY TO FIRST DRAFT

Rereading written notes taken on site helps recover the dynamic immediacy of the passing scene. The journal can be on your desk as a resource for your brainstorm of travel memories. For me, nearly the entire diary serves as a first draft, although I may prune parts and use them in other travel articles with a different market focus. As we see in the examples, some sentences from the travel journal can be directly inserted in travel articles. Some passages have to be substantially rewritten in order to preserve continuity and style.

The next chapter covers the structure and pace of a travel article. For those who are itching to get started, and already have a travel diary, it's time to make a typed transcription which will be your first draft.

The first step is to type the travel journal entries into your computer. Skip the personal passages that explore your private moods and musings. Using the block define and move keys for whatever word processing program you have, arrange related entries. This preliminary phase of typing and organizing material is easier on a computer.

If you are using a typewriter, try this organizational technique. Type travel journal entries onto separate sheets of paper, a paragraph or two per page. Leave lots of blank space. Sort the sheets of paper or cut and paste paragraphs so that related events are together. By using this technique, the writer who uses a typewriter should still come away from the transcription phase with a working draft.

At this point, I'd advise against spending a lot of time arranging the journal entries to create a sequence of events with a plan to make a story. Read chapter four on structure first, and do some of the writing exercises so that when you do start constructing the story, you'll have an idea of the appropriate journal entries to use that will tell the story within the accepted framework of a travel article.

I know that some people who read this book won't or can't wait to get started shaping the travel piece. If you are compelled to tinker with the draft of raw travel journal entries now, remember that memorable travel writing has the same ingredients as any stimulating prose: description that summons the senses, alerts the mind, triggers memory; details that pique curiosity; facts effortlessly woven into the textual fabric. Beyond that, travel writing strives to put the reader in the place. It's nearly an act of magic to construct brilliant prose evoking the spirit of a place. Consult any writing book on prose style and the advice is the same: Use simple construction, vivid description, active voice and mighty verbs.

To give you an idea about how the untouched journal entries become part of finished travel articles, here are excerpts from travel journals and the related paragraphs in published travel articles.

Freelance writer Chad Neighbor, who is based in Scotland, jots down the barest of entries in his travel notebook to serve as memory helpers. His diary entry about a stay in a cottage near a Scottish loch reads:

> Tigh-na-Coille. 150 ft from loch on part of promontr set off by burnlet. basic but thick walls up to 2 ft set tapering in rms upstairs. w-to-w carpets, well equipped, modern furniture but practical, gd dining table. fire already laid (by previous occ) no wood but good coal. many repeat vis sometimes neg. over 10 years of photos on walls from 1 of them. helpful comments from other occ on, walks, restaurants, attractions, wildlife, etc. bats. post bus goes by door. black wd of rannach across rd capercaillie. schiehallion. coal fires (no logs) comments on what's lacking (washmach). fortingall yews

These notes show a writer who needs just a word or two to summon the scene to mind. This system of note taking probably wouldn't contain enough information for a beginning travel writer. However, peeking into another writer's notebook gives an idea of the many ways that details can be recorded. While Chad Neighbor's notes seem to skim the surface, he does have lots of material. For example, place names that are difficult to spell were carefully written out, although missing some capital letters because of his hasty style. Many common words were abbreviated. Scene setting details were carried directly from the notebook to the article which ran in *The Washington Post*, July 31, 1994.

> The attractions of these superbly located cottages are only too obvious. The scenery tends to be first rate and, in our case, the 150-foot stroll to a private beach (even if wind and water made it far too cold for swimming by non-huskies) was irresistible. . . .
>
> Another quite different bonus of Forestry Commission and National Trust cottages is their logbooks, compiled by many years' worth of visitors. These are a valuable resource for new

arrivals dying to discover the best local tearoom or spot for spying a kingfisher. We followed the advice to visit Scotland's smallest distillery at Edradour near Pitlockry—a fascinating detour.

But the diaries also offer an absorbing chronicle. Some people have been spending certain weeks at certain cottages for 10 years or more and feel almost as if they're part owners. Indeed the excellent photos of Tigh-na-Coille and surroundings were taken, mounted and hung by a regular visitor there who thought the walls were a bit bare.

One of the most entertaining aspects of the entries was the complaints, visitors being clearly divided between those who expect all the modern conveniences and then some, and those who do not. There were complaints about the lack of a television, a microwave, a washing machine and, poor soul, a double boiler. . . .

You may notice that Chad Neighbor writes a line about the logs and coal for the fire twice in the notes. He saves this information for the end of the article, using it as physical and psychological closure. The last thing he does during the trip is lay the fire for the next visitor which is what he found when he arrived.

> One of the tests of a good vacation, of course, is how you feel when you leave your temporary abode. After our week on Loch Rannoch I felt relaxed, refreshed and more appreciative of one of Scotland's most spectacular areas.
>
> And, after laying the last fire in the fireplace (a tradition to welcome the next arrivals) and making our last chug down the driveway, I also felt sad to be leaving.

New York based travel writer Ann Jones shares her travel journal entry that became the lead and opening paragraphs for "Horse-Packing in Kookaburra Land" which appeared in *Diversion*, February, 1991.

> March 18: Drove Sydney—Tumut (6 hrs) thru central highlands of NSW—all rolling brownish grass & sheep & dusty eucalyptus—storm at Guilbourn—sandstone at Berrima—Tumut in a valley of green willow & poplar along a river—wide streets—tin roofed bungalows—dinner at Returned Soldiers League Club—Chinese buffet.

This rapid fire impression of her entry to Tumut became the opening for the finished piece.

In Tumut the hot place to eat is upstairs at the Returned Soldiers' League. The restaurant is a cavernous hall with all the warmth and ambience of an American Legion post, and the food is plain—the kind my grandmother called "filling"— but the price is right. Saturday night they lay on something a little special, like a Chinese buffet. That goes over big with the locals, since there's not a whole lot of Chinese food available, as far as I could tell, in the hinterlands of New South Wales, Australia's southeastern corner.

. . . I'd left Sydney that morning, heading southeast, for a leisurely six-hour drive to Tumut. The highway ascended a series of rising valleys to grassy tableland that seemed to belong only to me and the sheep—thousands upon thousands of them.

It was March, the end of Australia's summer, and the dry grass, the dusty sheep, and the road were all the same color, actually no color at all. Then, below me, appeared a big stand of green poplars along the Tumut River, and the road wound down among tidy tin-roofed bungalows, steepled churches, and plain-faced business establishments set wide along broad avenues laid out for the grander city Tumut once intended to become.

Notice the author's effort to relate the faraway place to the familiar: "ambience of an American Legion post . . . the kind my grandmother would call 'filling.' " The sketchy notes in the travel journal expand when Ann Jones uses them to summon memory to embellish the experience for the final rendering in the travel article. The note about "brownish grass & sheep & dusty eucalyptus" becomes more refined "the dry grass, the dusty sheep, and the road were all the same color, actually no color at all."

Ann Jones says she takes notes for her travel articles in three ways. "As I go, I jot quick notes, especially facts and people's memorable remarks, in a standard reporter's notebook that is always with me. At day's end or when time permits, I try to make a longer entry in a journal, summarizing the day, including descriptive details, and noting issues and themes raised by the day's events and conversations. (The excerpts included here are from her day's end travel journals.) I also often carry a pocket tape recorder to make quick notes to myself, conduct interviews, and record the noises of the place, especially animal and bird sounds and local music. I rarely listen to the notes or interviews, but I often replay the noises to bring back the feel of the place I'm writing about."

When I started using travel journal entries as the foundation for travel articles, the writing was rather formal and composed, as the following entries from a trip to Barcelona demonstrate. During the years since then, I've learned that it is easier to extract a first draft from travel journal entries that are focused on the details, atmosphere and scene. Rather than striving for artful sentence structure in the journal entry, craft specific descriptions that are rooted in sensual perception. Compare the choppy description in the travel journal entries for the Etruscan article discussed earlier in this chapter with these highly structured notes on Barcelona that eventually formed the basis for a destination article with a special focus on the architecture of Gaudi.

Today we hunted Gaudi's buildings. Beginning with the Holy Family Cathedral, still unfinished, and ending at Park Guell, a marvelous fantasy land high above the city where clean air is able to be breathed. The cathedral proved a wonder, high towers, a sand castle in pre-stressed cement. It may take another 50 years to achieve Gaudi's vision, certainly work is not progressing rapidly.

The candy colored towers are visible several blocks away. An amusement park perhaps, or a children's playground. No, Templo Sagrada Familia, the Holy Family Church between Calle de Provenza and Calle de Mallorca (north east of the Diagonal) at their intersection with Calle de Cerde. Still under construction after 100 years, this cathedral evokes the gothic spires and buttresses of churches of the Middle Ages, yet it is constructed with the humorous, even mocking, combination of materials that marks all of Gaudi's efforts. Fantastic/ marvelous forms, part nightmare, part joyous fantasy, crawl upwards to the four spires on each end of the cathedral. There is also harmony, however, the spires may look like a sand castle melting under the onslaught of the sea, but the design is wonderfully proportioned, superbly designed and completely in tune with human sensibility.

The effect of entering a building you do not realize is unfinished is remarkable. You wonder if this is what a war zone feels like. We pursued his work in downtown area, marching perhaps longer than desirable. Got a bus up to the park which relieved our legs. There we bought postcards, attempted a watercolor (stiff, amateurish) and watched school children play. The pure air was instantly remarkable and cleared my eyes and headache. We rested up, then walked the Gothic quarter before dinner.

The published piece opened with more drama and walked the reader through the building.

Jutting above Barcelona's skyline, the rosy colored towers could be the turrets of a transplanted Disneyland castle. Or a fantastic suspension device from a children's playground. Or the scaffolding of a movie set. Surely not a cathedral. But the sparkling pink towers do rise from a cathedral—La Sagrada Familiar, the Church of the Sacred Family, architect Antonio Gaudi's unfinished masterpiece.

. . . Visitors enter the church through a vestibule that resembles many other commercially successful places of worship: admission is charged; signs in four languages advertise a multimedia documentary about the building for an additional fee; a sales clerk offers souvenirs and postcards; the visitor's registry has comments in a dozen languages.

But beyond the vestibule, the similarity disappears. The nave, the choir, in fact the entire heart of the cathedral is an open-air construction site. Great blocks of pre-cast concrete, stacks of tiles and numbered pieces are laid about, not unlike Lego pieces, waiting to be fit together. A closer look at the four landmark towers reveals they are not pink, but gray concrete cones that culminate in mosaic glitter. It is the light, filtered through Barcelona's air pollutants, that makes the towers appear pastel.

An elevator whisked us and other visitors to a bridge connecting the two center towers. . . . Figures from a dream menagerie—reptiles, amphibians, mammals—crawled up the cathedral's facade, part nightmare, part hilarious fantasy: A tortoise at the base of a column stretched its mouth in a gasp, a lizard curled back on itself, dragons stared. . . .

Note how many of the phrases in the travel journal were used verbatim in the finished piece. The generalized statements have been sharpened into visual details. The detached tone has become more personal and shows the reader what is unfolding. Comparing the building materials to Lego blocks continues the playground fantasyland image established in the opening sentences. The structured journal entry mentions the improved air quality in the elevated areas of the city as it affects the writer, putting the writer at the center of attention; the published article describes the colorful effects of the air pollution and focuses the reader on the cathedral while conveying the same information about bad air in a more interesting way.

ARTFUL WRITING

Travel writers should be striving to communicate elegantly. We are the filter through which experience passes on a path to the reader. Our job is to describe accurately what we see and feel, not just reprocess factual information that is important to economists or trade brokers or the tourist industry. As your experience grows, you'll make choices about which trips to take and whether you'll pay for them yourself, seek expense assistance from a publication or rely on free junkets.

While on a recent familiarization tour to Curacao, I kept my usual travel journal, writing down my experiences and observations. I didn't worry whether I wrote down all the facts that reached my ears, knowing this work could be dispatched handily at the library. I focused on what my senses told me.

Take a look at the journal entry written during and immediately after a visit to caves:

Hato Caves. tunnels going off into rooms beyond. ribs of limestone. domes on ceiling. delicate columns inspired as Gaudi. path built about 4 years ago. humid inside—water seeking lowest point. Iron ore on walls. Cathedral area pock marked vault wishing well. Bat chamber—skunky smell—be quiet so they can sleep. Wear sneakers; watch head. Religious fantasy faces in the stone. In cafe: Unico music box locally made, maybe guide will play contratempo. handcrank, 150 years old. 45 hammers. 8 tunes on each cylinder. still made by 2 people on Curacao, 1 person on Aruba. gentle old rhythms of time gone by. sounds of guitars plucked or piano. Cactus grow like bushes. Near airport—wind generated electricity—new project backup power.

The journal notes became this segment of a travel article about Curacao, which was published in the *Toronto Star*, January 29, 1994:

> Another kind of underworld is experienced at Hato Caves, a series of cool natural caverns near the airport. The tour guide embroiders the quasi-historical spiel with Amerindian legends and religious fantasy. In the bat room, visitors maintain silence so the nocturnal creatures can sleep.
>
> Out in the bright sunlight, there's a souvenir shop/snack bar and a peaceful terrace. Turn the hand crank on the authentic Unico music box and the 45 hammers plink out a medley of island tunes. (Some music boxes are as old as 150 years.) The mellow brown wooden box is as big as a modern juke box. Gentle rhythms of time gone by conjure up a room of two-steppers and waltzers.

Using just the material in these few pages of my notebook, the story could have gone in several directions: the geology of the caves, interviews with the artisans still making music boxes, the wind generation project and how it affects tourism, the varieties of cacti.

The entries were hastily scribbled phrases that would remind me during the writing phase of what the caves were really like. I skipped or compressed the details of how old the caves are, what Catholic saints the rock formations resemble according to the locals and how many years it takes for a stalagmite to form. That was my decision, to pre-edit my notes by not writing down everything I heard so that I could concentrate on the feeling of being inside the cave. Knowing I could easily research the statistics about the age of the cave and the lifespan of a stalagmite, I didn't pay close attention to the guide's lecture. I also discarded the notion of miraculous images seeming to appear in the cave wall. The idea didn't fit with my own observations—the cave wall looked just like a cave wall—and the guide's remarks seemed rather coy, as if he wanted to foster speculation of the miraculous.

However, another writer with a different story slant could turn that bit of information into a travel story. Some editors expect travel articles to contain the basic scientific facts about natural phenomena like caves, volcanos, rivers or deserts. Other editors would jump at the chance to publish articles that reported hitherto unknown sightings of the Madonna in a cave niche. Apprising yourself of the requirements for your potential markets will help you select details even during the initial journal writing stage.

You may be wondering how you can know your markets if you are just beginning to explore the possibilities of travel writing. One way is to read several issues of the publication you plan to write for. Do the travel articles focus on facts or impressions? Another way is to make preliminary market research calls. Chapter eight, on marketing, delves into these points. For now, though, a reasonable guide for your note taking might be to consider that your strongest potential markets are related to subjects that interest you. That way, you'll be motivated to pursue the story to a conclusion.

It's true that at the beginning, the urge to write about everything will propel your pen. Take a step back, though. You know you can't write about everything your see and hear. Focus on what interests you, what piques your curiosity. Your experiences drive the story line. Your information gathering will have to hold your attention and later on, when the piece is finished, the reader's. Packing in the facts for facts' sake won't make a great travel article.

The content of the travel journal is deeply important to your success as a travel writer. Scribble down the impressions in whatever form your mind delivers them. There will be time when you get home to construct elegant prose.

EXERCISE 1

Build a list of verbs that relate to the place you plan to write about. Forget the blank piece of paper or the cursor blinking a taunt at you from the screen. Just plunge in with a list of verbs, then nouns, then adjectives and adverbs. Brainstorm about the place, history, landscape, people. Whatever comes to mind. Think action! Use a pen and notepad if the keyboard intimidates. Or tape record yourself free associating about the place. Save this list of words. Writing is communication. Whatever method you use to communicate your experience is valid.

EXERCISE 2

Take inventory of materials that you've gathered that will help in the construction of a travel article. This might include journals from trips you took in the past, scrapbooks, sketchbooks, menus, receipts, expense records, photos, letters or postcards sent home. These items may trigger memories that will improve your story.

Using any of these artifacts, write a paragraph or two about what you remember about the scene, the meal, the journey, or purchase related to the tickets or menus or whatever you've saved. If you have saved lots of items, then keep writing your memories as they arise. Fill a notebook with the feelings and mind pictures stimulated by the postcards or photos. Keep going until you have exhausted your memory bank. You'll be surprised at the wealth of material you have. This notebook can be the beginning of a travel article!

EXERCISE 3

Learn to write a useful journal entry by strolling around your hometown. Take time during a lunch hour, on the weekend or after work. In your notebook, jot down many words and phrases—bright, active, sensual words—to describe the people you see, places you visit. Don't think about grammar, spelling, punctuation or sentence structure. Leave a few lines or some blank space between each entry.

EXERCISE 4

Practice making the transition from raw journal entries to useful sentences and paragraphs for saleable articles. In the blank space between the notes you took about people and scenes in your hometown, use the jotted descriptions and observations to construct complete descriptive sentences. To develop muscular sentences using a variety of structures, try to avoid using the pronoun "I" and start sentences without using "The." Find powerful verbs that propel meaning.

EXERCISE 5

Use the phrases and sentences to write a letter. Pretend you are writing a letter describing the place to a blind friend or to someone from another culture. Try the exercise again, but this time, write the letter to someone who formerly lived here who you want to return. Explore historical possibilities by writing this letter to a famous person who has influenced the town in the past.

EXERCISE 6

Write a four-page or longer letter to a friend explaining a day-trip or excursion you recently experienced. Or report the events of a single day during a longer trip. The letter should bubble with your impressions, reactions and observations. When you are satisfied that you've told everything you have to say, go back over the letter with a red pen and be an editor. Cross out any references that only the friend would understand: personal jokes, asides, names of people the two of you know, etc. What remains could become a first draft of a travel article. Be creative; use picturesque words and sentences with verve.

Writers who are stymied with writer's block, which I think arises from fear of failure, often fritter away creative time by writing letters. I've certainly written my share! You can bypass inaction by writing productive letters which could flow directly into your travel article. Send a copy of the letter to your friend and solicit a friendly critique of your descriptive prowess.

Chapter Four

STRUCTURE AND PACE

Travel articles have the double role of conveying hard facts and transporting readers through vigorous description. In this chapter we'll delve into how to organize the article. Techniques for using journal entries for detail and story line will be discussed and we'll explore ways of communicating facts without straying from the focus of the story. We'll also work on finding a dynamic lead and building story momentum to a satisfying conclusion.

After you've written a long draft version of your travel article, using your travel journals or what you've recovered from memory, it's time to organize the article and keep the story line flowing so readers (and editors) will stay interested. A capsulized version of what we will be attempting is: Show the story like a movie, don't tell it.

I know that's a big order for a beginner to accomplish in early attempts, but if you keep the phrase in the forefront of your mind as you write and hew to the principle of the phrase, you really will learn to write visually. And that is what travel writing is all about. Print the phrase on an index card and keep it on your desk or taped to the top of your computer screen. If you find yourself stumped for the next sentence, look to the "Show It" card, imagine a scene in your mind and paint it in words. If you concentrate on writing descriptions that create pictures in a reader's mind, you will be writing toward your goal.

The outline of a travel article resembles camera directions for a film script. Using movie-making terminology, we might describe the construction of the travel article like this. Open with a sensation-filled lead with a strong hook to grab the reader's attention. Close-ups ground the reader in the specific location. Use special effects to parachute your voice into the narrative in order to establish a point of view and develop curiosity about the story in the reader's mind. Why did this writer want to visit this place, readers are wondering, and what happens next? Long shots fill in the historical, geographical and factual background. Mix with wide panning description to show the landscape and daily life. More close-ups woven throughout the story show detail that activates visual imagination and the senses. The ending wraps up the story by referring to anecdotes, scenes or situations described earlier in the story.

STRUCTURAL ELEMENTS

Now, let's look at the structural elements individually. We'll look at examples of the paragraphs that show structure taken from two published travel articles, one on Ischia that I wrote for *The Washington Post* and the other, which appeared in *Travel & Leisure*, on Paris's La Coupole restaurant by Peter Mikelbank, who freelances from Paris. The articles are reproduced on pages 229-235.

The Lead Frame

Many writers struggle to construct a lead before writing the story. Other writers allow the lead to emerge after writing a first or second draft. A few writers leave buried leads which sharp-eyed editors extract and place at the top of the article. However, writers at the beginning of their careers can't afford to bury their leads. If an editor doesn't see the point of the story in a glance, when the first sentence is read, then it is unlikely the story will make the cut and be accepted for publication.

The lead may arise naturally as you begin writing, or you can wait until the story is finished and find the lead as you reread the piece. Like cream, the richest part of milk, the lead may rise to the top. If you are having trouble finding a lead, don't stop and struggle. Write on. It can be futile to search for the perfect lead sentence without a story underneath. Sometimes you need to read the finished or nearly finished story before you can see what the clever opening line might be.

A lead sometimes jumps from the story content to summon a mood or transport readers through time or space. Quotations are good openers for travel articles that handle historic material. Intriguing opening sentences set the tone for the article. A lead full of promise and strength will keep the text floating high for several paragraphs. Alert audiences deserve chiseled and finished text.

A lead sentence that bears no relationship to the paragraph that follows can be stylish, but a risky business. Traces from the lead really should be woven into the rest of the story and show up at the ending, too. Clichés do not usually make strong openings; however, later in this chapter, there's an example where a cliché image framed a successful travel story. Leading with a personal reference might work if the reader can easily identify with the writer. Disappointment lurks under lead sentences that plod predictably. Involvement fades. Only the numb reader continues.

Where does that lead sentence come from? There are writers who can't or won't proceed with a story until the most wonderful lead in the world sings "Write me!" Other writers are confident that the best lead sentence will emerge as the story progresses. It's a matter of personal taste, talent and tenacity. People who are willing to sit and scribble drafts until the right lead comes waltzing should do so if it works for them. Those more comfortable going ahead with the writing and dealing with the lead later will have just as much success. There is no set rule for finding a lead.

One thing is sure about the lead, though. You must find it. Chances are the lead will sell your piece. If there is a mushy opening or no lead at all, your story is inside the return envelope and on its way back home within seconds. Elements of the lead might be the kernel of your query letter. Some writers send query letters that sell with just the lead, ripe with style and mystery.

The lead is the brains of your piece. If it reads smartly, the rest of the story will snap into place. Once you find the lead and nail it to the top of your story, go back over the whole story and see how you can trim or tailor it to fit the lead. Maybe there will be a sentence or two that needs to be added deep in the text or close to the end that will reflect the lead and enhance its power. Tweak the language or punctuation in the lead itself. Break the lead into two sentences. Try out various ways of saying the same thing until you are sure the lead is really a leader.

One way to identify a missing lead is to read the text aloud, or have someone read it to you. If there is an obvious lead buried somewhere, it will have a natural glow that demands placement at the beginning of the article. More than likely, it will be a sentence or two that stands out as the essence of your travel experience or condenses many impressions into a provocative nutshell. It may be a nugget of local wisdom, a description of a singular person, a moment in time, or a commonly held adage about the location.

Whatever emerges and works as the lead will also influence the ending. So don't lock placement for that sentence just yet. If you lack the lead, but you've already written an ending, examine it for cues to constructing the lead. The opening and ending work well when there is a relationship. Not exactly like twins or a mirror image, because constructing the lead and ending too alike can get a bit precious. There should be a strong supportive resemblance of mood, diction and subject.

The visit to Ischia opens with a lyrical orientation and a dash of science:

> From the slopes of Mount Epomeo to the gardens and vineyards at its base to the hot springs along the north coast, the Italian island of Ischia is a testament to the afterlife of a volcano.

The hook is all in "testament to the afterlife of a volcano." Readers have to think about what a volcano's afterlife means, which in turn conjures images of roaring hot lava. For refuge, the reader races to the earlier words and images about gardens and vineyards. Curiosity should be aroused; how did the island get that way?

The story about La Coupole opens with a quotation: "There is never any ending to Paris and the memory . . ."—Ernest Hemingway.

Immediately, the reader is in Paris, thinking about the past, memories and Hemingway, ready to hear about the Lost Generation and the Jazz Age. The power lies in using a quotation from a readily identifiable source. Hemingway shares common ground with a wide range of readers.

Learning to write a lead that snaps a reader to attention is a specific skill that has much to do with storytelling, conversation, humor and timing. A lead should almost always be short and captivating. When the lead is lengthy, the reader is presented with too much information to absorb early in the article. People read travel articles for pleasure, so the writer might consider using a lead that eases the reader into the mood. Although the lead is the opening to the travel article, it doesn't serve the purpose of the "topic sentence" in formal composition. In the lead of a feature travel article, it's more important to intrigue readers than to inform them of the substance of the article that follows.

A strong lead might set up a situation or a conundrum that will be explained in the body of the article, such as "The search for the gold market ended at the bank." The lead might unequivocally establish the writer's perspective which will be developed through the piece, such as "I hate beaches." Perhaps the lead highlights a representative aspect of the place being described, e.g.; "Wind owns the outer banks of North Carolina." Sometimes the lead is a question or a quote, which invites the reader to continue by provoking curiosity, e.g.; "Do you know how to sleep in a tomb?" The words in the lead sentence are punchy and graphic. Boldness and overstatement tend to be more interesting than simple observations. A useful way to approach the lead sentence is to decide to write one that has never been written before. The lead in a travel article presents writers with an opportunity to play with words and images, to experiment with voice and tone. Remember, brevity is a significant quality for tight leads.

If a reader thinks "So what?" after reading the lead, it has failed. Weak leads rely on comparisons to other places or experiences which might not have meaning to the reader. "We had the time of our lives in Disneyland; the kids loved it too!" Long rambling leads that describe the destination are particularly annoying. "Nova Scotia, which means New Scotland, is an oblong island north of Maine tucked along the rocky Canadian coast." Similarly boring is the writer who uses the crucial first sentence to discuss why or when the trip occurred. "I traveled to France in March, the off-season, in order to avoid the crowds and experience Paris authentically." This description should unfold in the body of the article, while the lead should tantalize and invite. Bland statements, sentences that report the obvious or merely rework familiar concepts falter as leads. The words in a weak lead sentence lack snap and resonance.

If you think you need to boost finesse with the language, here are some ideas for improving strategy with words. Study the headlines and opening sentences in respected newspapers and news magazines to see how information is presented cleverly and succinctly. Develop an appreciation for classic spoken comedy routines. Read the dictionary to refine your knowledge of precise word meanings. Cultivate original conversationalists and practice telling stories and anecdotes.

Ground the Reader

Early in the travel narrative, engage readers by placing them firmly on the ground you are describing. In the first two or three paragraphs after the lead frame, the goal is to get the reader to see and experience the same place you, the traveler and writer, have been. Occasionally the writer can achieve this in the lead sentence, but usually introduces the reader to specifics about the location in the dozen or so sentences after the first. The grounding paragraphs tell where the article is taking place, show a panorama of the landscape complete with geographic characteristics or other surroundings, discuss the season or climate and any other details that help the reader understand the story environment.

Consider this opening for a travel destination piece:

> From the slopes of Mount Epomeo to the gardens and vineyards at its base to the hot springs along the north coast, the Italian island of Ischia is a testament to the afterlife of a volcano. In the summer, this verdant volcanic island across the bay from Naples swells with exuberant Neapolitans on weekend escapes and other Europeans in search of sun, sand and spa. But the rest of the year, when Ischia turns from frenzied to sedate, it is even more seductive.
>
> *L.P. O'Neil*, The Washington Post, *April 5, 1987.*

The reader gets geography cues right away (island, volcano, across bay from Naples). We know what Ischia looks like and why people go to Ischia (vineyards, verdant gardens, hot springs, beautiful surroundings), what they do there (beach and spa life, wine and food), and a hint of what is to come (off-season visits are more seductive).

Look at the lead from a story detailing La Coupole in Paris.

> La Coupole had become Paris' Jazz Age widow. The grand brasserie was settling into decline—a once-celebrated beauty whose increasingly thick lipstick was excused as a dowager's attempt to preserve an impression of youth.
>
> *P. Mikelbank*, Travel & Leisure, *July, 1989.*

The writer makes it easy for the reader. The location, a time frame and mood are conveyed right at the top of the story. We know we're at the famous brasserie La Coupole, in Paris. We know it was at its zenith during the Jazz Age and that the restaurant has been in decline since. By using the metaphor of an aging beauty, the writer alludes to La Coupole's racy history.

Bring in the Writer

Ischia's third paragraph introduces the writer's voice and suggests why the writer is visiting this place.

> We were staying with friends in Ischia Porto, the principal town when Holy Week began and the extended family started to return to the island. The daughters living in Milan, Modena and Ferrara came to help their mother cook special wheat and ricotta cakes called pastiera, a process that consumed the better part of two days.

Although not specifically stated, the reader can easily guess that the writer is visiting the friends in order to participate in the preparations and celebrations of Easter Week. Leaving a slight ellipse in the information chain permits the reader to think and draw conclusions, an essential ingredient in clever storytelling. Would the same effect be achieved if the sentence went like this: "We were staying with friends in Ischia Porto, the principal town, to celebrate Holy Week with the extended family who were returning to the island."

The story about La Coupole does not include a paragraph about the writer's purpose. The length of the piece and parameters of the magazine's format dictate a tight focus. The article was written for a department, or column, in the magazine, and the subject was the restaurant rather than the writer's experiences in the restaurant. No "I" is needed. However, the writer's voice shines through the prose anyway in the choice of historical legends, vocabulary and most especially through that strong metaphor of the aging Jazz Age beauty.

Take a moment to look at the complete story in the Appendix. Is there an opening where the writer's presence could be inserted in the story without damaging the flow? How about toward the end when the reopening of the restaurant is described?

Close-Ups

Building on the lead's grab, these tightly constructed paragraphs convey mood, tempo, smell, sounds, physical description. They also plant clues about the rest of your story.

After orienting the reader in a specific place, it's time to narrow content and visual description. Select visuals that richly define your experiences and perhaps include a few facts. The close-ups should be related to the ensuing story, so choose well.

Here's a close-up from the Ischia story:

> On Good Friday, some of Ischia's citizens joined local priests and bishops and sailed to tiny Procida Island, between Ischia and the mainland, where the local people donned Roman-style robes, taking roles to reenact Christ's procession to Calvary. This can be a grueling procession—penitents, transported by the rhythmic dialogue unfolding between the priests' chants and the dramatic prayers and cries of the crowd, sometimes flail themselves with ropes or sticks.

Following through on the reference to visiting Ischia during the off-season, the story unfolds with incidents surrounding the Easter holiday. Instead of describing a church service, the scene stays outdoors, focused on a procession of penitents which was far more visually affecting and unusual. Accessible to anybody, the procession caught the spirit of a religious service without bringing the story inside a church. It gets the flavor across without making an opinion on the worship ritual, which is inappropriate for a travel article.

And at La Coupole, a detailed close-up:

> When "Monsieur Rene" Lafon opened the restaurant-cafe-dance hall in 1927, its awning was a brash red skirt on a broad terrace at the center of Montparnasse, the lively bohemian district. The newcomer's distinctive neon signature and frosted curls promising "Dancing" and "Bar Americain" attracted the quarter's young moderns. Legends and scandals followed.

The writer has the delicate job of transporting readers across the decades. He has described the restaurant as it was in order to communicate the mystique of La Coupole. The metaphor of the gallant faded beauty of the opening sentence continues: "brash red skirt . . . neon signature . . . frosted curls." The stage is set for the next paragraphs by teasing hints of legends and scandals.

Long Shots

Pull back from the close-ups for a few paragraphs and word paint in a broader way the history, geography or other specifics necessary for the unique story you are telling.

A wide-angle long shot paragraph from the middle of the Ischia story conveys history and geography:

> The island's fertile soil supports family farms as well as small market gardens. Before the early years of this century, when tourists began to include Ischia on the Grand Tour, most Ischians earned their livelihood in the olive trade. But around 1900, many olive growers began to replace their groves with more profitable vineyards.

Now, take a big screen look, the fourth paragraph, at the history and background of La Coupole:

> The appeal was not the simple fare (cassoulet, curry and seafood) but the magic circle, constantly spun wider. Dali, Man Ray, Chagall and Calder had favorite waiters; other neighborhood artists passed among tables sketching diners. Cubists, surrealists, dadaists and the Lost Generation writers claim corners of the legend.

Wide Panning Shots

To show the landscape and way of life, a travel story includes broad-brush description to fill in the background for readers. The pace of these cuts from long view to close-up, broad view to detail should vary, but not so often that the story rocks wildly from scene to scene. The end of one paragraph should flow easily into the beginning of the next. Learning how to properly pace a story takes some experience. The reader should feel guided and cared for, not shunted abruptly here and there for a quick scene. Try to linger on a few key scenes.

> Ischia Porto is the island's principal town, linked by a modern road to the three main beach resort towns of Casamíccciola, Lacco Ameno and Forío. Most of the 14,000 island residents live along the north coast, while the farm land and country villages are concentrated in the southeast.

Although the article about La Coupole is about one room, a

restaurant, there are still broad descriptive segments which paint a picture in the reader's mind.

> Resembling a large art deco room on an ocean liner, La Coupole's dining area casually achieved a crossroads-of-the-world reputation. It was an informal late-hours place where actors and kings met Rothschilds and rock stars beneath 24 frescoed columns—painted by the likes of Léger and Kisling in lieu of paying their tabs.

Ending

Think of the travel article as a piece of weaving. Through the piece, certain images or themes continue. That's the story line. In the Ischia piece there are several continuing threads: escaping the frenzy of Naples, Easter Week celebrations and the family. In the piece about La Coupole, the metaphor of the aging beauty unites the story elements.

The Ischia piece ends like this:

> Our sojourn under the fair skies of Ischia was the perfect remedy for the busy chaos of Naples. When it was over, we stood on the top deck of the ferry chugging eastward to the mainland and looked back at Ischia wrapped in a seafarer's sunset—red sky at night, sailor's delight.

The ending for the Ischia piece doesn't quite capture all the elements in the story, but it is rich with mood. It provides a literal type of emotional and physical ending because it describes a departure. And there is a reference to the chaos of Naples, a point raised in the opening. Perhaps the episodes with the family could have been referenced by expanding on "Our sojourn" or replacing "When it was over" with more descriptive concepts.

At the end of La Coupole, the writer again uses a quotation, this time from the present.

> "It's not the decor or food that makes La Coupole special," says one Parisian, leaning across a table in the revived shirt-sleeves-and emeralds atmosphere. "It's her conviviality that's unusual."

The romance is there. Who can read the words "one Parisian, leaning across a table" without flirting with sexy images? And the theme of the aging beauty revived finds a resolution in the final line. Like a lead, the ending can stray from the specifics of the story. If the paragraph evokes ambience, provides emotional or visual closure, or answers questions raised in the story, then the goal of wrapping up the story is accomplished.

CREATING A STRUCTURE

Now that you've gone over a couple of travel articles and seen how certain paragraphs accomplish what a camera does in a movie, we'll look at other aspects of structure in travel writing, expanding on the points discussed above. Structure also is created through the story line or narrative, the thread or threads of visual image or topic that run through the whole piece.

Knowing the basic structure of a travel article is important. You can't bend or break the rules until you know them. When I started, I analyzed published pieces, paragraph by paragraph, to determine how the story was told. I read a travel piece, about Tunisia I think, and jotted down on a legal pad what happened in each 'graph. Present time, geographic location, facts about the place, present time, flashback of the author's voice telling why the author is there, present time, historical information, anecdote in present time, historical facts and so forth. Striving to duplicate that structure, I wrote a travel article about Algeria which I had recently traversed by car. It was a coincidence that the two countries are adjacent.

Internalizing a structure enables the writer to bend the rules, to expand at length in an introductory anecdote, to digress with a personal association, to experiment with style. The order of close-ups, long shots, historical detail, flashbacks, etc., is completely variable according to the writer's urge and the expectations of the editor it is destined for.

A skilled writer will weave in the crucial points that the reader hungers to know: where, when, who, why, how, what. Remember a travel article's structure resembles the traditional elements of a news story, so you'll play with the order of those reliable questions.

WHERE = the place, grounding the reader in geography
WHEN = the season, grounding the reader in time, climate
WHO = the writer, to bond and identify with the reader
WHY = reason for the trip, the motive, also to identify with the reader

HOW = the process of travel unfolding, framework and story line

WHAT = the story detail, anecdotes and facts

Once the structure and the cinematic directions discussed in the two articles above have been assimilated and are fixed solidly in mind, the writer develops the skills to cover all the expected ingredients in a travel story. The temptation is always to "tell my story" as it happened. Linking the events as they happened in real time doesn't craft a story, however.

By creating a strong, organized structure—a conventional structure—you let editors know you are fluent in the technical basics of the trade. An article that rambles on about personal forays and ignores the need to inform readers early on in the text where they are and why they are there creates doubt in an editor's mind. Can this person write travel articles at all, wonders the editor? There isn't anything here to convince me this is a travel article. Reads like a personal reminiscence. Self-indulgence in the name of art is often just poor writing.

Of course, the precise order of the orientation paragraphs is a matter of individual style. Travel writing has a formula, the structure, but the writing shouldn't be predictable. The diction and words should soothe or challenge, not send readers to sleep.

THE WRITER AS PLAYER IN THE STORY

Beginning writing students ask how they can manage to tell the story from their point of view without having every sentence start with "I." Others wonder why newspaper editors shun first-person accounts of trips but do publish travel stories with the writer's voice figuring in the text. There is a difference between a first person travel story and a travel story in the author's voice.

This is how I explain it. The first-person account of a travel adventure written by the earnest novice relies on the chronological order of events or the purpose of the trip or simply the random events themselves to provide structure. Since the prose isn't elegant enough, generally speaking, to compensate for the absence of structure, the piece has a hollow feel; no voice, just the plaintive "I" moving around in a new place seeing and doing things.

The travel story with real structure doesn't have much room for the "I" to express itself in the first person. Too many other elements have to be communicated—the grounding of the reader, the close-ups, the wide-angle description, the history and geography. As we learned above, during the summary of camera directions, the writer's "I" has one specific place to appear after the reader is grounded and give the "why I went" signal for the trip's purpose. Then the writer almost disappears, although occasional reappearances that don't intrude are allowed.

So, the reader knows where the story is happening. How did you get there? This isn't the time to explain which airline flies to the destination being discussed in the travel article. Nor which road you drove or how you gassed up the car and checked the oil. Helpful details like those are usually contained in an information sidebar or box that accompanies the article. Such specifics can be woven into the text, but most are distracting when you are telling a gripping story. The question is really about why you are there.

Explaining *why* you are there may give readers their own motivation to travel to the same place and certainly a reason to continue reading. Share your travel motivation to heighten identification and gain reader sympathy. You want readers to feel friendly toward you, and to think that they too could be in Tanzania or Toronto, feeling the same thrills, discomforts, curiosity or disorientation as you are now communicating.

Many articles present information in a straightforward way, with the writer never making a cameo appearance. However, some of the best contemporary travel writing introduces the writer early in the story. The writer continues as a player in the action, where appropriate. For the duration of the story, the writer becomes the reader's guide and pal. The reader learns why the writer went to this place, how the writer felt and interacted. Although the writer's presence is not the focus of the story, judiciously worded explanations of the writer's point of view help tether the story flow. Telling the story with the writer as player helps strengthen structure.

Think about how you talk to a close friend about your trips. You the traveler have a role. Things happen to you, you participate in daily life at the travel destination. When you describe the trip to a friend, the narrative dominates and then you launch into an anecdote that involves you. In the written version, a tension exists between the personal events selected to reveal the writer's personal story and the background knowledge and panorama of the place, the narrative backdrop. How the personal anecdotal stories are presented makes the difference between an it-happened-to-me monologue and a thrilling travelogue.

UNFOLDING THE STORY

After locating the reader and filling in the broad brush of necessary information, the nuggets of the story unfold. Only you can choose what details go into your story. You want to paint a portrait of the place and might include some of these elements, displayed through your observations, mixed with facts. The details will show the reader what the place looks like, how the people live, what you observed. The elements you select will depend on the type of travel article you are writing—the size, geography, population, founding history, tribal beliefs, cuisine, religious traditions, agricultural products, trades and arts, climate, color of the dirt, system of government, and on and on. You must realize by now that there will always be too much material available. Part of the travel writer's skill is omitting information that is already widely known.

Let's say you're writing a travel story about New York City. No need, really, to replay the founding history or comment on the size of the population. Don't waste structural links on information that doesn't add to the story. On the other hand, if the travel story focuses on the impact of the huge population on you, the lone visitor from the hinterland, you may want to lead the story with the numbers. "New York City on New Year's Eve and it's eight million to one. I'm the one, overwhelmed and waiting for the clock to strike twelve." The population detail works in this story; in another it would be dead wood.

Continuing to write this hypothetical New Year's Eve story in the Big Apple, you'd cull details that supported the story line of being one against the masses, finding examples from your journal and memory of your woebegotten self, wandering through the tidal wave of humanity that culminates in Times Square around midnight. Maybe the clock theme could help determine what anecdotes you select, or, more likely, you'd notice while rereading your travel journal, that while in New York you were ruled by the clock and that's what led you to put the image in the lead. The allusion to sports scoring also suggests that the body of the story would contain elements that relate to scoring, victory or loss. The lead might be written first or crafted after a careful look at the incidents that are available to be put into the story.

How do you figure out which details go in and which are omitted or saved for another story? You already know the answer: practice, practice, practice.

Just the Facts

Facts are not seasoning to be sprinkled randomly through the text. They should relate and support your article and be necessary to your article. Sometimes facts can be the nucleus or turning point of a article. The almanac or encyclopedia may describe certain customs or weather conditions that your firsthand experience belies.

In the place-specific or destination story, though, idle fact-dropping is no more interesting than name dropping at a cocktail party. Tedious, in a word. Usually it takes a skilled stylist to use bald facts to steer a story; writers like humorists Dave Barry or P.J. O'Rourke come to mind.

Check out chapter six for the scoop on fact finding and how to use facts in your travel article.

TAKING A DRAFT VERSION TO COMPLETION

Compare the published and draft versions of the lead to an article about taking tea at the Ritz Hotel and with a rickshaw driver in Agra, India.

Published version:

> "Tea! Thou soft, thou sober, sage, and venerable liquid . . . to whose glorious insipidity I owe the happiest moments of my life, let me fall prostrate." Colley Cibber, "The Lady's Last Stake," 1708.
>
> This particular lady isn't quite at her last stake, but she can sing the praises of tea. I am thinking of two very different teas, one served in India, the other in London about a year later. Both were rich in ceremony and human connection, though vastly different in circumstance and location.
>
> *L.P. O'Neil,* The Washington Post, *January 20, 1991.*

Draft version:

> Taking tea is accepted the world-over as a social pleasure that refreshes the spirit as much as the palate. More people drink tea than coffee, beer or designer water. The shared

ritual transcends social status and income. Tea erases economic borders and binds wealthy London socialites to New Delhi beggars. A properly brewed pot of tea is rich with ceremony—the pre-heated pot, the measured leaves, the boiling water poured just so—whether the cuppa' tea is prepared in Soho or Kenya, Sydney or Kuala Lumpur.

The published version immediately involves the reader with the writer. Readers know they will be reading about (and traveling with) a woman who likes to drink tea. Specific references are made to the places that will be discussed in the story, grounding the reader early in the story. The paragraph goes on to create enticing questions in the reader's mind: What were the "vast differences" of the teas in London and India? What kind of "rich ceremonies" were experienced? Who else participated in the "human connection?"

In the draft version, more factual information is presented: "more people drink tea" than certain other beverages; "the pre-heated pot" and other details of making tea; "taking tea is accepted the world-over. . . ." But the writer is absent. The notion that tea is universally enjoyed and thus levels economic and social borders is presented impersonally. Maybe too much information is conveyed, leaving the reader with no questions that the story promises to answer. References to exotic places where tea is drunk does create a teaser for the reader, but a false one, because only Agra and London are actually discussed. Rather than grounding the reader and letting the reader know the location of this story, the introduction of other places confuses story focus and ultimately weakens structure.

Telling What Happened

Next, show what happened, but not so simply as . . . and then I did this . . . and then I saw that. . . . You've gained the reader's trust and attention by briefly introducing yourself and your reason for traveling. Now you have to back your*self*, the overreaching "I" or "we," to a minor role in the text. The story isn't really about you anymore, it's about the place and what happens there as shown through what you saw and experienced.

Readers want personal observation from an acute eye written with flair and contemporary voice. Stilted sentences, each one grammatically matched to its predecessor make for tepid, if technically correct, writing. Strive for voice, a narrative that includes yourself and your observations without relying on the pronouns "I, my, we" which can distance the reader.

These close-up scenes from "A Tale of Two Teas" allow the reader to step into the writer's shoes and experience the immediate surroundings. The writer is still present, but the reader has assumed the writer's eyes.

> Tea at the Ritz Hotel does have class. Under the high ceilings that simulate celestial heavens, the Palm Court conveys the illusion of spaciousness and wealth. The ballet of the tea service begins with waiters adjusting their cuffs and jackets and polishing the silver plate trays while guests settle themselves and eye one another with airs of expectation. To stately Britishers and tourists alike, this is life as it should be.

Later in the story, the writer has tea in Agra with a rickshaw driver. The writer is present, but not self-involved.

> At the tea shop, other customers slid away from the only bench to make space for us. A man who looked like a young Marlon Brando chatted with the proprietor, then left in a hurry. Children smiled and chirped, "Hello, lady."

STRUCTURAL GIMMICKS

There are so many ways to tell a travel story. Finding the right story line for you, one that is also a strong and unusual story line, is important. The story line is the spine on which the anecdotes or details of travel will hang. Earlier I used the comparison to a piece of weaving. The story line or several lines run through the whole piece and give readers, literally, something to hang on to. A vague or weak story line fades out or disappears when the writer rambles, strays off the topic, introduces too many variables and gabs about extraneous information. Think of a person talking who interrupts to discourse on a tangent, then returns to the main topic, strays to an unrelated anecdote, introduces another topic and strays from that one. Distracting, isn't it? In your travel writing, you will eventually learn to play with several themes or story lines in one article, but as you are learning, try to confine your details to a designated path.

You have many options available for mapping out a story, always using the basic movie camera directions explained at the opening of this chapter, but utilizing different themes. The story could have a geography focus and use the ecology or geologic evolution of a place to structure the travel experienced in the present. Or it could use a historical focus with flashback type description as in the story about La Coupole. Follow the footsteps of a historical figure. Use the built-in pattern of a celebration as the foundation for the story, one of the story lines in the Ischia piece. Tell the travel experience as a slice of local life as the Ischia piece also accomplished. Focus on food preparation, another process that allows for digression to tell the needed background details.

Using Clichés

Elsewhere in this book, you will read that clichés should be avoided like the plague. And that, savvy readers will recognize, is itself a bounder of a cliché. Perhaps a place is so thoroughly identified with a fact that it becomes cliché, "The rain in Spain falls mainly on the plain," "Bombay teems with crowds," "The jungle is steamy." Brave the pitfalls; write a travel story revolving around a cliché. You risk overdone images and well-worn anecdotes, but by sticking to your own experiences, you could emerge with a vigorous piece of writing.

When I proposed a story about searching for the underworld in the once notorious capital of vice, Singapore, the travel editor at the *Arkansas Democrat* (now the *Arkansas Democrat-Gazette*) audibly perked up. Singapore has such a squeaky-clean public image that a contrast to its past reputation is an obvious story mission. However, my angle was a tad different. A woman would be hunting for the remnants of waterfront iniquity that once made Singapore a lonely sailor's favorite dry dock.

> When the airless Singapore day fades into the humid night, the veil of sin descends. The red lights glow, the music pulses, opium burns and curtains are drawn. At least it used to, street-corner sages tell us.
>
> *L. Peat O'Neil,* Arkansas Democrat, *March 25, 1990.*

I found that the cliché had long ago evaporated. Today's Singapore is a sleek, prosperous, firmly regulated society. Its mainline vice: conspicuous consumption. By using a cliché as the frame for the story, I summoned dormant images from readers' subconscious; all those black-and-white films from the 1930s and 40s, spy novels and Somerset Maugham stories.

WRITING THE LONG DRAFT

Are you ready to write a long draft? Perhaps you've already started writing based on what you've learned in earlier chapters. I'll bet you have several two- or three-page drafts, forays into the world of travel writing. Or maybe you even have a long piece that you consider finished. Just for the sake of exercising your emerging skills though, take the time to really run the distance and write a long draft.

Block out at least an hour at a time. It may take several sessions to recall enough material for a full draft. Get comfortable. Close your eyes and think deeply about the journey you want to describe: your last vacation, a weekend getaway, a visit to relatives who live in another town. You could even think about one episode from the trip or a specific incident you experienced while traveling. Once you start getting images in your mind's eye, as soon as your memory starts flashing thoughts and concepts, start writing.

Describe everything you remember about a single situation. Sit yourself down in that cafe again and explain it to a blind child, spelling out the confusing and strange and bizarre, noticing the simple and ordinary. Describe the too-tight fit of a waiter's jacket, the stain of coffee across the lapel, the frayed cuff on the elderly lady's suit, the heat of sunlight outside the shade of the parasol, the sweat on the beer glass, the spilled espresso absorbed by the paper on the wrapped sugar cubes, the marks of the chair slats on the bare legs of the tourist as she leaves, the rattle of newspapers.

This is an exercise in training visual memory and selecting detail that shows a story so you don't have to say it. Will you use all this draft material? Probably not in one story, but somewhere you will. Once the scene is pulled from the memory etching in your mind and written down, you can use it. For a writer, experiences stored in memory are potential; experiences on paper or computer disc are reality. Don't fret if you've found the draft writing process difficult. Of course you have travel journal entries to rely on. Perhaps you transcribed your journal or selections from it after you read the discussion of travel journal writing in chapter three. Whether you write a long draft from memory or transcribe the journal entries that struck you as important at the time you wrote them, you will be jump-starting your travel article by keeping at it until you have many draft pages of writing. It may take you several sessions, or you may get it all down at once.

There are two reasons for writing a long draft. You'll have lots of material to select from as you choose details to tell the story. You'll feel a sense of accomplishment. Twelve pages of draft material churned out in a couple of days or a week of steady focused writing are more useful to a novice writer than two pages of highly polished writing. Why? Because an inexperienced writer's idea of polished writing might not be. Better to spend your time practicing the act of writing and committing your thoughts to paper than shining away at paragraphs that weren't outstanding to begin with. For now, aim for quantity; the quality should develop later.

Look at the actual journal entries and the draft when you start selecting incidents to construct the story. How you recorded the entries might jolt your memory; for example, a hastily written passage where the ink is running might remind you that the day was rainy, a detail you may have neglected to transfer to the story and just might be significant. You'll have to decide. The point is that the journal entries support the story line you've chosen and every incident you thought worthy of writing down deserves considering for the final story. Even if your travel log is just a notebook of jotted expenses, odd anecdotes, or a word or two about something you thought significant; it will be useful in writing the draft.

To speed up the writing process, I put almost every travel journal entry into the transcription and this usually serves as a first draft. Typical omissions include personal reflections, events or dreams that don't explain or enhance the travel story. Then I take the long transcription and mark it up, improving the language, crossing out extraneous information, looking always for the story line. Sometimes the story doesn't emerge until two or three drafts have been worked over. There have been stories that remained locked into a dull format for months until I reread them and saw that while the description was crisp, the underlying story lacked energy.

Draft after draft, there are travel stories that take time to emerge fully. Be patient and stick with your goals. If the draft you are working on seems to be stagnant, put it aside for a few weeks and crank out a long draft about another travel experience. Jumping from story to story may seem unfocused at first, but actually the change heightens your attention, and working on another project may improve your writing style. Even though the writer is the same—you—the subject matter will be different, and this should inspire your writer's pride to find new ways to tell the story. Each piece we write teaches us and influences our creative faculty.

EXERCISE 1
Words that convey extra meaning.
Write descriptive phrases, using adjectives and nouns that do double duty.

Example: To communicate the sensation of skiing in a driving snowstorm, consider these descriptive packages:

fluffy snow
cottony snow
puffy snow
or
knife cold snow
ice white snow
deceitful fluffy snow

All snow is fluffy, cottony and puffy but the second group of words communicate more than description. They convey physical feeling. The words work harder, putting the reader inside the writer's ski boots.

EXERCISE 2
Alone in a metro or train compartment late at night, you doze off, then realize the train has halted and the lights are flickering. Construct half a dozen phrases that communicate your startled state and the stopped train. Search for words that suggest fear and concern.

Examples to get you started:

The train hurtled into the threatening night; I dozed, unaware.
My sleep and the train died at the same time.
The train wheels ceased their lulling rhythm and my sleepy brain jerked alert at the soundless alarm.

EXERCISE 3
Construct an outline of scenes.

Using the movie camera directions described at the beginning of this chapter as your guideline, work with your long draft or transcription of travel journal. The typescript or printout should have wide margins to accommodate written notes or use stick-on notes. Read through the draft and label scenes. Which are close-ups, which are the long shots, which are wide panning scene shots? Mark where the reader is grounded. Mark where the author's voice enters. At the beginning, you may find that you've written only close-ups, descriptions of specific buildings, scenes or people or things you saw, and wide angle shots, general observations that sweep across the landscape.

If you have other typescripts of travel articles you've written, go over them and label them with the camera position they represent. Do you have more of one kind than another; for example, all close-ups?

EXERCISE 4
Selecting appropriate detail/Selecting relevant, intriguing facts.

Using the same typescript and a different color pen, or make a fresh copy if you prefer, read over the story and analyze what kind of story details you have to work with. If there are so many paragraphs or subjects that you can't find a focus, make a grid to analyze the material. On a separate piece of paper list general headings like animals, buildings, local people, plants, food, street life and so on. Obviously, you'll tailor the headings to the subject matter in your draft article. So, if the story is about a group horseback riding tour on a Cape Cod beach then the headings will reflect that—horses, tack, stables and outbuildings, people in the groups, the guide, plants, ocean, etc. Then write down these headings next to each anecdote or paragraph or however you have divided the story elements. When you've finished labeling, go back and read the headings.

To continue the example of the horseback riding tour, are there more headings about the people in the group than the horses? Do you have more anecdotes that feature the guide's salty personality than the scenery and the ocean? Use this analysis to figure out the story line. If most of the draft notes focus on the horses then the story line will revolve around them, although you'll use selections from the other details to keep the story interesting. This analysis technique may seem overly simplistic and obvious at first, but by breaking down the draft material into labeled paragraphs and anecdotal units of specific detail, you now know what building blocks are available.

EXERCISE 5

Write sentences that explain travel situations you experienced relating to buying tickets; long distance transport, theater, bus, metro, or any kind of tickets or permits for travel. Start the sentences without using any personal pronouns, including "I" or "we," but make sure the reader knows why you are there.

Example: The line to the desk for exit permits swelled and parted for the woman with the mud-stained backpack and a Labrador on a leash. That was me cutting the queue, intent on getting Barkley through customs before his vaccination expired.

EXERCISE 6

Write sentences that quicken the pulse of a story. Use action verbs. Do not use any tense or form of the verb "to be" (I am, you are, he is, I was, you were, etc.). The sentences describe people in a public place—a market, city hall, the beach, etc.

Examples:

1. Ripping aged leaves from heads of cabbage, the balding market vendor whistles an aria from Verdi. Shoppers pause and pretend to consider the vegetables, but their hearts thirst for the opera.

2. San Francisco's North Beach lacks sand and surf, but the local bohemians parade a fair amount of skin. Fashion comes in two colors here, black and leather.

EXERCISE 7

Write with a descriptive voice without starting sentences with the pronoun I. Remember that you can communicate voice without using "I." Strive to write simple declarative sentences.

Example: Outside the train window, sagebrush chased dust across the red dirt desert floor. Sure was windy, but the passengers inside the snug dining car couldn't feel it.

Chapter Five

STYLE AND TONE

A writer's style is as personal as a signature, memorable as a face, subjective as a name. The writer's attitude to the subject matter and to the act of writing contributes to the development of style. A travel writer demonstrates style in the lead that grips, artful description that makes readers feel like they are accompanying the writer, and the inspiring or funny close that ties the story together. Along the way, clever turns of phrase, verbal jokes, allusions, metaphor, contrast, vocabulary, juxtaposition and other tricks of the trade will keep the story moving stylishly.

Before writing can be assessed as having style, it has to be clear and competent. And the person making the assessment, in this case, the writer herself, really has to have some standards of taste and a knowledge of what constitutes style. So, crack open a college-level grammar review textbook or read Strunk and White's *The Elements of Style*. Do the exercises in the grammar text and take a red pencil to your own travel articles. Trade articles with a writing friend and ruthlessly correct grammar and sentence structure.

Reading what other writers have said about style can be useful in identifying or cultivating your own. Discover a model of elegant writing by choosing from what accomplished writers offer. Take a look for yourself in John Bartlett's *Familiar Quotations* or H.L. Mencken's *A Dictionary of Quotations* to get a feel for the variety of opinions on what constitutes style. Select essays, memoirs and diaries of respected writers whose words have survived time's test. The works needn't be travel essays to be worthwhile in your self-tutelage. While you are at the reference shelf, look up "style" in a dictionary. You'll see some variation of this definition from *Webster's* dictionary: ". . . a manner or mode of expression in language

. . . distinction, excellence, originality and character in any form of artistic or literary expression."

Style can be breezy, ponderous, sympathetic, humorous, poetic, satiric, academic, comfortable and so on. Although writing style seems an amorphous quality, it is composed of measured elements. Selectivity of content is a basic ingredient of a writer's style. Originality of voice and expression—the point of view—conveys style. And of course, the quality of writing technique is crucial to style. In a way, style can't be taught, because it is so individual. But a writer can practice experiments with phrasing, improve vocabulary and absorb techniques used by other writers. A writer can learn what isn't stylish, steering around elegant variation, studied irony and purple prose. More about those traps later.

In this chapter, we'll look at the elements of style that show the writer's imprint on the piece and examine ways to nurture stylish writing.

CRAFTING STORIES WITH STYLE

The best travel writing evokes a clear and vivid sense of place. Accurate descriptions of a place contain illustrative details, anecdotes about the people, and experiences felt by the writer all laced together with a nod to history and geography. The travel writer's first editorial task is to select travel incidents that show the character of a place in a story.

Developing style in nonfiction writing is a lot like developing a point of view for a fictional character. The details you select to tell the travel story should demonstrate something of the character who took the trip—you. When you first start traveling and looking at the world with a writer's eye, there may be a tendency to see everything and write down too much. Since you enjoyed your experiences, you feel an urge to pack all the details into a travel story so the reader can have the same experience. This approach doesn't work. The interesting travel story is carefully composed of selected details that reveal the writer's sensibility through details that affected the writer's senses. By strengthening your ability to pull the illustrative details from your journal and memory, and tell them with a consistent and distinctive perspective, you develop your writing style.

Consult the richly colorful entries from your travel journal. Or cultivate your memory through triggering your senses and looking at photographs and write down the memory pictures after your trip (as discussed in earlier chapters). You are now ready to select entries that will form the basis of the article and express your style. Difficult as it may seem at first, not every observation you record in your travel journal will support the story flow, nor be interesting or useful to readers.

It's agreed then: Style is a matter of selectivity, individuality and quality. Review the anecdotes and scenes from your personal journal of travel experiences. If you've already written a draft of your travel article, read it and pretend you haven't been there. Do you know enough after reading the piece? Are you curious to learn more? Do you have the information to start planning a trip to the place?

Put yourself in the reader's place: What would you want to know if you were going to take this trip? Read what other writers have reported on the place. And, you have the travel journal to work with. With a wealth of material in the background, you can start to focus on story content.

Here you come, fueled with a love of travel and appreciation for varied cultures, and it's natural to want to share everything you've observed and experienced, but selecting the right illustrative events goes to the heart of style. You can even deliberately leave out information to pique the curiosity of readers. But don't trick readers; if you omit a detail that figures in the story line, with the idea of spurring readers to the end, then you are obliged to return to that detail and explain.

To develop your instinctive writing style, try to write as if you were narrating the story, speaking to an audience while pictures unfold. Select incidents and descriptive scenes that are consistent with your experience. What impressed you? Are you including an incident because you think readers will like it or because it is meaningful to you? You can't second-guess the reader. If the encounter or particular description flows with your story line and sticks in your mind, then it belongs in the narrative. If you love an experience, it expresses your style. Later, after the story is constructed, you'll again streamline the material. Like a sculptor, you'll chisel away excessive facts, you'll sand off the surplus explanations and adjective-heavy prose. You'll use verbs that show your story.

I cut my beginner's teeth on a travel piece for *The Washington Post* about an overland trip across North Africa. I had written freelance travel articles for small papers and magazines, but this was my first major sale.

Mysterious and exotic, Algeria and the surrounding region offered many story angles. Too many. Doing justice to the story of driving across three countries, camping in the wild, shopping in markets and meeting local people could fill the entire Sunday travel section. Writers rarely get that kind of space and as a novice, I didn't deserve it. Readers don't relish wading through that many pages devoted to one story. So, I had to focus.

First, I selected one portion of the journey. Algeria was certainly the least known country of the three, and by limiting my story to Algeria, I increased the article's market value. Travel editors are curious about stories from places off the beaten track. Also, the timing had to be right; Algeria hadn't been involved in political unrest or international incidents for several years. There was a window of opportunity for a travel article. Since the mid-1980s, however, Algeria has again been experiencing internal strife; a travel article about the region might not sell today.

In constructing the article, I selected anecdotes that would illustrate my story premise or thesis. I wanted to show that Algeria (sometimes portrayed in the news as a haven for political extremists and a potentially dangerous place for Americans) was a friendly country with warm, sympathetic citizens. I cared deeply about writing an accurate portrait of the people of Algeria. My personal style is rooted in developing and enhancing human connections and I tend to be impressed by small, unexpected acts of kindness. Thus, I strive to have my writing style reflect that orientation. I had no shortage of encounters with helpful strangers in Algeria, but a balanced story needs adversity too, so I deliberately included material that showed how difficult Algeria can be for travelers.

Here are the incidents that told the story: (1) during a frustrating and heated confrontation at the border about auto insurance, a guard exchanged money for us and gave extra so we would have enough to purchase obligatory auto insurance for the duration of our stay in Algeria; (2) reaction of local men to a foreign woman entering a cafe; (3) man walking on the road who called out a welcoming greeting; (4) young man who bought bread for us; (5) dairyman who provided a new bottle for milk because I had none for refilling; (6) shepherd who sang as he moved his flock around our tent at dawn; (7) boy who invited us to join his family if it rained on our tent during the night; (8) conversations in a store while waiting to buy scarce, expensive food; (9) women who sold eggs at the side of the road.

All of these incidents demonstrated how Algerians lived their lives and reached out to strangers. Many of the encounters served dual purposes. The first warns readers of the bureaucratic difficulties endemic in this part of the world. The second and ninth hint at the lifestyle of Algerian women. The sixth and ninth show rigors of rural life. The eighth and ninth provide information about tough economic conditions.

Other encounters recorded in my travel journal were used in the "Ways and Means" section of the story, the sidebar of travel facts that most travel editors require. My guideline for placing incidents inside the story or in the "Ways" section was this: If the item related directly to the story action of driving across Algeria, it would be fodder for the main story. If it was handy information for anyone going to Algeria, the anecdote was classified to the "Ways" sidebar. Some of the incidents that were appropriate for the main story, I chose to compress. For example, a meeting with the American consul was condensed to one sentence about how rare it was for Americans to camp in Algeria. Why omit the consul's useful comments about economic conditions and the complicated status of women? Because I had already identified incidents that showed the difficulty of obtaining food and the hardships endured by women. Better to devote the space to dramatic encounters with local Algerians than U.S. embassy staff.

Similarly, a conversation with an Algerian woman at the bus station became a note in the "Ways and Means" section on transportation options. She was well-informed about bus travel and had sound advice for visitors. I was tempted to include her in the story because she was one of the few Algerian women who relaxed enough to chat with me, but my interaction with her didn't provide a direct link in the story line about driving across Algeria.

Some of the material contained in the journal of this trip was completely omitted from the travel story. For example, I could see no useful purpose in describing an incident I saw in Algiers. There was a Soviet naval vessel in port one day and the foreign sailors were cutting a wide path for themselves on the promenade along the docks. They were also attracting the attention of several young Algerian women dressed in sleek French jeans. Their progress was observed by the groups of Algerian men lounging around lampposts and cafe tables. Feigned (or real) insults were exchanged and a few men pressed close to the sailors, but no international incident ensued. Sure, this was interesting to watch and had potential for illuminating the society, but it probably belonged in a story about the port of Algiers, not in a story about camping and driving in Algeria.

One way to test the interest value of your experiences is to give friends and family a rundown of your travels and note which anecdotes hold their attention. Compare what events you selected for your story with which ones elicited questions and deeper interest from your audience. Watch your audience and remember how they reacted.

Telling a lively story with flair is challenging work. In print, the task is even more demanding. There is no opportunity for eye contact, gesture or feedback from the audience. The onus is on the writer to keep the narrative moving at a consistent level of literary skill. Story momentum is easier to maintain when the links in the tale are all uniquely interesting. Hit the high spots, incorporating the incidents or experiences that elicited the most interest from the audience when you talked about your travels. Most of all though, you are selecting and defining what affected you and appealed to you. Personal writing style depends on confident, individual taste.

THE WRITER'S VOICE AND POINT OF VIEW

Style is a matter of tone and voice. Will you, the writer, mock yourself? Is humor your strong suit? Will the story touch a deep emotional nerve? Do you have cross-cultural bonds to establish or can you tell the funny side of experiencing other cultures? An anecdote can amuse or offend, depending on how the story is told. What is your attitude to the place you are describing? Your biases and opinions about your experiences there will influence the writing style that emerges as you compose the article. Were you changed? Disappointed? Surprised?

Establishing voice and tone early strengthens an article. Readers will want to stick with this voice because the tone is friendly or funny or smart. The words are cleverly chosen, juicing the reader's mind. Phrases that sound familiar resonate with the reader, making the reader feel included. There is no single correct writing style to achieve tone or voice. There is only the one right way for you to say what you know. The following examples were selected because each has a distinctive tone and you hear it immediately. They were written by travel writers who enjoy what they do and want the reader to be interested and entertained.

Some daring writers use a pun for an opening to establish attitude and voice:

> This is no mickey mouse enterprise. When completed, the amusement park and resort called Euro Disneyland will be one-fifth the size of Paris, family entertainment on a scale the continent has never seen.
>
> *Peter Mikelbank*, The Washington Post, *March 31, 1991.*

This writer pokes fun at herself:

> Scanning the Dutch countryside last month revealed, in addition to the typical windmills, bicycles and dykes, a somewhat more unusual sight: me in a car.
>
> *Jill Rigby*, The Toronto Sun, *July 29, 1990.*

> What a concept; two weeks in another town with someone you love and all the time in the world to explore their psyche and physique. Oh, and have fun.
>
> *L. Peat O'Neil*, The Washington Post Magazine, *January 12, 1992.*

Again, we hear a bit of humorous sarcasm. The voice seems like that of an acquaintance with the rhetorical question opening. The mood is established with the allusion to the romantic movie title *Two Weeks in Another Town*. There's fun in the alliteration with the psyche and physique. It adds up to a breezy, quick style.

Writing with style may involve shifts in time, perspective and mood, although not so often that the reader can't follow the story line. The writer may hint at what is to come, as shown below:

> It's Saturday night and the cafes and bars in the centre of town are packed. The Netherlands is playing England in an international soccer match and television sets draw crowds in almost every place.
>
> I've been looking for a jazz bar called Take Five. Just over the bridge, turn left, go about two blocks, turn right, you can't miss it, I was told.

So I have been walking along cobbled streets, through alleys, around corners, without much luck. It's about 10:30 and the sun has not been down for long. Some of the narrow, dark, side streets are devoid of traffic—not even a bicycle—so I move along quickly. In another city, I might be afraid but I have been assured that the streets are quite safe.

Donna Laporte, Toronto Star, *August 11, 1990.*

Do you hear the voice? This opening sounds like a letter from a friend: easy, familiar. The style is relaxed and chatty. The writer quotes the directions received earlier, shifting between place and time. But, this is how people actually talk; the voice is natural. You can see the scene, even if you don't know precisely where it is. And, just for the fun of it, the writer has put a clue in the opening paragraph (international soccer match) that you might expect will turn up later in the story.

Engaging writing establishes personal mood. Although this paragraph opened an article commenting on travel magazines, it would work with equal success at the top of a travel article about a man who breaks away from the pack and dares not to try and recover lost boyhood:

A man can grow weary of men's travel articles, and for a very specific reason: They are basically all the same article. The subject may be vineyard-hopping in Sonoma or kayaking in Norway, but what it's really about is a man pursuing the one fantasy all men share: that with a little money and time, a map and a Swiss army knife, we can recover the lost freedom of boyhood.

William F. Powers, The Washington Post, *November 6, 1994.*

These leads establish right at the start that a certain voice will tell the story. The reader knows something about the storyteller from the start. That familiarity takes the reader by the hand and says "Come along, you'll have a good time if you read me."

Style might involve what is left out of the opening, or a comparison to establish an understanding of what exists.

This writer uses what is missing to describe the setting:

Five golfers, each of whom can strike the ball brilliantly, are standing on the first tee at Tour 18, staring at the face of a lighthouse straight down the fairway. The hole is supposed to look like the 18th at Harbour Town, the great course at Hilton Head, only there's no ocean along the left side of the fairway, just a swamp, because we're not in coastal South Carolina but rather suburban Houston, in what used to be an oilfield.

Joel Achenbach, SMITHSONIAN, *August, 1993.*

Lively, bright writing keeps the reader surprised:

When the last ferry leaves the island, when the deer come out of hiding and the fog spreads like cream cheese across San Francisco Bay, the ghosts of Angel Island are said to gather at the old Nike missile site to resume their fighting— Miwok Indians, Russian fur traders, Spanish pirates, Chinese detainees and German prisoners of war.

Denis Collins, Men's Journal, *November, 1994.*

Fog like cream cheese? Surprising simile, but it works. When you cast about for an image to use in a comparison, be original, as this writer was. Steer clear of preposterous similes that distract the reader and detract from the story.

Stylish writing jolts curiosity:

A few times a year, I go looking for the good place. "Get out," the voice says. "All these parking meters, espresso bars, TV channels, people. Get out now."

William F. Powers, The Washington Post, *May 24, 1992.*

Bankruptcy is an awful thing. In 1990, it became an American brand of purgatory; many considered it a payback for an era of greed. For me, bankruptcy ushered in a time of personal grieving, searching and guilt. . . . At least I hoped for another chance. . . . And trail cooks spend a lot of time on their knees.

Patricia Lewis Sackrey, The Boston Globe, *August 14, 1994.*

OK, we're wondering after reading the example above, just what *is* the good place? The writer has gotten our attention. We know why he is traveling and what he is looking for. By elliptically contrasting the "good place" to parking meters, espresso bars, TV channels and people, the writer establishes a question in the reader's mind. Where is this place without cars, TV and people, and how can I get there?

And in another example, the question arises: What does bankruptcy have to do with a travel article? The reader is curious about how the road from bankruptcy led to being a trail cook. Note how humor lightens a potentially difficult subject. The writer calls bankruptcy "an American brand of purgatory" and summons the same metaphor with the phrase "trail cooks spend a lot of time on their knees."

IDENTIFYING BORING WRITING

How does a boring paragraph begin? Could this be one? Probably not, because you're already wondering just what kind of sentence introduces boredom. Though not the most original question ever asked, it does engage your mind. If the reader is thinking about the ideas presented, then the text doesn't fulfill the first element of boredom: lack of engagement.

Boring writing lacks surprise. The sentence rhythm is repetitious, the words are predictable and sound like other sentences and phrases that we've heard before. The next word or turn of phrase is what we expect and the writing risks losing the reader.

Boring writing lacks a natural voice. It is removed from the way people talk and think, and is self-conscious with a poky dedication to traditional phrasing or an artificial high-minded diction. At the risk of losing your interest, here are a few of examples of weak style:

> Upon completing our repast, we surveyed the piazza and strode with purpose through a throng of layabouts to the morning's artistic quest, St. Mark's Cathedral.

Perhaps this writer thinks he is a 19th century teacher on the Grand Tour. Unfortunately, scores of novice travel writers affect a style like this. Words that time and custom have relegated to infrequent usage (repast, surveyed, strode with purpose, layabouts, artistic quest) should be used sparingly in contemporary writing. Alliteration (through a throng) has its usefulness, but leaded into this already ponderous sentence, it has the effect of choking the flow.

> The rolling green hills of Prince Edward Island are all that a bucolic place should be.

> New Orleans is the capital of Jazz, a good time rhythm and blues town.

In both sentences, the end is a vague restatement of the first part, which deflates the image. Sentences that rely on generalities ("all that a bucolic place should be," "a good time rhythm and blues town") lack style and information.

The key to holding a reader lies in the construction of the lead and the next few sentences. What engages a reader's full attention? Ask yourself when you read travel articles: Do I want to continue with this writer or am I tired already? The top of the story sells your piece and grabs the reader. Use a gimmick, an anecdote, a story, a quote, some phrase with universal appeal. Ask a question, state a fact, inflame curiosity, be bold. The more original the lead, the greater the survival possibilities for the story. Before writing your own story opening, take a moment to review the section on leads in chapter four.

Of course the goal is to write lively and entertaining prose. Readers who are involved in the material expect to be served juicy text. And you, as the involved writer, should want to produce your best.

So, how about that boring paragraph? The sentences are constructed alike and sound similar. The writing style is flat and ordinary. The pace and tone rarely change. The vocabulary is limited and repetitious. The diction is pedantic and tired or thick and overwritten. The reader stops before the end. This paragraph is boring.

SELF-EDITING

Fancy adjectives, frivolous subjunctives and obscure personal witticisms are no remedy to flat writing. Humorous asides inserted whimsically with the idea that they create voice almost always fail. Elegant words are not necessarily the ones with the most syllables or snob appeal. Sometimes simple words, used with imagination, create a more unified story.

Now, fish out that story you've been working on this week. If you don't have a project in process, pull out a draft that you've set aside to work on later. Read the article aloud and listen to your voice. Better yet, record yourself reading and play the tape back for the true effect. Take a highlight pen and mark all the verbs. Make a list of them. How many are truly action words? Replace the verbs that don't demonstrate motion or activity. Rearrange sentences so they are in the active voice. Passive voice places the subject as the receiver of the action while active voice has the subject as the doer of the action. For example, I drove the car (active voice). The car was driven by me (passive voice).

Next, highlight the adjectives. Do they pile up before nouns like a chain reaction car crash? Knock off one adjective if there are two for a word. Are the adjectives specific or bland qualifiers? Does the adjective immediately summon a mental picture? Shift the descriptive work to the verb and the noun itself if the adjectives are overly familiar. English overflows with words exactly appropriate for every circumstance. Adjectival props show a reaching writer. Qualifiers sap the strength of a sentence. Are you comfortable and confident that what you are hearing is muscular, verbal, evocative, resonant English? Does the article need to be rebuilt or should it just be tuned up?

Polishing tedious material is not an editor's job. It's our job. We writers have the responsibility to ourselves and to our readers to craft prose that informs and enlightens, educates and inspires. Our writing is our self, our mind's expression. Let's resolve to shine our writing before sliding it into the mail chute. Guaranteed, no editor will be spending time wrestling with listless words and a thesaurus. The manuscript that needs that kind of work spends its shelf life inside the return envelope. Editors sometimes will suggest rearranging paragraphs, insist on stronger transitions, and help with continuity. They've also been known to make a few cuts, sometimes without even consulting the writer! But rare is the editor who will devote any time to helping a writer who is boring.

Developing a style, writing with punch, choosing simple, elegant words are a writer's heft. If they are really original words, written with verve, you get to defend them when editors want to change them. However, cooking up fantastic prose is work, even if you are saturated with talent and skill.

Life is being celebrated every day in countless different ways. The traveler is the go-between, bringing news of wondrous events to eager ears back home. The travel writer goes one step further, discovering, experiencing and then sharing impressions with an audience. Your description in the article expresses your wonder and the truth of your experience, but you must search for language that reaches a broad audience.

In trying to avoid flat writing, some novices assume the wide-eyed tourist's narrative. Sorry, no room for "Gee Whiz" in the travel writing genre. Examples might be: You're traveling and you see a fabulous sunset, an experience most humans on this planet have had. You rave about the colors in the sky, but what's so unique about a pretty sunset? Or, let's say you've never seen a certain activity—the changing of the guard at the presidential palace in Athens, or a fire-walking dance, or a pig roast. Though the perspective is personal, a keen eye for action and nuance and some knowledge of ritual archetypes and myths will bring balance to a story about cultural performances.

Perhaps some of your readers know these rituals well. Prune the "gosh" and "golly" type observations and language that expresses astonishment at what may be ordinary and commonplace experience. Just as you rigorously cut phrases rooted in prejudice, cliché and condescension. Artful understatement grabs more reader attention.

Sublime writing is not in all of us all of the time. But everyone who diligently plies the pen or keyboard will surely someday turn a magnificent phrase. Meanwhile, there are legions of efficient, interesting sentences informing and pleasing readers. Keep in mind that there are also lots of badly written, boring sentences out there, too.

You make the choice as you construct a piece. Will each sentence carry its share of the story line? Or will you overlook a few dead sentences, even though they weigh down and sink the piece? Learning to self-edit is perhaps the most difficult part of writing, but improving that skill is the fastest track to developing a recognizable writing style. Each time you sacrifice a marginal though beloved sentence, your style tightens and improves. The work of rewriting, cutting and moving sentences is the heart of the process of becoming a skilled, professional writer. Always pause to read aloud and listen for the continuity of the voice.

Settling for less than sublime writing does get the job done. After all, you want to get the piece finished and out to the editor who expressed interest in your query. There is a point somewhere between half-baked, lazy writing and the best writing you've ever done that will realistically be your median effort.

Strive for muscular sentences that carry a story on their shoulders. Editors don't call it "moving the story along" for nothing. With writing practice, training the imagination and reading selectively, the serious writer will create the oft outstanding, occasionally arresting and usually saleable piece. That's why reading excellent writing is so important. A unique personal writing style develops with its roots in literature.

FINDING THE RIGHT WORD

Precision in language is an art and a skill. Selecting words of determined meaning will toughen writing. For example, I've seen many travel articles that contain a sentence resembling one of these below. The writer obviously intends to communicate that the resort or destination has an array of activities. Because the presentation is flat and predictable, no meaning is carried in the sentences. No real information is conveyed. No image comes to the reader's mind; the words and space are wasted. It's the print equivalent of radio dead air. Take a look at these sample sentences. The goal in this hypothetical travel article about a destination resort is to inform the reader about the range of activities. Write a critique for each of these sentences.

1. Daily activities boards list a host of things to do here, including swimming, golf and croquet.
2. Daunted by the activities menu, I lazed by the pool all day.
3. What a fabulous array of things to do! I found activities for every taste, including the palate.
4. There are many activities such as sports, dancing and sun bathing.
5. Imagine a place where there's plenty to do for everyone.
6. You'll find sufficient diversion.
7. There's no lack of entertainments, whether you're a doer or a watcher.
8. Things are happening here. Lots of things, as long as they are all sports.
9. Visitors can choose from activities such as horseback riding, tennis, golf, swimming, croquet, water sports, aerobics classes, and just sitting back and watching the world go by.
10. At breakneck speed, we worked our way through the activities menu. By the end of our three-day marathon, we'd sampled twenty athletic diversions, not one of them in the pool.

Here are my critiques:

1. Questionable use of the word "host." A host is a person.
2. Stylish with use of humor.

3. Gushy writing. Could use the second sentence.
4. Unrefined, flat.
5. What's this, the land of volunteers? Everyone "doing" for everyone else.
6. Says nothing.
7. Ambiguous, could be improved.
8. Vague. Attempt at humor falls flat.
9. Laundry list and clichés.
10. Visual and communicates information.

Why do we need to use precise language? Because although description is intensely personal, the end product is intended for a varied audience. Striking, zippy language reaches a broader range of people and retains interest. You want your writing to endure, don't you?

Why settle for worn-out phrases when a personal imprimatur is called for? Hack out those dull clichés. A good test: If you've seen or read the same series of words recently, the phrase is lurching to the wrecking lot of dead metaphor. Don't drive clunkers; test drive fresh words and innovative comparisons. Elements of humor always win out over bland statements of fact. Audacity, boldness in point of view grabs attention. Don't forget exuberance and gaiety.

Writing is a visual process. Words catch the eye before the brain. A string of long, heavy words is difficult to read and retain. Short, brisk words paced in sentences that roll off the tongue are preferable to cumbersome, otiose, convoluted conjugations. A few well-crafted sentences will attract reader notice far more than long-winded bombastic material that overwhelms the reader.

Nouns are naming words and must be specific to show what is happening. Verbs are action words. But even action words can be inactive—passive voice verbs avoid responsibility for action by deflecting the source of the motion. Active verbs give momentum to a sentence. Readers can see the action by picturing a person, place or thing doing something. If you want to create visceral prose with tensile description, rely on verbs, not adjectives.

Using Foreign Words

Travel writers are painters trying to be both believable and creative at the same time. Travel writing has to appeal to people who have been to the place and to people who have never been to the place. Your idea about what makes the place unusual drives the story. The words you choose to express that experience elevate the quality of the story or doom it to the commonplace.

One way to capture the mood of a foreign place is to use words from that country in the text. Food, native dishes, special drinks featured in the story in the original language re-create an authentic mood. Some words like cappucino, espresso and baguette are in current use. Strive for words which create curiosity and ambience without being impenetrable. Brioche instead of round French roll; risotto, not rice in sauce; minestrone, not vegetable soup.

Explain foreign words with pronunciations in brackets or quotation marks once or twice in an article, but limit this format, as it can defeat a reader. If there are many foreign phrases in your story, make a glossary for the sidebar.

Words that are rich with sound, the he-haw-he-haw of European ambulances, vroom-vroom of motorcycles in a city street, the ka-thunk, ka-thunk of a train track, thuck-a-thuck-a-thuck-a of tires on stone-paved streets, add texture to the article. Try to jot down the sound that accompanies an experience, then you'll remember the ting-a-ling of a pedicab's bicycle bell in an Asian street or the chucka-chucka of helicopter blades over Hawaiian volcanos.

CONNECTING WITH THE READER

Enable readers to visualize themselves in your story. Use words with which they can identify. Keep your audience in mind. Know who you are writing for and use language appropriate to the subject matter. Remember that we writers are competing with other information sources—television, radio, computer bulletin boards, information databases. And we are writing for people with limited time and, in some cases, a disinclination to read. Writing for nonreaders who are in a hurry means that the text has to appeal quickly so that the reader will persevere. Because statistics tell us this average person doesn't read very often, that individual may not have a high level of attention or retention. I don't think this means you should "dumb down" as the educators say, but rather, smarten up. Use words that are stimulating rather than soporific. Make readers work, but not too much.

Help the reader along. Don't leave holes that raise distracting questions. Tweaking curiosity doesn't mean leaving nagging ellipses in the story line. As William Zinsser said in a lecture to Washington Ed-Press members in 1994, where each sentence ends, the next should pick up the thought and the story line. Don't leave readers hanging—take them by the hand along each phase of the story.

Sidebars and boxes help the reader get factual information so the story can concentrate on experiences and visual description. Use charts for cost comparisons or to explain information. Keep the story moving; don't get bogged down in lengthy explanations that the reader can grasp by a quick look at a table or graph.

If you throw in facts that rank size or frequency or some other characteristic, such as longest river in the world or oldest restaurant in Paris, put in a reference or comparison that is accessible to your readers. For example: a river so long that if it were straight it would stretch the length of the Mediterranean Sea; a restaurant in Paris that opened when George Washington was a young surveyor. If it's the second deepest lake in the world, note which one is the deepest. When a fact is important enough to include, define it fully so that the meaning supports the text.

LETTING THE READER DISCOVER

Readers of mystery novels will recognize this technique. The first three chapters of a mystery reveal clues and information that may provide the key to the solution. The travel writer can "plant" clues in the early part of the story to entice readers to continue reading. This isn't trickery, but rather a narrative device designed to heighten the sense of drama.

The lead for a travel story about Kamchatka, in the Russian Far East, shows this technique:

> When I found the spoon, I was walking behind Gorsha's lumbering beige horse, my heavy backpack roped to its saddle. I happened to look down and found a tablespoon with a pretty scrolled handle embedded in the soil. The spoon bowl faced up. I pried the spoon from the weeds and dirt and stashed it in my pocket, then scrambled to catch up with the group. It would be a while before I learned the meaning of this find.
>
> *L. Peat O'Neil*, The Washington Post *(to be published)*

If you do plant clues in the opening, make sure that you return to the information later on in the story. When a question is raised

in the reader's mind, it is only fair to supply an answer. To resolve
the unfinished question about the spoon I found by story's end, I
could write the answer within the story without specific reference
to the opening. Or, I could write, "Remember the spoon I found?"
and proceed to explain. How the answer is woven into the text is
a matter of a writer's style.

STYLES TO AVOID

Learn what isn't stylish and steer around writing traps such as
overwriting and overstating (purple prose), elegant variation (studi-
ously searching for synonyms), irony (a distancing device pointing
out incongruities between appearance and reality) and eccentrici-
ties in language (slang).

Overwriting

Overwriting, the so-called purple prose, seduces newcomers. Do
you write with the idea that the more words you pile on, the richer
the writing becomes? Think of all those descriptive words as fat
that need to be trimmed from sentences. Weigh your words. Do the
sentences seem flabby and circuitous? Are your valid and succinct
observations lost and obscured in the incoming tide of bubbling,
steaming modifiers, written in convoluted, compound sentence
structure with mixed metaphors and uncertain subordination, so
that no one can understand the defined, objective point to begin
with? Like that sentence you just read? Cut to the quick. Avoid
repetition; use simple expression rather than complex diction; select words and phrases appropriate to the material. Find a single
word to replace two or more imprecise words. Make word choice
appropriate to the material.

Cut out generalized catchall words like nice, fine, wonderful,
one of the most, among the best. Be specific: prim, porcelain, elec-
tric, riveting, midnight blue, crumbling. Verbs show, nouns tell,
adjectives focus or distract, adverbs qualify or confuse. Watch those
adjectives and adverbs for true meaning.

Be wary of stilted diction, pretentious words and artificial writing. A house is not an "edifice" or a "place of residence." Walks
and performances begin; they don't "commence." Precipitation is
rain, snow or sleet, not "inclement weather conditions." People
talk or shout; they don't "opinionate" or "discourse."

The quasi-English academic voice often affected by novice travel writers isn't a natural voice, unless you are a British professor musing about your peregrinations. Check your travel article for words that are pompous and out of place. Could you read this article to a group of friends and would they recognize your narrative style? Give it a try; read a few of travel articles including one of your own to friends and don't reveal who wrote them. Could they identify your work by listening to the narrative voice?

Elegant Variation

Do you find yourself searching for synonyms for words because you don't want to repeat the same word over and over? I do, because mining the language for ever more clever ways to say the same thing is part of the challenge of writing. Using synonyms is an accepted stylistic tool, but the search for a different synonym or descriptive phrase for every word in an essay can easily be overdone. This is called elegant variation. You've fallen into this stylistic trap when words trip over themselves in an effort to be different from their earlier appearance in the text. When the effort to find a different word becomes overworked, awkward and obvious, then the writer has gone beyond conscientious stylistic variation into the dreaded elegant variation which isn't elegant at all.

Here, I've rewritten the opening of a published article so that it is an example of elegant variation:

> Mount Rinjani, a dormant volcano, is swathed in Indonesia's daybreak. The gauzy mist of dawn arises from the volcanic crater. In the early morning light, I've worked hard to get to the top of Lombok's humped black lava-strewn incline, more than two miles up. But my aching legs and shoulders are small payment for the spectacular sunrise view at the peak. Down in the cavity, the waters of Segura Anak are ethereal in the hazy break of day, and I thank the mythical resident goddess for giving me the fortitude to complete the ascent at first light up the formerly volatile mountain.

It actually was written for publication like this.

> Mount Rinjani is swathed in the gauzy mist of Indonesia's dawn. I've worked hard, and yes, even suffered, to get to the top of Lombok, more than two miles up, but my aching legs and shoulders are small payment for the spectacular view.

Down in the crater, Segura Anak is ethereal in the hazy morning light, and I thank the mythical resident goddess for giving me the fortitude to complete the ascent.

Note, in the first paragraph, how many different words are used for morning—daybreak, mist of dawn, early morning light, sunrise, hazy break of day, first light—each one different, most of them superfluous. Words used to describe the volcano are resolutely different with each reference: Mount Rinjani, dormant volcano, humped black lava-strewn incline, volcanic crater, peak, cavity, formerly volatile mountain. Yes, there are synonyms used in the paragraph that was published, but the words don't break the story flow and when the "gauzy mist of Indonesia's dawn" is repeated as "ethereal in the hazy morning light" there is a change of perspective from standing on top of the volcano and looking outward to a view on top and looking down into the heart of the crater.

Irony

Irony distances the writer from the material. Ironic comparisons use words that create a discrepancy between their meaning and the use in the sentence. Irony is writing one description while clearly the truth is entirely different.

In the shantytown, each family matriarch guarded her palace from a throne on the porch.

I was welcomed to the village, although I don't know how the chief discovered I was an American. Was it my digital watch or the laptop computer?

Irony can sound like a joke that you had to be there to appreciate. Occasionally, an ironic sentence can enhance the material, for example, as a rhetorical question. But the ironic voice sometimes does not stand the test of time. Ironic statements rust. The joke or key that makes the statement clever one year may have been rendered moot the next. Don't you want your articles to be read and understood in the future? Before using irony that is specific to a time or place, ask yourself whether a reader will understand it in five years. Ironic comments on yourself or companion may not be fully understood by readers. If you finish up the description or story with a lame "well, you had to be there" then the story doesn't bear retelling.

Eccentricities in Language

Yesterday's hepcat is today's dude is tomorrow's what? It's risky to use slang words that limit your writing to a particular place and time. Slang also infects diction. How many articles have you read where the writer uses the construction of stating the information and comparing it to itself with a "well" surrounded by commas. As in: "The band played Sousa just like, well, a marching band—loud and brassy." Not a day goes by that I don't read an article which includes this construction. It's already stale; how do you think it will sound in ten years.

Dialect and jargon, when used at all, should be integral to the story line. Avoid substandard English such as double negatives, profanity, illiterate forms. Sentences constructed in local jargon with regional witticisms may fit in a story about that region, but the same diction or word choice could leave other readers baffled. When I wrote a piece about Maryland's Eastern Shore, I included the phrase "Mer-lan as the locals say" to give readers an indication of the local accent. However, continuing in the regional dialect could become tiresome.

Don't make up words. Though it may sound cute to you at first blush, made-up words can be stumbling blocks for readers. Cruise the dictionary and thesaurus for words. Use American English and standard spelling. Review the finer points of diction in a grammar handbook.

EXERCISE 1

Practice writing with various points of view. Writers with a well-developed point of view acquire individual style. Improve your writing style by playing with different points of view, attitudes, vocabularies and goals.

Describe an episode from a recent excursion in your city or a journey farther afield. Rewrite the scene in several different tones and voices, using the basic information contained in your first version, or adding more details or anecdotes as you recall them.

Write the scene from the point of view of the building. Or, what does that prominent statue, the motionless military general on the horse, see? Cast the scene in a historical light, writing with the vocabulary and style of that earlier period of

---

time. Another version might describe the scene humorously. Try writing the travel episode as a war correspondent might— with staccato short sentences and no pronouns. Pretend you are reviewing the destination for a convention of New Age healers; how would that person describe the scene?

After you've written the scene from various points of view, go over the text and highlight or underline sentences, phrases or words that show the particular style or perspective you were striving to create. Read each version: Is the tone consistent? In the humorous piece, does the reader feel that a funny person is telling the story? Does the version written with an historical perspective lose its tone because of contemporary jargon?

EXERCISE 2

This exercise can be used as a warm-up for those times, regrettably frequent, when writers just don't feel like getting down to the writing. The idea is to stimulate innate love of language, gain confidence and expand visual vocabulary.

In a column on the left side of the page, make two lists: verbs (action words) and adjectives (descriptive words). Don't think, just write. Let the associative powers of your subconscious mind direct the flow. After you've filled a page, go back and craft sentences using the words. Focus your attention on the place you'll be writing about as you construct the sentences. Try to have no sentences that begin with an article or a pronoun.

EXERCISE 3

Using visualization techniques, find the high spots of your trip by going back to the selected site for a sense-memory trip, a visualized walk-through with attention to sight, smell, sound, taste, touch. Writers recall travel memories and write with the inner eye. Remember your personal discoveries in order to convey a sense of wonder to the reader.

EXERCISE 4

Communicate information through omission or allusion, leaving something for the reader to discover. Write a page or two about a travel experience. Read the piece over and identify ways of telling elements in the story without explicitly setting forth every action or experience.

For example: The soundtrack during breakfast on the veranda explained why these islands are called the Canaries.

Are we ever told that birds were singing during breakfast? Not exactly, but you have the information.

EXERCISE 5

Build descriptive phrases for specific people and places. Focus your inner eye on a person you've observed many times. Or, go out with your notebook and find a person to watch. Describe the person's gestures, appearance, facial expressions, manner of communication, etc. Write phrases or sentences, whatever is most comfortable for you. Do the same thing with a building to capture the overall appearance and specific features, the relationship of the building to others on the block, and other aspects that catch your eye.

EXERCISE 6

Write a list of "double-duty" verbs—verbs that create the illusion of affecting the senses concretely, e.g., scrape, reek, drum, lumber, plough, careen, slaughter, drizzle).

EXERCISE 7

Practice writing sentences that express originality in the writer's voice. For example, the following paragraph has no pronoun identifying the writer; however, the voice conveys a sense of the person's indignation and feelings of self-reproach.

"Humiliation is an effective teacher. No one tries twice to use a metro ticket on the regional rail system in Paris. Survive the embarrassment of the ticket-taker nattering loudly about illegal rail rides at the expense of the French people. Extract the proper fare from your wallet and buy the right ticket. Attempt to explain in French that the signs are not clear. Protest that the entry gate accepted the wrong ticket and admitted you to the regional rail system. Complain in English, whine in French. Cry the crocodile. All to no avail. And to top it all, there's still the matter of paying the fine."

Chapter Six

FACT CHECKING AND RESEARCH RESOURCES

F acts—a definition. From the Latin root, factum, a fact is that which is done, according to *Webster's New World Dictionary*. A fact is a thing that has actually happened or is really true, the state of things as they are, reality. Travel writers deal in facts, things that have happened, and facts, the state of things as they are.

In this chapter, we delve into facts; where to find them, how to store them, how to check them, and how to weave them into your article with style. We'll look at collecting data before you travel, while you're on the road and what to do with it when you get back.

GET ORGANIZED!

Whew! I've just crammed the file cabinet drawer closed again, shoving crumpled maps behind brochures and clippings from magazines. I found the brochure I needed about boat rides in the Everglades, but what a struggle to extract the file and then shove it back in the drawer. Don't get me wrong, my files are organized, one for each country, state or city, but there is just too much material. Once again, I make a silent promise to purge my travel files of outdated material.

Does that sound like you? Files so full of material that you can barely find what you need, stuffed so tightly in the drawer that you couldn't add new material without pulling something out? If you're like me, you probably need to devote an hour or two to file weeding.

Storing reference material in an easily retrievable system is a time-saver for a working travel writer. Build a personal travel reference resource collection as soon as you decide to be a travel writer. Save travel articles, brochures, maps and other material that will assist research and writing. Keep only the most recent material.

Smart travel writers know that many printed brochures are updated every year or two. Once you've finished writing and your editor is satisfied with the work and fact checking, I'd recommend keeping source material for about six months to a year after publication; occasionally a reader may write with a question that you need to research before answering. If you intend to restructure the story and sell it elsewhere, you may need to consult the research material again or seek updated sources. When a year has gone by, you probably aren't going to take the time to rewrite the story and the material is starting to lose its useful shelf life. That's when it becomes clutter.

Writers who are reluctant to let go of source material should think about whether keeping the old stuff is holding them back from writing about fresh subjects. Before you toss everything, ask yourself if you could get the brochure, article or guidebook again easily. Ask yourself if the material is still up-to-date and useful. If it isn't, pitch it.

Articles that have appeared in newspapers and magazines after the late 1980s can generally be retrieved from electronic databases. Newspapers and magazines published earlier are usually stored on microfiche in libraries if the originals are not available.

BUILDING A ROLODEX OF TRAVEL INFORMATION SOURCES

Every productive phone call you make to a person working in the travel industry is a potential contact for fact checking. I save business cards and staple them on large Rolodex cards. A filing system using 3" × 5" cards would be just as handy. Some writers prefer to store address and phone information on a computer disc or with each story file. Whatever information storage system you use, organize it and stick to it. Sorting through stacks of cards or slips of paper with names and numbers on them will slow you down. When you need to check a fact, you need to have the resource person as close as a phone call.

When you call tourism industry officials for information on a particular city, state or country, ask who you can call for assistance with questions. Get names and numbers of people in the photo department of the tourism office; you may need to request photographs to illustrate a story. In the beginning of your freelance career, you may have to ask lots of questions to find the right person to handle your research needs. Your telephone manner will either enlist the help of strangers or alienate them, so work on developing a pleasant, conversational style. Choose the time of day—morning or just after lunch—and the day of the week—Tuesday through Thursday—when office workers are usually less harried. There's more information about how to build your travel writer's Rolodex in chapter nine.

PRE-TRIP RESEARCH

The predeparture visit to the library is crucial. Select books on the history and geography of the place, and guidebooks and photo essays for visual inspiration. Consult recent newspaper articles and travel articles which may be stored in the vertical file area of the library reference section or may be available on electronic databases or microfilm. You are reading to develop your understanding of the destination, to internalize what has been written about the place already.

You can read too much, saturating your curiosity, and drowning your natural alertness in pre-digested facts and other people's opinions. This pre-trip reading should be a preview, an introduction. Try to read something written about the place at another time, such as an explorer's diary, or a visiting eighteenth- or nineteenth-century writer's essay, or reliable guidebooks like Nagel's or Baedeker's written decades ago. Look for basic concepts about the history and culture, so that when you are on-site, your mind will make connections. When you dine, you'll remember what you read about regional cuisine, farming or fishing. If you attend a cultural event or religious ceremony, your background reading will have prepared you to appreciate what you see, perhaps even begin to understand it. When a conversation starts with a local resident, you'll be a more informed participant. Fiction set in a certain locale can also be a source for understanding its atmosphere.

Well in advance of the departure date, call the state or national travel offices and ask for maps, guidebooks and information about hotels and cultural centers. Many tourist promotion offices have toll-free numbers. State travel offices are usually based in the capital city. Foreign tourist bureaus are located in New York City, Los Angeles, and other major U.S. cities.

There's an advantage to scanning maps in advance. Before I embarked on my first extended solo journey, I pored over maps of

Europe, learning place names and figuring distances. I intended to take advantage of a first-class Eurailpass by staying overnight on the train and needed to pick destinations that were far enough away to last all night. My father, an architect, taught me to memorize portions of city maps so that I could wander without burying my head in a map and labeling myself a tourist. With the map planted in my mind's eye, I roamed around confidently. Warning: Don't try this without a map tucked in your pocket which you should consult if you are feeling lost or uncertain. Studying maps in advance can lead you to historic and cultural sites, parks or markets that you didn't know about and could have missed.

Some foreign tourist board offices provide material written in English, which may not be available on site. If you are going to an international destination in turmoil recently, call the overseas travel advisory hotline at the State Department for a safety update. Talk to people who have traveled or lived where you are going. They know the special places that visitors miss and can recommend accommodations and restaurants. They also may provide the names of friends where you are going, as discussed in chapter two.

DURING THE TRIP

While you are traveling, gather facts wherever you are. It can be extraordinarily difficult to recover specific information after you return home. Collect anything not available from tourist bureaus or travel agents at home—pamphlets, local newspapers, business cards, flyers. Realize that some of the printed material or brochures you acquire may contain outdated or inaccurate information, so make corrections if you can verify changes on the spot. Another hurdle is that printed material may not be in English. When you enter a museum, public landmark, restaurant or other sightseeing venue, check posted hours on the door or ask an attendant. If you are in doubt, verify information with the local or regional tourist office. Write down the names and titles of your sources in your notebook or journal.

I remember being stymied after a long research trip in the Mediterranean. I intended to write about visiting prehistoric caverns during a month's residence in Malta. Later, when I sat down to transcribe my journal, I found pages of interesting entries about what the caverns and carved rock rooms might have been used for. I vaguely remembered conversations with the bus driver on the way to one group of caverns, comments shared with other visitors and the speculations of an archaeologist who happened to be in one ruin while I was there. The notes, however, were all jumbled together without attribution, my own ideas running in between comments from others. Ultimately, all I could do was summarize: "During several conversations that included a visiting archaeologist, a local bus driver and other visitors. . . ." The Italian archaeologist may have done important relevant research, but I neglected to get her name or affiliation. The only fact I could state without hesitation was that none of the information came from signs, brochures or pamphlets on site. There weren't any. However, that may well have changed since 1985 when I was there, and it's possible that information is now easily acquired on site.

Even if you don't think you are going to write about a place or event, gather information while you are there. A helpful organizational tool is to carry large lightweight mailing envelopes, address them to yourself and send brochures and papers back by printed matter airmail. I've sent packages to myself from many countries and never lost one. Send by registered mail if you like, so there is a written record that follows the packet. Obviously, don't mail valuables, but extra clothes and papers can safely be sent home to lighten your burden. If you are writing on deadline or must submit your piece immediately after return, it's best to keep important reference material with you.

WHY CHECK FACTS?

An unfortunate criticism of travel writers is that we don't adequately check facts. We've all read articles that seem familiar because the facts used to support the story are the same as someone else used in another travel story. Sometimes factual information has been lifted from other published material, often without regard to context.

For writers in a hurry, it's tempting to use the same facts presented in a tourist brochure or on a Web page. You may think it's a safe bet, but consider how embarrassed you'll be if it turns out those "facts" are inaccurate. Since many foreign tourist bureaus produce brochures in their own language first and then have them translated, the margin for error is wide. Even when there isn't a translation step involved, why subject your work to the mistakes of others? Use up-to-date standard reference books as source material; you'll be amazed at the facts you'll learn! Be aware that even the most reliable sources can change.

Facts are rooted in a provable universe. They can be verified by readers, so make sure the facts you use are checked first. When facts can't be verified, they probably aren't facts, but speculation, gossip, myth or innuendo. Fortunately the English language is full of qualifying words that allow us to communicate information without wagering our integrity. They should be used sparingly, of course, and only in situations where you can't verify information that you feel really belongs in your story. Qualifying words and generalizing phrases that blur the edges of absolute statements are: includes, said to be, believed, according to local legend, at the time I visited, etc. Using these phrases saves you from the embarrassment of presenting incorrect information as gospel truth.

Plagiarism

There's also the issue of plagiarism in "borrowing" information from other travel articles. If you use another writer's words in your article, you have to acknowledge that with an attribution. Using the same fact, date or historical anecdote that is in the public domain isn't plagiarism, but using the same wording as another writer is wrong. In academic publications, the acknowledgement of another writer's work is contained in a footnote. Travel writers simply put the excerpted material in quotes and include the author's name. Or, use a variation of this: As (Name of Writer) described it, "...." Before using quotes from another writer, think about whether you can say it better yourself. Opening or closing a travel story with a quote from some notable person is a useful technique to focus reader attention. The body of the story should be entirely your own work.

USING FACTS

Because facts are such an integral part of our stories, we should be creative in choosing fresh facts, or at least presenting them in original ways. When we've worked so hard to craft the travel narrative from personal journal entries, it would be a shame to haul out the same tired old facts used by every other travel writer. Story narrative and structure still guide the choice of information; style will shape presentation of the information.

After telling the general facts that ground the reader in the location, focus on one or two factual aspects of the place that enhance your experiences. Relate any additional facts to the story line. During the editing process, when you are rereading the piece, take a hard look at the facts. Perhaps you could improve the flow of the story by organizing helpful facts in a sidebar. Are there any facts just thrust into the story—facts for fact sake? Consider cutting them out. Facts should support your story narrative.

One way to convey factual information and sustain the story line is to describe how you learned a particular fact. For example, in a piece about Christmas in Santa Fe, you can effortlessly communicate a bundle of facts about the city's founding days by telling the origin of the holiday candle illumination in the civic buildings and cathedral.

Writing exercises at the end of this chapter will help you turn ordinary sentences about facts into more lively sentences that support story flow.

Avoiding Errors

Large circulation publications have proofreaders, copy editors and researchers who scrutinize an article as it makes its way into print. Errors of fact are usually caught during this process. Be aware that your research sources, particularly on the Internet, may contain errors. It doesn't improve a writer's credibility when mistakes are perpetuated, so double-check all facts yourself. Bear in mind, at smaller publications, one person may have to handle many editorial tasks and not have time to do fact-checking.

TIMELINESS OF FACTS

Rapidly changing information and long publication lead times mean that writers have to be particularly sensitive to the timeliness of facts used in a travel article. Historical evergreen facts—those that endure despite political, social and physical changes—are obviously more useful for extending the life span of your story. But their utility and accessibility means they probably have appeared in many articles. Those well-cooked chestnuts may not add anything to the story line.

Even though the facts you select come from reliable reference sources, you'll have to be alert to political, social and physical change. When the Berlin wall fell and the eastern European countries emerged, imagine the flurry of fact checking and word changing that had to take place to make upcoming travel articles conform to reality! Earthquakes and other natural events may alter the landscape. Competing religious groups may affect political or cultural hierarchies. When you are writing about a country in the throes of transition, pay close attention to the facts selected to support the travel story. Strive to explain when information may change between the time you write it and the time it is printed. Bring your experiences and the facts you've selected into focus with reality. For example, you visit a museum that is under renovation and certain exhibits are closed, but they may be open again by the time the article is published. Why not focus entirely on the renovation and its benefits, because the exhibits will be open again by the time the article sees print? Or consider another way to cover the situation by communicating the experience of the moment and what readers will encounter in the immediate future. Tell what it was like to see hidden glimpses of art masterpieces through the scaffolding of a construction site and how eagerly visitors await the unveiling of the new exhibits.

The stability of facts can be fragile, although we usually think of history as being inflexible. Earlier in this chapter, you were advised to find and check facts in standard reference books. And indeed, most current reference books are reliable. Facts culled from an encyclopedia, almanac or history book, such as the date a city was founded, by whom, or the architect of a particular building or the number of acres in a national park, would seem to be unchanging. But consider that there may be competing legends and two or three dates related to the founding of a city. Acreage in national parks may be augmented or subtracted or the purpose changed. The architect of a particular building may be revealed in time to be one of a number of people who were responsible for the project.

What's a conscientious writer to do? If all information is viewed in constant flux, then there are no real facts. When information endures as fact for long periods of time and is recorded in well-established reference sources, then it has generally been accepted as fact. Recent editions of established reference sources can be depended upon. The facts in the most recent edition of the *World Almanac* or the *Encyclopedia Britannica* are probably fairly current. When controversy surrounds a subject or a date or border is in dispute, then the reference book should include a statement to that effect. As the primary researcher, the writer then has a duty to pursue the information further, seeking other, more current sources. For help with current, reliable research sources, seek the advice of a reference librarian at your local library.

All this fact checking probably sounds like a tremendous amount of work, but don't be intimidated. Your travel story will be rich with personal narrative with a few facts worked into the story line. If you gathered information carefully while you were traveling, then the fact selection process is fairly streamlined.

Bob Jenkins, travel editor of the *St. Petersburg Times* has worked in writing and editing roles at newspapers for almost thirty years. Jenkins has these comments on facts in travel articles. "It's troubling when writers send articles that are out of date," he says. "In January 1994 I received a query from a writer I'd worked with before to reprint a story that had run in a national magazine." The story was a service piece about national discounts for senior citizens—an airline coupon book. In St. Petersburg, where so many older adults live, the story would be useful. The writer accepted Jenkins's fee and the story ran in February with a chart provided by the writer detailing the prices for the discount coupons.

"I personally had to answer sixteen phone calls from local people who were upset because the charts were wrong," says Jenkins. "The numbers had changed after his story ran the first time and he hadn't bothered to update. We lost credibility and as it turned out, the difference in the figures was only a total of $28 per coupon. He could have sent me a note that said this ran in September and the numbers need revising. It was four months out of date when I got it. Travel agents were upset too because they had to tell their customers the prices printed in the newspaper were incorrect." Jenkins also tells of an experienced writer who reported in a story about Rome that the Colosseum was closed for repairs. "We printed the story and two days later I got a call from someone who had been there ten days ago who had been inside the Colosseum. I called the Italian Government Tourist Office and they said the Colosseum was closed intermittently. The writer had wandered up, seen the doors closed and the scaffolding and assumed it was closed all the time and it wasn't."

"Even professional freelancers can make mistakes in judgement and timing. I believe the travel section has to be like any other section, accurate and have the pros and cons of situations. If a place is dangerous, alert people. If you can't drink the water as in St. Petersburg, Russia, tell people. If there are muggers and beggars on the streets of Dublin, say so."

Jenkins believes fact checking is a duty of the writer, not the editor. "I've got shelves full of guidebooks which are six months to two years old and I can go to them, but I have not got time to fact check. I really think that people who pretend to be writers have to basically do their own fact checking."

Indeed, time constraints are a perennial problem at almost all publications. Fact checking is labor intensive, time-consuming, and tedious. In an effort to streamline the fact-checking process, some publications ask writers to include photocopies of original source material when the manuscript is submitted.

Despite everybody's best efforts through the editing process, there may be occasions when articles are printed with errors intact. When that happens, there are remedies. If the error is substantial, the publication may run a correction. If the writer sent incorrect information, the editor may think twice before accepting future submissions. Letters to the editor sometimes illuminate errors. The writer or editor may respond in the letters column explaining or apologizing for the error. The best way to deal with errors is to prevent them.

The writer's responsibility is to include only information that is personally experienced or verified, preferably with a second source. Whether you write without pay for a moonlight mini-press (also called a "zine") cranked out on the photocopy machine at your editor's day job or contribute travel articles under contract to a multinational publishing giant, you the writer are responsible for the truth in your writing. If in doubt, leave it out.

HONESTY AND FACTS: RECORDING FACTS IN YOUR JOURNAL

The process of constructing travel articles from personal journal entries has a distinct advantage over writing from memory. Like a reporter, you have a notebook full of description, dialogue, personal observation. Because it is a journal and a diary, you also probably have reflections, musings, fantasies and digressions. As you record events in your travel journal, be scrupulous about writing down what actually happened. When your thoughts and words enter the world of fantasy or speculation, make a note about the transition. "I'm wondering," or "I dream," or "My musings are." Later when you are transcribing, you may not recall when your writing shifted from reality to projection or outright fiction. As a conscientious observer, you are serving up a version of events as you saw them to readers who did not. Your experience shapes the description. An element of strong travel writing is the personal point of view. Just make sure you report what you saw, not what you think you saw. So, if you aren't certain about the details, ask questions.

Countless times, I've neglected to ask questions about things I've observed. Those incidents are shrouded in mystery and supposed explanations. Sometimes the unexplained can be included in a story without unduly affecting balance. But when the scales are tipped in one direction or another, the travel writer has a particular duty to seek truth and balance.

I remember an incident I observed in Moscow in the spring of 1993 when the former Soviet Union was struggling toward democracy. Leaving a hotel lobby, I noticed a police car parked outside with an interesting insignia on the car door of St. Michael spearing a dragon. In the back of the car a man was seated between two uniformed officers. I walked toward the car with my camera elevated but another policeman waved me away. I gestured to the camera and the insignia on the door and the policeman allowed me to take a quick photo. I assumed that he waved me away because of the scenario inside the car, but on reflection I realize there could be many reasons. The obvious one is the police didn't want anyone photographing what appeared to be an interrogation. But perhaps the man was an undercover police officer, or someone being protected. Perhaps the situation was dangerous and the police didn't want a tourist around. Or maybe it is routine policy—a holdover from stricter Soviet rule—to wave people with cameras away from police cars, but because I was a tourist, he allowed me to photograph the insignia.

In any event, I couldn't honestly surmise that my first impression was the truth of the matter. And therefore, I couldn't include the incident in a story without showing the range of possible explanations. Of course, I could write about the encounter without any of my speculations, letting readers draw their own conclusions. But choosing to use that encounter in a story carries some responsibilities. Why would I select that incident to describe my travel experiences in Moscow unless I was trying to communicate some impression about the local police? Once I decide to write about what happens to me, the duty of honesty and balance should push me to determine the truth of the incident or to convey the range of my explanations. I shouldn't allow potentially false interpretations to color a reader's impression.

GENERALIZATIONS AND FACTS

Know the difference between your impressions and "true" facts. Watch for outdated and biased notions. There is no need to perpetuate impressions and images that no longer exist. Spain and Italy were once routinely characterized in guidebooks as inefficient countries where the water was tainted, the food greasy and the accommodations grimy or the service slow. Greasy food is international. Slow waiters and indifferent cleaning staff can turn up anywhere; they aren't national or ethnic characteristics. Religion and other cultural hallmarks are always evolving. Check your biases and stale attitudes.

We all have opinions, but it is important not to convey personal bias as fact. Strive to show both sides of a situation. Steer clear of stereotypes, unless your experiences truly justify perpetuating an overworked image. For example, almost every travel article I read about North Africa trots out the tired image of visitors being hounded by freewheeling guides, touts and salesmen. How many times does the reading audience need to hear about pestering salesmen rampant in Moroccan markets? Is that really the strongest impression that the travel writer carries forth? My experience was that a couple of engaging teenagers offered to show me their uncle's rug shop. I never saw dozens of market flacks dogging my heels whenever I stepped out.

It's easy to unconsciously rehash what other writers have set down, to blow our real experiences up to fit stereotypes. I sometimes wonder if strenuous pre-trip reading might unduly influence what scenes we focus on. Striving to record events accurately and in a balanced context enhances the reliability of the travel diary with its lines deeply rooted in reality. If we write down what actually happens in a timely fashion, the nuance of the moment won't be lost or skewed in retrospect. My journal reminded me that herds of street vendors didn't hound me in Morocco; only a couple of mild-mannered fellows made contact during a week.

FACTS AND WRITING STYLE

Travel writing has creative latitude. Travel articles aren't news stories. Aesthetics—the style you develop as you write—may allow the omission or rearrangement of the sequence of events or compression of detail. After all, the story does have to move along at a readable pace. Including every fact and every aspect of your experience detracts from the construction of a strong travel article. We've touched on this topic in chapter five during the discussion of style and omitting information to allow the reader to make discoveries.

Whether you account for every moment of your travel experience in a chronological fashion or roam around disregarding time is a matter of style. I tend to favor telling the story and letting chronology slide, as long as readers aren't misled. Pursuit of style shouldn't cause you to forget the truth of the facts. For example, if you start the story at the end of your journey, explain it to the readers. Otherwise you run the danger of confusing them vis-à-vis geography and transportation routes. The voice in the story needn't go over every connecting detail, but it has to hold together. The threads you lay down should connect, but how you connect them has to be intriguing for the reader, effortless to read.

A student in a writing workshop asked me to critique a detailed article about her trip to a South Pacific island. Because she wrote about every meal, beverage, taxi ride and hotel room, I felt like I was plodding through her appointment book or expense log. You can include details about one or two meals if they feature an interesting encounter or special food. It would take an extraordinary cab ride to make the content cut into a travel article. Data about hotel rooms, meals and beverages goes in the sidebar about transportation and finances. There are clever ways of informing readers how you got from here to there, what you ate and where you stayed. Check out the exercise section at the end of this chapter for ideas.

Balance and Personal Experience

Travel is: glamour, freedom, learning, self-exposure, self-knowledge, new people, luxury, trial, difficulty, challenge, achievement and endlessly interesting.

Travel represents all these things to me. You can make your own list. Every reader of travel articles has a similar collection of words that characterize travel. What a wide brave spectrum of ideas we travel writers are dealing with. Remarkable, isn't it, that travel can bring both happiness and difficulty, and often at the same time. In some ways, it is like an intimate human relationship, evolving as it happens, never stagnant, always kinetic. True travelers are involved in the act of travel to the point that it becomes a state of being. Travel is movement and meditation. Travel is a pleasure but also is charged with attitude, emotion, experience.

The travel writer plays with the personal point of view to make a story engaging, but tries to be balanced in presenting that impression of a place. What travel means to you will determine the experiences you choose to write about and how you present them, both in the journal and in the finished travel article. Watch your choice of descriptive words for the attitudes they carry and the subtexts they suggest.

Sometimes the events we actually observe are so implausible that they seem to be a figment of the imagination and read like fiction. I could hardly believe what I was reading in Spaulding Gray's piece about seeking a psychic healer in the Philippines. A combination of horror fiction, travel narrative and detective thriller, the story ran in the November 1993 issue of *Conde Nast Traveler*. I had the opportunity to ask Spaulding Gray about his article and he said he wrote it as he experienced it, but that memory is always a filter. When reality seems preposterous, give the reader reference points for understanding so that the story stays firmly inside the boundaries of nonfiction.

Clichés Are Not Facts

European countries are often depicted as cultural treasure troves where commerce is second to art—a cliché that limits and misrepresents modern Europe. How many times have we read statements in travel articles describing Asian countries as mysterious and secretive, populated by Zen practitioners who value meditation and ancestor worship more than money? Aren't these outdated erroneous clichés? Don't fall into the trap of ignoring contemporary politics, industry and trade. The southern United States isn't just known for its down-home cooking and warm hospitality. What about its literature, landscape, football and industry?

Word choice can convey hackneyed images. Search for new ways to describe. Cultivate simile and metaphor for description in your narrative. An unusual comparison may be more evocative than a string of fancy adjectives. Where the water is sparkling blue, the parks are green and verdant, the sky full of luminous clouds, the market bustling, the babies cute or squalling, the women fragile but strong and the men virile but gentle, we have entered the land of cliché. That's the one country a travel writer avoids.

RESPONSIBILITIES OF A TRAVEL WRITER

People read travel stories for many reasons. To get ideas for vacations, to travel vicariously, to confirm their own experiences, to contrast their own experiences, to learn about the world. A travel writer's work may influence opinions and affect decisions about spending money and time, and that imposes a responsibility to create honest and clear prose.

Travel writing necessarily includes staying at hotels, using various transportation systems, eating in restaurants, engaging the services of porters, maids and other attendants. When reporting on conditions at hotels, resorts, cruise ships, restaurants and other packaged travel and entertainment experiences, it's important to remember that the experience is wedded to a particular time. If your assessment is extreme in either direction—just too wonderful or too awful—consider that you'll have to check your perceptions. Circumstances might well change for the next visitor. Fact finding through judicious questions and research will cover some of the unknowns in order to present a balanced assessment. Balance is necessary in criticism and in praise, so if you, the writer, have a terrible experience, you have a duty to reexamine the facts or redo the experience. On the flip side, do you really believe your three days of paradisiacal splendor at that secluded resort on Maui will be the same for the next visitor?

Even if your experience was heavenly, ask probing questions about what could go wrong and how it would be handled. What does the hotel in the tropics do if there is a power outage and the air conditioning fails? Suppose the swimming pool has to be closed; does the hotel offer alternative recreational facilities? If the meal is undercooked or otherwise displeases the guest, will the chef offer another entrée? Will the restaurant charge for the meal anyway? Like any reviewer, the travel writer explains what happened clearly, not raising specters of failure and predicting consistent problems, but displaying a willingness to look at the good and the bad in a given situation.

Although free travel is also discussed in other chapters, now is a good time to mention that a travel writer's credibility depends on balance and honesty in recording the facts. If you are offered a free trip or a cruise, or a free stay at a fine hotel and nothing goes wrong during your entire trip, you really must consider whether the service and courtesy you experience would be the same for the average reader of your article. Are room upgrades offered to other guests? Do all cruise passengers receive a welcoming fruit basket in their cabins? There's no reason to go out of your way to find fault just to prove your endorsement can't be bought, but seek the facts that your readers need. Be guided by your responsibility as a communicator of facts, as well as your impressions and observations.

Some experiential truths can be distasteful. If you've been robbed during your trip and if crime is a problem experienced by many visitors to that place, include a note about being watchful of personal items in the "ways and means" sidebar accompanying the article. Did you fall victim at the market to a scam artist who seemed to sell you a heavy vase, but later substituted another box with a carefully wrapped rock inside? Let readers know what to expect and how you reacted. Conscientious travel writers share this knowledge so readers can avoid similar problems. Don't forget discretion. Every experience you have may not be appropriate for a travel article. If you've overindulged in the local firewater, you might want to spare your readers the details. But you may want to include a friendly warning about social drinking with the natives.

TIME AND TRUTH

Travel is all about stopping and starting, yet travel articles present a story as a continuous narrative. Writing style allows latitude for skipping literal physical movements—how you get from here to there—so that the story flows in an engaging fashion. Some travel articles and books are composed from experiences gathered during several journeys to the same place. It's up to the writer to explain the sequence of events or whether the information was gathered during different trips. Some travel writers are scrupulous about placing events in an accurate time frame; others present several visits as a continuous journey without an explanation. A traveler who has experienced the rigors of long months away from home in a relatively tough environment might resent this omission. Passing off legs of travel as a continuous experience, implying a personal involvement and dedication to extended travel that apparently didn't occur, leans toward misrepresentation. It's one kind of journey to come and go from a difficult country like China with intervals of ease in the west, picking up the narrative thread as you return. It is another kind of journey to stay in that country for a year or more—as long as the story takes to unfold.

When your travel story is based on several visits to a place, it is politic to say so in an early paragraph. Your work will likely be richer and more detailed when you have several opportunities to explore the destination. Writers who return to a place to examine the effects of time's passage usually explain their purpose in the article, helping the reader understand the special motive, which may be tinged with personal nostalgia. When you've been a resident of the place you are writing about, it adds credence to your travel piece to mention that intimacy—assuming, of course, that the explanation enhances the story.

EXERCISE 1

Fill in the blanks with all the words that come to mind.

I think Europe is _____

I think Alaska is _____

I think Asians are _____

I think the western United States is _____

I think Central America is characterized by _____

I think Africa is _____

Study your phrases or words. What directed you to select those particular words? Do you see bias in your lists of words? What about stereotypes? Are you influenced by experience or by television or film images, books and conversations?

EXERCISE 2
Fact selection.

Facts should move the story along. Facts that inhibit story flow or stop the reader short need to be rephrased so they fit in the narrative. Take a copy of your article and, using a highlighter, mark every phrase that contains a fact. Mark sentences that include dates, historical information, names of leaders, etc. The piece shouldn't look like a flood of marker color. If it does, start cutting facts. Read the sentences before and after each sentence that contains a fact. Does the information hang together and relate?

EXERCISE 3
Making ordinary facts lively.

These groups of sentences contain the same facts presented in different ways. Be attentive to the visual images that come into your mind as you read the sentences. Which do you enjoy reading?

Example A:

- Washington, D.C., was a wet lowland between the Potomac and Anacostia Rivers when Pierre Charles L'Enfant, a French architect, started to design the city in 1791.
- In 1791 the French architect Pierre Charles L'Enfant first saw the swampy river delta that he would transform into the new nation's capital city.
- The year is 1791. Slapping mosquitos, the French architect Pierre Charles L'Enfant looked in dismay on the swamp that he would have to transform into the capital city of the United States.

Example B:

- The Villa Borghese in Rome was the private retreat for Cardinal Scipione Borghese, who commissioned the marble building in 1613 which now is a public art gallery.
- Rome's Villa Borghese, a marble palace commissioned by Cardinal Scipione Borghese in 1613 as a suburban retreat, now houses an art collection open to the public.
- When the aristocratic Cardinal Scipione Borghese commissioned the Villa Borghese in 1613 as a pleasure palace for himself and his retinue, could he possibly foresee that the

elegant marble rooms would be open to the art-loving public three centuries later?

Select several facts about the last historic landmark you visited. Write a basic declarative sentence or two using the facts. Then manipulate the sentences. Turn the information around so that the facts are still present, but rework the information until you have sentences that create nearly visible scenes. Then, try your hand at writing a vivid factual sentence about the founding of your hometown or city. Reconstruct a scene like the two examples above.

EXERCISE 4

There are many ways to inform readers how you got from here to there, what you ate and where you stayed. If you've traveled recently, describe an evening during the trip. Tell about traveling to the restaurant, the components of the meal and what happened through the evening. If you haven't a fresh travel memory, describe an evening out in your city or town.

After you've finished writing, use the highlighter to mark all the pronouns at the beginning of sentences (I, we, our, you, he, she, they, it). Wherever you have used pronouns, revise and rewrite the sentences so that prepositional phrases, subjunctive clauses or verbs lead your sentences. Reread your text and notice the difference. Is the second version more visually interesting than the first one?

EXERCISE 5

Pretend you are a gossip columnist. Write up the same trip or outing using the suggestive language of a "people" column. Be daring! What happens to the text's meaning? What would happen if travel articles were constructed from biased impressions about a place?

Chapter Seven

TRAVEL PHOTOS

W hen you page through a magazine, what commands your eye? Ah, of course, the photographs. Brilliant though the writing might be, the eye gravitates to images. Images help communicate words and ideas. Visuals help readers see the story as it unfolds. Masses of text are difficult for recreational readers. Photographs, illustrations, quotes pulled from the story and other graphic material help improve the visual quality of a printed page.

WHEN ARE PHOTOS REQUIRED?

Writers usually don't have to provide the illustrations for stories that will appear in major magazines and newspapers. Such publications have photo editors and art directors who are responsible for selecting illustrations and photographs and arranging the page layout. Many newspapers and smaller magazines do expect the writer to provide photographs with a travel story. During the query phase, clarify what the editor expects. Ask what format the images should be: slides, negatives, prints.

If you have appropriate photographs, sending them along with the story enhances its marketing appeal. The editor can buy the story and photos in one package, saving time and resources. When the story describes a remote place where photographs would be difficult to acquire, the writer should make an effort to take high-quality photographs while on the journey. Submitting a story about an unusual destination without photographs might affect an editor's decision adversely.

Photos should relate to the story line. Generic shots of monuments or beaches won't be as eye catching as unusual scenes with people in action. Deciding which photos to use is the editor's job, so if you are going to send photos, send lots of them. Include tightly focused shots of crowd scenes, broad shots of the landscape, details of buildings, and portraits of people and animals.

Think of photos as a series of visual stories. For each location that you plan to feature in your story, capture a series of photographs. Shoot an opener that sets the scene, details that expand on the ideas and ending photos that wrap up the mini-"story." To illustrate your entire article, you would have many series of mini-stories that can be grouped. For example, in Curacao, I noticed teenage boys with elaborate haircuts, designs shaved into a short crew cut. I took photographs of the boys sporting these haircuts. But to really explore the visual storytelling possibilities, I should have sought out a barber that does the special designs and taken pictures of boys getting their hair cut. Photographs that display the whole sequence of events are more useful to editors.

TAKING PHOTOS FOR TRAVEL STORIES

To get started, equip yourself with a 35mm camera and use it before you venture forth on a research trip for an article. Test the various features and settings on the camera. Take pictures with the different exposure settings and write down what shutter speeds you used with each shot. Log photos in a notebook so you know what you shot, who is in the picture, the address, and any other details you can report at the site. Number or letter each roll of film and put the number on the receipt from the photo processor. When the film is developed, notice what settings worked and which were over- or underexposed. You don't have to be a professional photographer; with modern automatic camera equipment and an imaginative eye, it's possible to sell your images.

Take many pictures. The first thing to learn about taking photographs to illustrate travel articles is that you can never shoot too many pictures. And no matter how many rolls you do shoot, only a handful of pictures will be acceptable, let alone superb. In other words, a writer who is an adequate photographer will still produce only a few photographs that can be used in publication.

Since photos can be an essential selling point to an editor, travel writers need to be competent photographers. Develop your visual sense, take lots and lots of pictures and upgrade your picture-taking skills. Look at the types of pictures used in your favorite magazines or books.

Try to improve your odds of success by taking perhaps ten times as many shots of a given scene as you normally would if they were snapshots of the family. By walking around the subject and studying all the possibilities, you increase the odds of shooting the most interesting angles. Imagine what a scene will look like in print. Look through the camera lens, checking the potential for each scene. Kneel down and shoot up toward the subject or find a vantage point where the scene can been photographed from above.

Standing and shooting the first scene you see will yield photographs that everyone else has taken: "Point and shoot" rarely produces a fresh image. But making images more complicated doesn't necessarily mean you'll have better photographs. Until you have refined your skills, just take lots of pictures. Realize that no matter how many years you've been using a camera, taking pictures for publication is quite different. Admit your limitations, difficult as that may be. Accept that you'll probably have to discard many shots. Then loosen up and click that shutter.

There will be times when you can plan your picture-taking in advance. If you know you are going to write about five different landmarks or buildings, then you know you should take pictures of them all. Offer an editor options. Take distance shots and close-ups of details. Walk as close as you think is appropriate then move in three feet more. If the weather is unreliable, take the planned pictures at the first opportunity that you have good light. Late afternoon and early morning offer fine opportunities for good contrast. When the sun is high, the light can be too intense, burning out the image you are striving to photograph. Make several visits to the place, if it is close to home. Photographs don't have to be taken at the same time you actually visit the landmark to gather information for the article.

In addition to planned photographs, you'll need other photographs to illustrate a travel story. Especially prized by editors are photos that evoke spontaneity. Wander around the area detailed in the article you are writing; when a human interest scene catches your eye, take many photographs from different perspectives.

Photos serve a dual purpose. They will be illustrations for your article and they'll help you remember what happened on the trip. Photos supplement the travel journal and help you recapture the scene in exquisite detail. Pursue a particular topic by taking photographs of the subject wherever you go; for example, parked bicycles or haystacks or unusual store windows (watch out for your reflection in the glass) or poodles or barber shops. That series of pictures of taxicabs from around the world might be the basis for a travel article or even a photo book someday!

Action Shots

Another reason for taking many pictures is that you'll develop reflex abilities to quickly grab that one shot that won't happen twice. I remember being in Agra on a busy market street. I was just looking around, perhaps writing down my impressions or sketching. All of a sudden I heard the deep throb of a motorcycle engine. I didn't hesitate, but yanked out my Minox 35mm camera and aimed at the street. Two motorcycles with sidecars were roaring through town. I clicked the shutter, advanced the film rapidly, and of the three pictures I took, one sold.

The motorcycle street action didn't appear in the text of my story, which was about having tea with a rickshaw driver, but it did illustrate the commotion of street markets in Agra which I had discussed. The speeding motorcycles showed the vicissitudes of street life much more vividly than a pretty picture of colorful vegetables at a market or a cloth vendor's stall draped with saris. If your story has action, the photographs should complement the text by showing motion.

As you travel, think about what scenes illustrate the mood of the place. Take photographs that capture the essence of the location. Is it serene, bustling, empty, crowded? Are buildings imposing, charming, neglected, cared for? Do the people in public smile, laugh, scowl, chatter? Seek photographs that tell a story, people interacting, people watching each other, animals eating, sales transactions, children playing together. Photographs of historic landmarks that feature a caretaker trimming trees or a costumed guide leading a tour or an artisan at work are more interesting than static shots of a building or statue.

Photographing People

If there are people in the photo, check to see that background trees or telephone poles aren't growing out of the top of someone's head. When you look through the viewfinder and you aren't pleased by the scene, shift your position to adjust the perspective.

People are best shown in a context rather than posed. Tell your human photo subjects to look at each other or what they are doing rather than at the camera. Take photographs of people working or playing—cooking, fishing, weaving, making a bed, gardening, kicking a ball, skating, plucking a harp or bowing a violin. Sometimes, though, an artfully posed group of people tells volumes about a place. For example, a line of Italian villagers staring at the camera suggests their ritual of sitting around near doorways or in cafes passing the time of day.

Crowd scenes show the ambience of a place, but are difficult to photograph effectively. Photos that work in crowds are close-ups; medium shots with few human heads. Take vertical frames because you don't know what the layout will be. A vertical frame will have fewer people in it but still convey the density of the gathering. A horizontal photo with many people in it loses the specifics.

Your own appearance in the travel story and relationship to the story line suggests that photos of yourself would support the narrative. Action photographs of yourself may be useful; posed snapshots are not. Take photographs of yourself or your family involved in an activity featured in the travel article—climbing the mountain, tasting wine, riding the pony, stepping onto the ferry. Photographs of yourself shouldn't look posed, any more than the pictures you take of others should be posed. Learn how to use the remote shutter release feature on your camera. Prop the camera on a bench, wall or rock to capture yourself in mid-stride against the natural backdrop of a public setting.

Though it's tempting to take photos of yourself next to a distinctive landmark or in the foreground of a stunning landscape, those photos are for your personal use. Such pictures look posed and stiff. If you don't have a remote shutter release feature, then you'll have to ask someone else to take them. Do you really want to hand your camera over to strangers to take pictures of you? The result is usually a fuzzy overexposed long shot of unidentifiable people dwarfed by a monument or staring starkly at the camera. Rarely do photos of posed people taken by amateur photographers work for publication.

Other Tips

Think of the photographs you take while traveling as art, not snapshots. Create a composition in your photographs. Most people who look at the article in print will look at the photos first. You have the opportunity to make visual accessories for your story. The photos should be strong, inviting and inspire curiosity so that potential readers become actual readers.

Strive to put the focal point of the picture just above or below the center horizontal line and just to the right or left of the center vertical line. Frame the subject with an arch or wall. Use natural entry points such as a path, a road, or a break in the trees to draw the viewer into the picture. People's eyes move into the center of interest. Include road signs, markers and other visual cues in your photos to help a reader understand the location. Signs can even be the subject of a photograph, especially if they are humorous. Remember to get close enough to the sign so that it fills the viewfinder.

Think about contrast, Linda Halsey, the travel editor at *The Washington Post*, once told me as I was embarking on a long trip through Asia. And try to get close-ups of everything. Landscapes just don't show up very well in black and white. To "read" properly, each frame has to have distinct light and dark tones. Before taking a picture, I learned to imagine the scene in black and white. Would the subject show up, or was it in shadow? Was the background too busy for the subject to be distinguished?

For a picture to sell to a newspaper, it also has to have action, movement, and help tell the story, either the one you're writing about or a related incident. Magazines need the same illustrative subjects and usually have demanding technical requirements for their photographs.

Though beautiful to behold, seascapes and landscapes don't hold a reader's attention. In some ways, lovely scenes are the visual equivalent of gushy writing. The eye craves people or activity, even a boat on the horizon to fix humanity in the picture. People want to study pictures that tell a story. Select views with people, animals or buildings to add interest and stimulate curiosity. Even if these particular features aren't mentioned in your story, and they don't have to be, any action in the picture enhances rather than distracts or deflates the story. There is a temptation to show everything in a picture, to squeeze in the whole market, all the folk dancers, the breadth of the mountain range. Focus on the small rather than the broad sweep; for example, one hill, one tree, a corner of the garden, or a small portion of a market stall. Fill the frame. Pictures that are two-thirds sky or sea will have to be cropped anyway—all that light space is deadly for contrast in print—so why not anticipate the editor's frustration and aim your camera fully at the subject, trimming the bland before shooting.

You don't have to show the entire thing. Viewers can extend a wall or a porch. If the subject of the picture is compelling, the eye will be satisfied with the detail. Your best test in reviewing your proofs or negatives is how your own eye looks at the pictures. Are your memories swaying your judgment? Try to look at images objectively. Does the picture tell a story? Are you curious about who is in the picture and what they are doing? Is there anything in the picture to identify it and locate it in time or place? You don't want people to think, "Oh, that could be anywhere."

Improve your photography skills by enrolling in photography courses at a university, community college or arts center. Study the works of other photographers, starting with travel magazines and books. Learn from what photo editors at major magazines have chosen to illustrate their pages.

OTHER SOURCES OF TRAVEL PHOTOS

Before sending out photographs, ask yourself: Will these photographs help my writing or hurt the presentation? What do you do when none of the pictures you've taken relates to your story line? Or when the technical quality of the photographs isn't on a par with your story? Turn to stock photo libraries, tourist bureaus, chambers of commerce and other photographers.

Tourist Bureaus

When I'm hunting for photographs to illustrate a travel article, I turn first to my own photo files and then to tourist bureaus or to the city's chamber of commerce. These offices are concerned with publicizing the merits of their state, country or city and generally are eager to help writers and editors find appropriate photographs.

Nearly every foreign country that encourages tourism has a tourist information bureau, generally in New York, Miami or Los Angeles, or a similar office affiliated with the country's embassy in Washington, D.C. For photos depicting U.S. destinations, consult the press relations section of state tourism or economic development departments which are usually in the state's capital city. Every state in the union and many cities and counties have employees devoted to developing and maintaining photo collections of scenic and historic landmarks, tourist attractions and the people of the respective region. If a state tourist office doesn't have the photograph you require, ask where you might find it. Perhaps the article is about a specific institution or landmark. Contact the administrator of the institution and ask for assistance in locating appropriate photographs to illustrate your piece.

Photos from tourist bureaus are almost always provided without charge. Sometimes the photos are offered on loan, and you may be asked to sign a receipt promising to return the pictures after publication. Tourist bureaus and similar institutions always want a credit line to appear with the photograph that identifies its source. If a credit line isn't already typed on a strip of paper and affixed to the back of the photograph, write the caption, which describes the scene in the photograph and the credit line, which acknowledges the photographer or source of the photo.

For example, a photograph of the statues of the lions outside the Art Institute of Chicago might have a caption: "Lions guard art treasures inside the Art Institute of Chicago" and a credit line: "Photograph courtesy Art Institute of Chicago, 1995" or "Photograph by Phoebe Shutter, 1995, courtesy Art Institute of Chicago." If the city of Chicago's tourist office loaned the photograph to you, the credit line might read "Photograph courtesy City of Chicago, Graphics and Reproduction Center, Photograph by Phoebe Shutter, 1995" or a specific City of Chicago department such as aviation or parks may also be listed in the credit line. The specifics of credit lines vary from place to place. When you obtain the photos from an institutional source or a government office, ask for the preferred wording for photo credits. Be sure to send a copy of the published piece to the office that provided the photos and return loaned materials.

Photographs provided by a tourism bureau are generally the product of professional photographers, so the image resolution is high. However, some tourist bureaus tend to keep photos on file for many years, so the scenes may be dated. Before sending out photos with your article, look at them closely. Automobiles and fashions change. Buildings are razed and new construction changes the landscape. That busy street clogged with traffic in the photo may have become a pedestrian walkway; the park entrance may have been redesigned. Always check to be sure that the images you send with your story relate to the text.

Some photos held in the files of tourist bureaus have been used over and over again to illustrate travel articles. These stale images do not enhance your chances of selling a travel story. A travel editor usually wants unique images, photos that relate specifically to the story under consideration. Take your own photos or travel with a skilled photographer, so that you can offer uncommon photographs with your article.

Professional Photographers

Usually the photo editor at the publication will undertake searches for photographs through stock photo agencies. The expense involved usually makes it prohibitive for a freelance writer to use stock services. Charges for research start at $50 and escalate. Then there is the fee for each photo used, not to mention the financial responsibility of hundreds of dollars per frame if the photo is lost. Your best bet is to use photos taken during the trip by yourself or another photographer working with you.

Rare is the writer who takes a picture as well as she crafts a paragraph, so a source of free photographs snapped with professional precision is an asset to any writer. Make friends with photographers. If you meet a photographer during your travels, get his or her name and contact information so that you can approach later if you need to get photos of the landmarks you've visited.

A popular vision of the photojournalist is the adventure bound intrepid story catcher, cameras slung over khaki or leather jacket, who rafts down roiling rivers, leaps onto helicopters and glibly talks entry to the inner sanctums of foreign dignitaries. While there are doubtless many weather-beaten photographers capturing the images that inform us of the world's culture, few are travel photographers. It's tempting to confuse the romance and adventure of news photography as depicted in popular culture vehicles such as movies and television programs with travel photography. The tasks are different. Travel photographers capture timeless moments that will illustrate portraits of a place and its people. News photographers seize the action of the moment. Travel photographers also try to capture immediacy and spontaneity in the picture, but the emphasis is on representative moments rather than news events.

WHAT CAN GO WRONG

Most of us worry whether airport security scanners will affect film adversely. Take a lead-lined film bag along if you are doubtful about the efficacy of the X-ray machines in the region where you will be traveling. But in some remote airports where security staff might not be familiar with lead bags, your luggage may be opened and searched or subjected to more intense X-ray scrutiny. Don't put any film in checked baggage. In most of the industrialized world, the scanning machines will not affect film, but repeated X-ray exposure may cloud unprocessed film. I usually carry exposed film in a clear plastic bag in my jacket pocket or tote bag. At the moment I pass through the metal detector, I pass the bag of film to the attendant and walk through. Usually, I have no problems with this system, but then there was the time in Brussels when I was severely chastised by a security guard who insisted the film had to go through the X-ray device. The bottom line is: Heed the instructions of security personnel.

My photo horror story occurred during an outdoor trek in Kamchatka, a peninsula in the Russian Far East across the Bering Sea from Alaska. With a camera and dozens of rolls of film, I thought myself well equipped for weeks of rafting, trekking and touring in the wilds. Imagine my chagrin when after days of snapping photographs, I realized that the shutter wasn't actually moving when I released it. Had a water spray damaged it during the rafting, or steam while I shot pictures of geyser eruptions? Perhaps the camera had been banged around in my daypack.

I never did determine the source of the damage to the shutter mechanism, which was repaired upon my return home. Fortunately, my travel mates had snapped photos aplenty and generously offered to share their pictures. I paid for processing duplicate slides and photos and had enough images to illustrate several travel stories. But though their photos were interesting and of high quality, the images weren't my own. The experience made me more attentive to monitoring the state of my cameras.

LEGAL ISSUES

There is the matter of legal or political restrictions concerning taking certain photographs. Find out in advance if you will need written permission or a license to take photographs in churches, shrines or archaeological sites. It is also wise to remember that at various times and places, some countries regulate the importation or export of unexposed or exposed film, camera equipment and accessories. Again, if you are unsure what the rules are, get the information before you start traveling. Ask if military structures and equipment or airports and official buildings of various types are off-limits to photographers.

If you are concerned about legal repercussions arising from photographing people, use model releases. You have the right to take pictures of anybody who is in a public place. You don't have the right to invade people's privacy by going into their homes and photographing them without permission.

A model's release form states that the person in the picture knows you are going to take it and that you can use it any way you want without compensation. Bringing out a model release form might cause some people to ask for money, since they probably hadn't considered that you might be taking the picture and then selling it. I haven't yet paid anyone for taking a picture. Most people are delighted to have the attention. Sometimes I'll get a name and address and send a copy of the photograph after I've returned home, a nice way of thanking someone for helping your travel photojournalism career.

If someone seems hesitant or downright hostile about having a picture taken, it's best to back off. Some photos shouldn't be taken. Consider whether the photograph would be an invasion of privacy. Find out what would be considered good manners among the people you are visiting. Put the shoe on the other foot: How would you feel if someone started taking pictures of you? Is your attitude condescending and rude or conciliatory and interested? Friendliness, honesty and good manners are the principles that should govern photographing people.

STORING PHOTOS

Photographs, negatives and slides have to be stored carefully to prevent injury or deterioration. Various storage systems are available from photography supply stores or mail order catalogs. Options include plastic storage sleeves for negatives and slides punched for insertion in loose-leaf binders, file boxes with glassine wrappers for negatives and boxes for slides. Whatever system you choose, make sure the materials are archival quality to preserve the photographs.

When you take photographs, jot down details in a notebook with the frame number from the film. This is extremely important to remember because you will have to write captions for the photos if they are used with your article. After the film is processed, label the slides or number them, keyed to a typed list that identifies the subject, date and place. Many photographers remove bad frames from the returned film right away, so a blurred or overexposed shot won't find its way into a presentation.

Doubtless you'll accumulate photos from other sources—from other photographers, tourist bureaus, and public relations firms. Make sure there is a caption, credit line and date for every photo in your files. It is surprisingly easy to forget the details, and a photograph you can't identify is no use to you or an editor. Cultivate a habit of labeling photos and slides as soon as you get them.

While working on travel stories, consult your photo files to see what resources are available. Once you know what photos you've taken or have on hand, you may tailor some details in the story to correspond to those photo images.

THE MECHANICS OF SUBMITTING PHOTOS

When you make an exploratory marketing call, have some notes on what photos are available so that you can answer intelligently when asked "What photos do you have?" As you discuss your story ideas with editors, or in your query letters, offer to provide photos for the story if the editor is interested in the article. Before submitting photographs with your article, find out what kind of photographs are expected and what form: color, black and white, slides, negatives, prints, transparencies or contact sheets. If the publication is concerned about writers and photographers taking complimentary press trips, let the editor know if you have taken the photos for a story while on a subsidized trip or have used your own money.

Remember that if you send manuscripts and photographs on an unsolicited basis, you do not have any financial recovery rights if the photos are lost. That means, unless an editor has told you that the publication wants to see your article and photos, either on spec or under contract, you are sending unsolicited material and run the risk of loss. Most reputable publications make a sincere effort to return unsolicited material if a stamped, self-addressed envelope was enclosed. At the minimum, if you are sending unsolicited slides or photos and want them returned, label each photo with your name and address and provide an envelope for their safe return.

Your name and address goes on the back of each photograph, or on the cardboard holder of each slide that you took and are submitting for publication. A rubber stamp or address stickers are useful for labeling photographs. If you aren't the photographer, put the correct name and address on back of each picture or slide frame.

If you are making simultaneous submissions of your travel articles, sending out photos to many editors can get expensive. An alternative to submitting photos or slides is to send a sharp photocopy of the picture so the editor can get an idea of what is available. Photocopy the pictures or make color photocopies of the slides, adjusting the copy exposure so the images aren't too dark. Send the photocopies of photographs along with the story or query letter. If the editor is interested, then you can send slides, prints or negatives, whatever form is required by the publication.

Cutlines or captions are typed on paper and attached to the photograph. For slides, type the captions on a separate piece of paper keyed to numbers which are written on the corresponding slide. If you leave caption writing to the publication, you increase the possibility of errors. Do it yourself and the editor has one less task. As stated above, if the photo was provided by an agency or institution, the photo credit should acknowledge that fact. Use the wording provided by the photographer, tourist office or agency or a variation of: "Photo by (name of photographer)" and/or "Photo courtesy Malaysian Tourist Bureau," etc.

If you haven't received the images a month or so after publication, call your editor and ask when you can expect the photographs to be returned. Editorial departments are chronically understaffed and overworked; perhaps the photos are on a desk waiting to be sent.

Don't assume photos were misplaced by the editor. I embarrassed myself in this way once. Two months after publication, I couldn't find the negatives for a story about climbing a volcano on Lombok, Indonesia. I self-righteously assumed the illustrations hadn't been returned to me and called the editor to complain. He insisted that all photos had been returned with tear sheets of published articles to the writers for that particular issue. I doubted, I whined. He suggested that the materials might have been lost in the mail, although that had never happened before, or perhaps they had been lost at my end, i.e., on my desk! An orderly hoarder of rough drafts, supporting brochures and finished articles—you've already heard about those crammed file drawers—I couldn't believe that. A couple of years passed. One day a manuscript page slipped between my desk and the wall so I had to move the desk to retrieve it. In the crevice between desk and wall was an envelope containing the missing negatives along with two copies of the published article. I phoned the editor at once and apologized; we had a good laugh.

Photographs are rarely lost in the mail, but it can happen. You may want to take these special steps to guarantee safe return of irreplaceable photos. If you are concerned about photos going astray in the mail, provide an addressed return envelope with the forms for return receipt requested or certified mail which have to be filled out by the person mailing back your materials. Include the appropriate fees in stamps or prepaid postage reply coupons with a note requesting that someone at the publication fill out the forms for this extra service. Or, open a Federal Express account and ask that your materials be sent back using overnight service. In practice, most publications pay for return postage for photographs relating to articles they are printing. Of course, if the editor requires slides or prints, you could send duplicates and not worry about whether they are returned.

A more common legal problem concerns the copyright for photographs taken by you. If the negatives or prints aren't returned, there is always the possibility that the images will be used again, possibly uncredited and unpaid. The chances that a reputable publication will use photos without credit or payment is rare, but it can happen, usually because the publication thinks the photos belong to it. Again, always stamp your name on the back of prints and write your name on slides so there is no question of who is the photographer and copyright owner of the images.

Quality Control

What if you don't like the editor's choice of photographs? Perhaps the photo was published reversed or cropped in a way that you don't like. Do you have recourse? Not really. If the error misrepresented the article, for example if a photograph was used that doesn't relate to your article in any way, you could ask that a correction be run in the publication that explains that the error was editorial and not the fault of the writer. Such problems are so rare, though, that you shouldn't consider them a real issue.

HINTS FOR TRAVEL PHOTOGRAPHERS

1. Have a definite objective for the photographs. Take pictures that support and illustrate the places you are writing about.
2. Keep equipment simple and in good repair. Choose filters and extra lenses with your experience in mind. Gadgets just weigh you down.
3. Patience is important. So is an ability to see the humor in situations and laugh at your mistakes.
4. Learn as much as you can about local laws and customs before you take pictures of people.
5. Take lots of pictures. You'll be lucky if 10 percent of them are visually sharp and contribute to a strong narrative.
6. Put in a fresh roll of film if you are approaching a situation where you know you will be taking lots of pictures. How will you feel if you have to stop midway in the ceremony to change film? Let a couple of unshot frames go; film is inexpensive compared to the impossibility of recovering pictures you miss.
7. Cushion equipment from bumps and falls. Dust, sand and salty air, extremes of heat and cold, rain and fog are all difficult for the camera.
8. Check and clean photo equipment before departure and each day during the trip.

EXERCISE 1

Using your crisply honed observation skills, take notes about published photos. Page through glossy travel magazines. What do you see? Are the pictures taken from unusual angles or did the photographer use a natural frame such as an arch, trees, or a window around the subject? How many close-ups, or distance shots illustrate each article? Can you see what is in the background? Do people look posed or natural?

EXERCISE 2

Using the draft you wrote for exercises in chapter three or four, evaluate what photographs you would need to illustrate the article. Read the piece and highlight subjects that are inherently visual—people doing things, colorful markets, animals, children, details of buildings or monuments. If you have already taken photographs related to the draft, go through them and select a dozen shots that relate to the story, illustrating the character of the place and its residents. Weed out any photos showing posed people staring stiffly at the camera, blurred scenes or those taken from such a distance that the subject is difficult to see. Are the photos a mixture of close-ups and medium distance shots, verticals and horizontals? Are there people in the photographs? Is there drama or dialogue in the photos—people looking at each other or moving toward something?

EXERCISE 3

With a draft or finished travel article about a place close to home, go out and "shoot the story." Take six or more rolls of film and really concentrate on getting every possible photograph. Bracket the shots, shooting at the recommended f-stop and one up and one down, so that you have various light exposures. Even if it's a struggle to find a hundred or more possible photographs about one travel subject, the exercise will push you to be creative, and to watch and wait for unique photo opportunities.

Chapter Eight

MARKETING TRAVEL ARTICLES

Marketing requires preparation and focus. You are selling your work and your experience. You'll need to do some research before contacting editors. Read the story and make a list of magazines and newspapers that you believe are likely to publish your story. This is not a list of where you wish the story would be published, but a realistic summary containing perhaps a dozen publications. You could start the list with the travel or leisure sections of the papers in your hometown or the closest city. Put this list aside to work with later.

Look over the types of travel articles detailed in chapter one. Into which category does your piece fit? There's a chance it may fall into several categories, which will broaden your marketing prospects. Skim the travel section of a current edition of *Writer's Market* or other indexed guide for writers who are selling articles. Read the listings and identify which publications are seeking travel articles in the categories yours fits. While in the market research phase, I use stick-on notes to mark publications listed in the market guide that might be interested in particular travel articles. Or, make a list with the relevant page numbers for easy reference when you are preparing the envelopes and cover letters.

FINDING YOUR MARKET LEVEL

Another facet of marketing is selling your past experience, convincing editors that you have the "right stuff," the ability to produce the quality of writing they seek. Your strongest tool in marketing yourself is your clips. Copies of published articles show editors that you are capable of writing for their publication.

Beginners have a dilemma. Without clips, they can't reach an editor, and if their work doesn't get to an editor's eyes, they won't ever be published and get clips. However, the clips can't be from just any publication. When the published pieces have appeared in papers or magazines with comparable circulation or advertising bases, then the editor may be more disposed to take a look.

Consider this: Every writer was once a beginner. Every writer started small, with a first acceptance for publication. And that first sale raised pulse levels and expectations. The thrill of the first acceptance letter or phone call ranks as a major life experience for the writers I've talked to.

Though it was twenty years ago, the thrill of my first magazine acceptance letter hasn't worn thin. *American Antiques* accepted my query about a special interest destination story featuring Maxfield Parrish's house, Wells Woods, in New Hampshire. The house had been renovated and opened to the public as a bed-and-breakfast inn. I had stayed there, paid for my lodging and interviewed the owner, mentioning that I hoped to write a travel piece. At that time, my publication history was thin—a couple of brief essays published in newspapers, sports and movie reviews for the *Varsity* newspaper at the University of Toronto while I earned a B.A. in English. The antiques piece was my first magazine sale after I'd decided to make my way as a freelancer. The $25 (yes, really!) payment didn't begin to cover expenses, but it created an endless horizon on which I could imagine future successes.

You know your writing is solid, has flair, grabs a reader, but your published words have appeared only in newsletters and small periodicals or weekly papers. Face it, the *New York Times*, *National Geographic*, *The Washington Post*, or *Conde Nast Traveler* probably aren't going to publish your first travel article. Don't waste their time and yours by approaching the large circulation magazines and newspapers until you have achieved a certain level of publishing success in your field. A writer's early sales nearly always appear in small papers, regional or local publications or specialty magazines.

A strongly focused, expertly developed, vividly described travel article that is printed in your hometown weekly with a byline is a worthwhile clip to have in your portfolio. Or maybe you contribute an interesting short review of a resort hotel to a travel newsletter. In the full-length piece, a range of your writing skills will be displayed. In a short review, command of snappy vocabulary will be featured.

You might not be paid for these first few publication credits.

Perhaps the editor will offer you a free subscription to the paper or newsletter. At this point, the goal is to collect a few published clips to serve as leverage into larger circulation publications. Strive to amass a variety of publication credits—long and short pieces with your byline on them. Of course, you'll take every assignment or offer of publication that you can. Don't underestimate the value of a big display in a local publication.

Remember that list of publications you wrote earlier? Are there any local papers or magazines on the list? Rework the list if you have set your sights too high.

MOVING UP

Regional travel markets are wide open for novice travel writers. Creating story ideas and writing about locations close to home has a couple of advantages; you'll be writing about what you know, always a solid bet, and you'll be developing stories and acquiring published clips at minimum expense. Writers from the region have an edge over out-of-town writers that editors of regional publications appreciate. Your experience and firsthand knowledge will be trusted.

Breaking into the regional travel market requires research. You'll need to know what publications are in the marketplace. Troll newsstands and local bookstores. Look for scenic magazines that showcase the region. Don't overlook Internet-based publications. The on-line version of the local newspaper may use freelance content for its Web site in addition to the articles that appear in the print version.

Ask the local tourist board, chamber of commerce or visitors and convention bureau for the names of regional publications. The state economic development bureau or commerce department should be helpful. Tourism is big business nearly everywhere, and counties, states and cities are eager to help promote regional travel. As a travel writer, you help them do their job.

Analyze what kind of travel stories are regularly published in these magazines. Are all the travel stories about country inns or bed-and-breakfast hotels? Is family travel the focus, or sports or specialty outdoor adventure travel? What kinds of advertisements appear in the magazine? How long has it been published?

Be aware that some regional magazines start up and disappear in a year or two. About ten years ago, I remember preparing three travel stories for a Washington, DC, regional travel magazine. The editor accepted the stories and told me she would keep them on file to be used when the timing was right, certainly within a few months. Normally, that would be a legitimate arrangement, as long as the stories weren't held indefinitely. As a relative beginner, I didn't think I could ask to be paid on acceptance, rather than upon publication.

After a couple of months, I called to find out when my articles would be published. The editor told me there had been a change of publishers, a warning that something was amiss. Soon I learned that the magazine was folding and all the assets were being absorbed by a new publication. Since my stories were still on hold and could be considered assets, I sent certified letters to the new publishers, withdrawing my stories from consideration. Allowing my work to remain under consideration any longer, without guarantee of publication, seemed risky. Further, I was not impressed by the way the publication dealt with freelancers, and I thought I could market the three stories elsewhere.

Is a clip from a publication that no longer exists useful? Yes, if the writing is good, because the clip stands on its merits. The same goes for work that appears in giveaway newspapers, newsletters and limited circulation publications. If the writing is solid, your talent will show.

Novice freelance travel writers can expand their portfolios by writing brief items for large circulation publications. While analyzing publications and becoming familiar with magazine formats, you'll notice that most publications have a "front of the book" or "back of the book" section composed of one to four pages of short items. Sometimes the sections have bylines at the end or after each item. Using the masthead as a guide, determine whether these items are written by people on the publication's staff, by contributing editors or by freelancers whose names do not appear on the masthead. Many magazines also feature one-page essays written by freelancers that appears on the last page, another opportunity for novices in search of publishing venues.

Since there is no space to develop a mood or story line, every sentence in a short piece has to be sharply focused. The items may be short, but a writer can put considerable effort into creating a meaty paragraph or two. An argument could be made for specializing in short items, because the pay scale is often surprisingly generous for this length, at least in the major travel magazines.

Consider, though, that a long piece in a regional publication might be a better clip for your portfolio than a two-inch squib in the roundup travel notes page of a national magazine. When sending out examples of your published work to editors, you'll want to include some full-length stories. When an editor reads short blurbs, there is scant opportunity to assess a writer's ability.

NETWORKING TO MEET EDITORS

How do you know if your writing is good enough? When are you ready to move up to a new level of publication? Seek advice at writing workshops or courses. If a manuscript critique is offered at the workshop, take advantage of the professional input. Attend writers workshops and conferences where local editors are speaking. Working editors sometimes teach courses at local colleges and universities. You could enroll and improve your writing while making valuable professional contacts.

Do you hesitate to approach an editor and introduce yourself? They wouldn't be at the conference or teaching a class if they weren't eager to meet writers. No need to tell your life story, just present yourself and ask if the editor is seeking new writers or interested in reading manuscripts. Ask whether a query or a finished piece is preferred. You might ask for the editor's card; offer your own. Usually the editors will remember you if you are brief and organized. Fix your name with the story topic in their minds.

Follow up within two weeks. If a query was suggested, send it, along with samples of your published work. If the editor asked for the complete manuscript, send it off, topped with the strongest lead you can muster. Make sure you enclose a self-addressed stamped envelope (SASE) and a cover letter mentioning your meeting during the class or conference. If the piece is rejected, send a query on another topic, and so on. Should you feel that you aren't making headway, perhaps you are aiming too high. Try a publication with a smaller circulation and work on your writing skills. Try editors again when you have fresh material to offer.

WRITING THE QUERY LETTER

This brief letter presents an idea to an editor and asks if the editor is interested in reading the finished manuscript. Most editors prefer queries. Letters save time, allow the editor to see if you can present an idea succinctly and hear whether you have a voice. If the tone of the query letter is flat and lacks personality, what will spark an editor's enthusiasm?

Communicate the story idea and how you plan to develop the focus. The editor may respond with a "go ahead, on spec" which means that you can go ahead and write the piece and the editor will at least read it. "On spec" is not a contract or an offer to buy your story.

Working editors have neither the time nor the inclination to offer critiques of unsolicited material. Cover letters asking for advice or begging for corrections or critiques generally herald the insecure and amateur writer. It would be a waste of time for an editor to read further with a pitch like that.

Once in a while, a query letter or unsolicited manuscript captures an editor's interest and attention. Perhaps, if it strikes a chord, the writer will be called and asked to rework the piece for publication. Put your best work forward and hope that you hit the editor's desk on an easy day when she's in the mood for prospecting new talent.

PRESENTING YOURSELF ON PAPER

During my years at various departments in *The Washington Post* newsroom, I've opened thousands of letters with manuscripts. A remarkable number of the letters announce that the story attached is the "greatest piece of writing you'll ever read," "a perfect solution to the nation's problems" or that the article is "exactly right for your publication." Confidence is a useful quality to have, but those types of statements are silly. There's no need to explain why your article works; editors will know whether it will or not.

Correct business manners are noticed. Braggadocio and extreme informality may adversely affect an editor's reaction to your letter. Self-stick notes, index cards, or scribbled lines on scrap paper are not query letters. Sending photographs of yourself, brochures describing your achievements in another field, letters of endorsement from former employers and other material unrelated to the manuscript you are selling does not enhance your professional image.

Presentation is important. The query letter that is read by an editor is the well written one, the brief, straightforward one. Use plain white or ivory paper. Forget about arty notepaper or greeting cards. Bright colored paper or fancy letterhead will not compensate for bad writing. What impression does an editor get from hot pink envelopes, manuscripts with seductive photos of the author paper clipped to one corner, business cards sprinkled with glitter and letterhead embellished with cartoon logos? None of these cute tricks sell travel articles to editors. And unless you've met the editor, addressing a stranger by first name could be considered presumptuous. I'm amazed at the number of manuscripts that arrive without self-addressed stamped envelopes or even a return address.

Check spelling and grammar. Computer spell-checking functions do the job, up to a point; you still need to review the spelling of proper names and place names, as well as read the letter once again before sending just in case grammatical errors were retained in the piece after revision. Computer spell-checking functions rarely recognize correctly spelled words that don't belong in the text. Are you positive about the spelling of the editor's name?

Use the established business correspondence format. If you are unsure of how a business letter should appear, consult business writing guides in a library. Briefly, this is one standard format: Put your entire return address in the upper right-hand corner, if you aren't using printed letterhead, which isn't necessary and doesn't really impress anyone. Type your phone number with area code just under the return address. The inside address goes on the left side of the letter and includes the name of the editor, the name of the publication and address. Under the inside address, type the salutation such as Dear Mr. or Ms. (name). The body of the letter follows. On the right side, aligned with the return address, type the complimentary close, such as Sincerely, or Very truly yours, leave a few blank lines for your signature and type your name. Don't forget to sign the letter.

Would you believe that freelance writers send queries by fax without a return address or even a telephone number? I've seen computer-generated letters arrive unsigned. If you send out multiple queries and use a mail merge function of a word processing program, read each letter over before mailing. What message does it send when a letter is properly addressed on the envelope, but the text of the letter is directed to another publication? Then there was the hapless writer who left the last rejection letter paper clipped to his manuscript. Imagine the chagrin when he opened the envelope to find two rejection slips—ours and the one from the last magazine he sent the article to.

These kinds of errors signal that the freelancer is sending out simultaneous queries or submissions, which is fine if that information is stated in the text of the letter. When a query letter has a grammatical or spelling error in the first line, do you think an editor reads further? Mistakes like these show carelessness.

Other errors freelancers make in their query and cover letters include: offering to change the article before the editor has even read it (the writer has no self-confidence); suggesting the editor can revise the article (of course they will; that's why they are editors!) asking for a job and pitching story ideas in same letter (don't confuse the issue; get an editor interested in your writing before asking for a job); over-explaining expertise and credentials (the writing should stand on its own); sending a draft of an article instead of a finished manuscript and offering to fix it if the editor is interested (take pride in your work; send out work you believe is polished); presenting manuscripts or story ideas that are similar to what the magazine or paper printed recently (once a topic has been addressed in its pages, publications usually wait before featuring the same idea or place again); sending a fuzzy photocopy or a print-out that is faint or difficult to read because of single-space typing or insufficient margins (editors don't look at manuscripts that are difficult to read).

Some writers enclose a list of all the magazines and newspapers where they have been previously published, but a list doesn't tell an editor how you write nor the length or substance of your pieces. Such lists are distractors when you are proposing a story idea.

Better than a list of publications are two or three samples of your published work. Present them with pride and style. Photocopies of your clips should be clean and clear. Arrange the columns of your published story so the photocopy reproduces only your own work, not the other stories on the page. Cut and paste or tape the publication name and dateline to a backing sheet so that it will appear with the text of the story on the photocopy. If your story was on the front page of a section, fit the masthead into your photocopy by using reduction keys on the copier. But don't reduce the print so much that it becomes too small to read. Blurred or faintly printed photocopies also annoy editors.

On the other extreme, the overly neat, plastic-encased portfolio of your complete works sends the message that you have too much time on your hands. Simply make clear easy-to-read copies and staple the pages of each story together, paper clipping them all to a cover letter. Make sure the clip holds them securely and that the self-addressed stamped envelope that you enclose is large enough and has correct postage for return of your clips.

So, how do you ensure your query letter or the cover letter with a manuscript is read? Be brief. Use the crisp lead from your finished story as the opening in your letter. Offer the completed story to the editor, state how long the article is and whether you have photos. That's it.

PREPARING THE MANUSCRIPT FOR SUBMISSION

The goal is to present the whole package as a complete story ready for an editor to buy and print. The manuscript should be easy to read with dark type, double spacing and wide margins. Include a self-addressed stamped envelope for return of the manuscript or a self-addressed postcard for the editor to inform you of the status of the article. Include photographs or slides in transparent protective holders and with their captions.

Make sure the cover letter has your name, address, telephone numbers and social security number. Put the same information on the first page of your manuscript, just in case the letter and manuscript are separated. Paper clip the manuscript pages together. Always number the pages; some writers type their name and a word describing the story in the top right corner of each page. For example, if I were to send out a story about the Chesapeake Bay Region of Maryland, I would write "O'Neil/Chesapeake" at the top right of each page.

Each publication has its own guidelines about length. The travel story length that is most saleable falls in the 800-1,200 word range. Even if the writer's guidelines state that articles of 1,000 words are acceptable, many publications prefer shorter material. Learn how to write tightly and keep articles in the 700-800 word range.

A travel writer who knows an editor's preferred story length demonstrates research ability and an understanding of the editorial process. Only a certain number of column inches of each page are devoted to text and photos, headlines and other filler. The rest is earmarked for advertising, much of which is determined well in advance. That is one reason why editors are confined to predetermined story lengths. The other is that today's readers have a low tolerance for lengthy articles, no matter how fine the writing.

To make your own estimate of a publication's standard story length, count the number of words in one inch of a column of printed text in the body of the article. Then measure the number of inches of columns that are the same width throughout the article. Each publication has its own design signature, which may mean larger or smaller than standard typefaces and nonstandard column widths. Often, the opening page of a story will have very large type for the first few words, or the words may string across the whole page. Count these words individually then add to the word estimate derived from measured text. Don't include photographs or headlines or large-typeface quotes (pull-quotes) or other filler material when determining the total length. Multiply the number of words in one inch by the full length to get the approximate number of words in the piece.

When you start researching markets for stories you've written, confirm your estimate of preferred story length with someone on the editorial staff by saying something like this: "Seems to me most of your roundup stories are about 700 words and your destination stories about 1,400 words. Do you have flexibility with length?" When discussing the details of editorial needs, always determine whether the sidebar (a box or column of information usually containing prices, addresses, and other dry information that would interrupt the flow of a story if included in the text) is part of the total word count or extra. Sometimes, a sidebar can be sold separately from a story to accompany related articles by other people, so if your piece is turned down, offer the sidebar on its own.

Always be certain that there are no grammatical errors or misspelled words. Proofread, spell check and fact check your manuscript. Are the numbers transposed? A common error is to write the current century for events that have taken place in the past (e.g., 1948 for an event that took place in 1848). Computer-driven spell-check programs do not always discriminate in matters of grammar. If you are weak in antonyms and homonyms, make it a point to read your story again after using the spell-check function. Words may be spelled perfectly but used incorrectly.

Proofread manuscripts and cover letters twice. Ship the articles to newspapers, perhaps two dozen at a time. If the manuscripts are returned with a form rejection letter, read it carefully. Sometimes publications change editorial needs and what was rejected today may be useful at a later date. Take note when the publication's form letter indicates they aren't considering any freelance material. You'll want to update your records and strike that publication from your mailing list.

SIMULTANEOUS SUBMISSIONS

Submitting your travel article to several editors at once is acceptable as long as the circulation areas of the publications don't overlap. Submit the same story to a paper in each city. Write on the top of the first page of the manuscript: "This is a multiple submission in noncompeting circulation areas."

The cover letter for this mass-marketing effort should be short and to the point. Avoid cute openings like "hi" or " good morning." Put the story lead in the first or second paragraph of the letter to pique the editor's interest. Add a few words about the subject of the travel article and mention any hook for that particular publication, any special connection to that paper's readership. If you are producing the mass-marketing cover letters on a computer, make sure that you carefully tailor the letter for each publication.

After an article has been published you usually have the right to resell the work to other markets if the reprint rights have reverted to you after publication. Before reselling a story that has been published, clarify what rights the first publication purchased and keep notes on what rights you sell to each subsequent publication. Most publications reassign the rights to the writer after publication, generally after a brief period—three to six months, sometimes a year. If you have a contract, read it. If not, and you are in doubt about your resale rights, check with the publication that bought the story first. Chances are that you own the rights and can market the story again and again. Remember to update information that may have changed.

APPROACHING EDITORS WITH YOUR IDEAS

Once you have a dozen or so published credits in regional periodicals and papers, you'll want to start sending out travel article queries to large-circulation publications. Query only after you've read at least two or three copies of the publication. Familiarize yourself with the types of feature articles and what departments appear in every issue. Read the masthead. Who publishes the magazine? Is this an in-flight magazine? If so, take note of the destinations served by the parent airline because those places will be featured in the magazine. One reason for reading several back issues of a magazine is so that you won't propose a travel article idea that appeared in a recent issue. Another reason is to cultivate a feeling for the magazine's preferred style—bright and breezy, fact oriented, sophisticated, humorous. Note whether the writers are well known or freelancers like you. Scan the brief bios at the end of the features for this kind of information. Some publications have a contributors page just after the table of contents. Does your experience parallel that of the freelancers whose work appears in the publication?

Contact magazines by mail and ask for editorial guidelines and a sample copy. Call local magazines or newspapers and ask to have the guidelines and a sample issue sent to you. While you are on the phone, get valuable information from editorial assistants. Ask whether they use freelancers, which editor reads articles, are articles held for consideration and for how long. If the person you are talking to is receptive, pitch the idea; you may receive practical advice about how to proceed in your marketing effort. Ask if you should query or send the finished piece. Verify correct spelling of names and titles.

Keep in mind that the publication's budget year plays a role in freelance assignments. Editors who have money left in their freelance budget will be ready to spend it before year end. Hit them in September and October with "fire sale" stories—material that is ready to run. Of course, year-end marketing also smacks into freelance budgets that are exhausted. If the editor likes the piece, you may be put on hold until the new budget year. Consult the editorial calendar that you've requested from the publications you plan to write for. Holiday and seasonal pieces are lined up well in advance. Winter destinations are sold in late summer and fall. Approach editors about summer destinations in late winter and early spring. Get the jump on other writers by pitching your travel story ideas early, or send the completed manuscript.

Don't call or E-mail editors unless you've received favorable response to your queries. A rejection letter with a personal note provides leverage for further conversation. You could try calling editors you've met at a writing workshop, but until you have attained a certain level of experience and a track record of publication credits, don't annoy and alienate editors with phone calls and electronic mail. The exception, of course, would be publications on the Web and publications that invite E-mail queries.

Telephone Etiquette

I know there will be readers of this book who consider themselves ready to approach editors directly, people who overestimate their abilities and relish the personal connection of a phone call over the slower pace of a query letter. If you must call to make a query, I suggest sending a fax. Be brief and polite.

Time your fax or call. Find out what days are busiest and whether a call is even an option. Many editors just don't have the time to take phone calls from writers. If you are an established writer with many publishing credits in national magazines and big urban newspapers (Chicago, Los Angeles, Seattle, Houston, Minneapolis, Miami, etc.) go ahead and call. If you are a newcomer and have a few published clips from local publications, write a query or send the complete story. Of course anyone can try to contact an editor by phone, but be warned that editors don't like interruptions. The phone call query may even harm your chances for acceptance. Editors like to review queries, proposals and unsolicited manuscripts when they have the time. If you are willing to risk a call, target your marketing calls to editors who will likely be interested in your work and at publications that you are professionally ready to write for.

If you are cold calling, as the sales managers say, find out who is the appropriate editor for the type of writing you do. Before you launch into your pitch, ask if the editor has a minute for you to present a story idea. A few minutes is all you can expect, even if the editor isn't busy. Brevity will help your case. You've written out the story idea already and have selling points to repeat if the conversation evolves. If the editor is busy, ask if you may call at another time.

Don't call on deadline. I can't think of any editor who would accept a call from a freelancer during deadline time. So find out beforehand when the crunch comes at the publication you are contacting. Obviously, a weekly travel section is under tighter time constraints than a bimonthly magazine. Calling first thing Monday morning or the last business hour of Friday night doesn't make much sense either. If you insist on calling, time your calls for hours when people are relaxed—midmorning or early afternoon.

Although you are just one of hundreds or thousands of freelancers who approach a given publication in a year, there are two kinds of freelancers who are remembered vividly by editors—the professionals and the pests. You can be a novice and still demonstrate professional qualities by your neutral but friendly language and voice tone, your considerate attitude and your concise presentation. Your awareness of editorial needs shows that you've done your research. If there is time for a conversation, listen to what the editor says and ask specific questions about editorial deadlines and time constraints. The pest, on the other hand, questions an editor's judgment, boasts, is coy about story ideas because the editor might "steal them," exaggerates past experience and makes a rambling presentation. The pest refuses to believe that the editor has actually rejected the idea and calls back again and again.

In constructing the points for the query conversation (for example, if I'm pitching a travel story about seeing Paris as it was during the Belle Epoque), I'll cite recent movies or plays or novels that are set in this time period and I'll have a list of restaurants, hotels, buildings and certain streets that capture the fin de siècle. If there is a centennial date (1898-1998), I'll have it ready. I'll know what hotels of that period have been renovated and which celebrities stay there. I'll be able to tell the editor what restaurants in Paris would give readers a sense of that time period. In short, I'll have done my homework before contacting an editor. The research I do will be useful anyway for writing the article.

If the editor isn't interested, but seems willing to talk for a minute, turn the call into an informational interview. Ask what stories the publication does need. Find out what subjects are submitted too often, what they have on file. Ask if you may send story ideas in the future. Don't get flustered and fold your cards just because your first idea received a rejection. You've met your goal by getting an editor or an assistant on the phone. You'll reap information that will be useful in future queries.

Remember, each time you talk to someone inside the publishing industry, you gain experience, confidence and information. Before you call any editorial office, make a realistic assessment of your level of achievement and be prepared to present your ideas succinctly.

WORKING THROUGH REJECTION

How a writer reacts to manuscript rejection ranges from assuming a Zen-based calm (it didn't sell here; so it can sell elsewhere) to a competitive stance (now I'll have to try harder) to weakened self-esteem (must be something wrong with me or my work). Don't take manuscript rejection personally; every writer has had a manuscript turned down.

One benefit of working on assignment with a contract is the kill fee. If your piece is completed according to contract but is ultimately not used, you will receive a kill fee which is generally a percentage of the total contract amount. Most freelance assignments are on spec, though, which means kill fees are fairly rare for novices. Whether you get a kill fee or not, you still have to think about marketing the story elsewhere. One thing to remember about rejection—it gets easier as your experience grows. What might feel devastating the first few times eventually won't affect you at all.

When I first started sending out query letters and manuscripts, I saved my rejection notes in a tattered file folder. I'd heard stories of writers who saved every rejection letter they'd ever received, presumably to make a success all the sweeter. I would browse through those rejection letters and savor the few handwritten notes of encouragement from editors. Then one day, I decided that brooding over rejection wasn't healthy or productive. I burned the letters. Remarkably, I began to sell more proposals after that. Did getting rid of the rejection letters serve as the catalyst for my turnaround? Perhaps it was just the logical upward climb after years of practice.

If you've received several rejections for a manuscript you considered a sure sale, it may be time for a serious reevaluation. Let rejection of your manuscript send you into the editor mode. Reread your piece and ask yourself if the writing is fresh and enticing. If comments were noted on the manuscript or in the rejection letter, heed them. Have a friend or colleague read the piece and offer a critique. Consider joining a writer's workshop and work on the piece in a group setting. Or, leave the manuscript for a while and work on something else with a clear mind. You'll return to the rejected piece later and be able to breathe new energy into the prose.

An article may be rejected for myriad reasons. Some of these reasons may be related to the writing, or to the publication's editorial plans, or to factors that neither the editor nor the writer knew when the idea was originally proposed. If the writing itself is the problem, perhaps the tone was off. Too cute, too snide, too scholarly, full of insider's jargon or just plain ordinary. The diction and syntax might not meet editorial standards. The vocabulary may have been too common or too pompous or affected. The length could have been a factor. There are many reasons why an article doesn't meet the editorial mark, and though some stories can be reworked, usually editors decide not to put in the effort.

Assuming you researched the market and were fairly confident that the publication would be potentially interested in the subject matter, and even assuming that an editor had given you the go-ahead to write the piece on spec, an article still may not be accepted. Perhaps the piece read too much like an article already in the works at that publication or was similar to a story that recently appeared in its pages. Perhaps the publication changed its focus, or redesigned its format. Maybe there were staff changes. Finally, though you may not like to admit it, maybe the writing just didn't make the grade.

If you didn't research the market and just sent the piece out blindly, it's very possible that your piece fell outside the scope of the publication. Market research is never a waste of time.

Working through rejection means staying focused on your goals. You still have to find a publisher for your article. Use the writer's market guide, consult the marketing list that you've drawn up and seek new publications. Cast your marketing net a little wider.

Getting past rejection should also propel you to the manuscript. Comb the piece for a fresh slant which may make it attractive to another publication. Check your prose for zing. Does your voice shine through the text? Will the reader learn something, be surprised, have an emotional response?

The worst thing a rejection letter can do is stop you in your tracks. Don't quit writing and don't lose momentum. Get together with a writer friend and have an editorial jam session. Critiques can be done by mail or in person. Sometimes we writers are too close to the piece and can't see stylistic problems or technical holes.

Here's a handy motivator to keep on the marketing path. During the market research phase, write down on an index card or legal pad the dozen or so places you plan to send your piece. Pre-address mailing labels, if you are so inclined. Note the date when you send out the story to the first choice, second and so on. Note the date the manuscript is returned and any comments. If you are meticulous about expenses, record postage and photocopy charges related to each submission. When the manuscript comes back (if it is returned) note the date and send it back out at once, bearing in mind seasonal needs and making sure each manuscript looks fresh and doesn't have smudges and curled edges. By keeping the article in circulation you maximize success and sustain your motivation. Eventually, the acceptance date for each article will occur with a minimum number of submissions. Soon the first place you send the article will accept it!

MARKET RESEARCH AND TRAVEL TRENDS

Before selling a product, the salesperson has to know what it is. The same theory applies to marketing travel stories. Decide which category the travel article is in before attempting to identify the markets to tackle. See chapter one on types of travel articles for ideas. Sometimes a story fits more than one type of travel piece—weekend escape and outdoor adventure, holiday peg and family outing.

Be clear in your own mind about what makes the article unique. Check in the *Readers' Guide to Periodical Literature* to see what other publications have printed similar stories, and when. Identify the particular slant or hook that makes your article timely. Perhaps a recent news event relates to your article. For example, a metal helmet from the settlement at Jamestown, Virginia, was excavated in 1994; an enterprising travel writer would use that discovery to sell a travel article about the colonial settlement.

Next, line up all the publications you plan to contact. And within each magazine or newspaper, target which editor would be interested in your article. Many newspapers and magazines have separate sections for travel and weekend getaways or family activities; you want to be sure you are approaching the right editor.

During your research, you may read about a publication that seems appropriate to contact. If you've never read a copy, you should write and ask for a sample copy. Some publications offer free samples, asking only for a self-addressed stamped manila envelope; others request payment for the magazine plus postage and handling. A friend or colleague may alert you to a publication, but before sending your story, verify that it is in print. Countless publications fold, and data in the reference directories may be stale. Consult the *Writer's Market* or other reference guide to magazines and newspapers for address information. If available, obtain the phone number; perhaps there is an 800 number. Then phone to verify the name and address of the current editor.

Broaden your search for potential markets. While the annual *Writer's Market* is useful, every other freelancer is using it. I research information about new publications in the annual directories to magazines and newsletters published by firms such as R.R. Bowker, Gale, Ayer's and the like. There are several periodicals directories listed in the Appendix. Almost every reference section of a public library will have one or more of these massive multivolume directories. Look under the heading of Travel & Tourism to see what kind of publications are listed. Chances are you've never seen these publications on the local newsstand. Some are trade publications, others are limited circulation, or promotional. Look upon all of them as potential markets, especially for a writer looking to enter the travel writing business. Other headings to check include Transportation, Leisure, Recreation, Hobby, etc. Just paging through these directories should give you ideas about places to sell your travel pieces.

Travel newsletters are a potential market. Many are completely written and edited by one or two people whose names are on the masthead. However, newsletter publisher-editors have many rainmaking duties, looking for advertisers or new subscribers and they may well need freelance editorial assistance. With the thousands of specialty newsletters available—travel, hobby and sport, regional groups, ethnic heritage associations, arts and languages—there are lots of possibilities for selling travel-related articles.

Experienced researchers know the standardized subject headings, then they can look up these topics in any reference volume. During your market research phase, you'll consult a variety of directories in search of publications to buy your work. Look beyond the categories of "Travel" and "Hospitality Industry." Note subject headings for further reference; for example, if "transportation" doesn't yield any potential magazines for your travel articles, then try "transport" or "transit systems." Library of Congress subject headings are used by most libraries. If you locate a good travel book, check to see what subject headings are listed on the copyright page. Those same headings might be useful in locating categories of magazines or other books related to the travel industry.

Follow trends in leisure travel by talking to travel agents and your sources at the tourist boards. What attractions are people visiting? Is regional weekend train travel increasing? Study the advertisements in newspaper travel sections. Notice what package tours are featured. Stay abreast of business trends in the tourism and hospitality industry. If three new airlines are offering discount fares from New York to Florida, wouldn't that tell you that a travel article about budget travel in Florida would be on top of a trend? When *The Wall Street Journal* reports that a major auto rental company is inaugurating a super luxury car class, there just might be a travel story in the making.

Travel trends also relate to news. After a hurricane has demolished the coastline of a Caribbean island, it's hardly likely that an editor will be needing a travel story featuring that place. Tourism has probably fallen sharply. When a year or two has passed, and the island has rebuilt its hotels to prepare for tourist visits, think about selling a story on the rebirth of tourism.

WHAT THE EDITORS SAY

I talked to a few travel editors and asked their thoughts and advice for novice travel writers. All of them are interested in fresh talent and lively writing. The travel market is wide open for a gifted writer.

Patricia Keegan is founder and editor of *Washington International*, a bimonthly publication for the international community in the nation's capital. Keegan's paper has grown steadily for the past eight years. She buys travel articles, interviews and stories which show a flair for words and sensitivity to the world scene. "I don't care if a writer has never published anywhere if the writing is good. I'm looking for writing from people who will help the paper grow and they are paid accordingly. The commitment has to go both ways."

Elaine O'Gara of Winterbourne Press has edited several travel newsletters. Her biggest gripe is being sent a single-space faintly printed dot matrix manuscript. "It seems so basic. Those go on the bottom of the pile. Writers should read the publication first and edit their own work before sending it to an editor."

Of the newsletter market in general, O'Gara says, "Many are written in house; the editor puts it together from their own travels or press releases." The newsletter field is pretty crowded right now, says O'Gara. "I can't think of any aspect that isn't covered. With desktop publishing it's easier."

She advises freelance travel writers who are considering starting their own travel newsletter to "talk to other newsletter editors and go to the reference libraries and find out what newsletters exist. Don't put lots of money into it at the beginning." O'Gara's marketing strategy included sending sample copies to newspaper travel editors of newspapers and magazines.

Michael Shoup, former travel editor of the *Philadelphia Inquirer* and longtime travel writer, shares these comments on freelance travel writing. "Study what the newspaper or magazine publishes and try to learn from that. It will give you an indication of what we do. It's going to be tough as a freelancer placing a story in a newspaper, but if you fail, the biggest thing is to try again."

In marketing travel articles, the "right place, right time" factor plays time and again. Shoup explains, "Say I've got an international piece on the front and I need a national or local story and across my desk comes a story about country music in Nashville. A week before I wouldn't have bought it."

He advises beginners to be persistent, and if they have any talent going for them, they are eventually going to get in. "Just don't give up if someone says no to you; send back more stories. I don't think my skin is thick enough to be able to handle the number of rejections a successful freelancer has to handle in order to become successful."

The *Inquirer* needs writers to contribute regional travel stories, such as a weekend journey. "It's tough to get good ones and we're always scratching. We'll pay more for it." Weekend journey stories in the *Inquirer* have stretched as far afield as London and the Bahamas. "As far as possible, but basically, Vermont to Virginia, the Mid-Atlantic to western Maryland. These are destination stories which address the simple fact that many people go away for the weekend by car."

Shoup points out that networking skills are important in marketing travel articles. "Contacts are important; use a reference name if you have one. I'm more inclined to take a look at a manuscript from someone whose name I've placed."

Shoup complains about people who've never even looked at the newspaper before sending manuscripts to the paper. "You have to go to the library and try and get an understanding of the stories we run."

He advises beginners, "There's always one success, so try. Maybe someone is a good writer, but not published in many places and pops up out of nowhere. That material stands out. It doesn't have to be gripping, just a printable story. I scan the cover letter and I read the first few paragraphs and I know in thirty seconds." Novices betray themselves with laboriously long cover letters and overwritten leads, says Shoup. "Adjectival diarrhea. I never even look at them if I get a long cover letter. Let the story speak for itself. If it's good I'll recognize it."

"People have no idea of the volume we receive, maybe one hundred manuscripts a week, so I don't have time to look at every one, nor play journalism professor," grouses Shoup. But there is hope for beginners, "I can get ten thousand stories that aren't well executed and one that is, so I never say never and never say no. I sympathize vastly with people out there trying to write. Recognizing the dearth of money, we encourage writers to resell it somewhere else. I'll tell them to call another editor."

The general pattern with freelancers, Shoup has discovered, "is that you find them, encourage them, and tell them they made the cut. They get better and then they disappear because they are writing for other publications. You always hope there is someone else around the corner." With all the submissions, Shoup admits he rejects stories that are perfectly printable. And the great majority of the *Inquirer's* best travel stories come from staff writers. Shoup says, "Our guidelines are: send me a good story. If it is, I'll recognize it and put it in the paper."

Once in a while, a busy editor does take the time to play "journalism professor" and evaluate a rejected article then tell the writer what went wrong. Julian Jones, a former vice president at the University College of the University of Maryland, recalls his first attempt to sell a travel piece. "Morrie Rosenberg (former editor of *The Washington Post* travel section) took the time to make comments on how I should change it. The manuscript looked like a freshman essay, all marked up. I was furious and stuck it in a drawer. When I cooled down a month or so later, I made those changes and he bought the story."

What was wrong with his travel article? As might be expected, the piece had been written in an academic style and didn't follow the structure or style of a travel article for a general audience. The value of a strong, generous editor is extraordinary, says Jones, who continues to write travel articles on a part-time basis. "That kind of personal attention is rare."

Bob Jenkins, travel editor at the *St. Petersburg Times* for the past eight years, receives manuscripts from beginners. "And from lots of writers who probably don't think they are beginners but no one has taken them aside and told them they need help."

"Overwhelmingly, there's too much first-person writing of commonplace experience," says Jenkins. "If the events are happening to a group, they aren't unique." The writer should compress the narrative to pass along information and save individual perspective for personal experiences that fit in the travel narrative, says Jenkins. "Obviously people write about their experiences in the first person. When it is a truly unusual experience, the writer may put himself in the picture."

Another weakness Jenkins sees in freelance manuscripts is "gushy writing—'Oh what a beautiful sunset.' As William Zinsser says, If you write correctly you won't need adjectives. The right word will be there. If the water is turquoise, say so, not 'alternating between shades of blue and green.' "

"Writers tend to rave on and on about the buildings and the mountains, but I think we do need to focus on the people. Too many people write as if they are looking out the windows of a tour bus." He suggests that taking photographs of people may be an intrusion in some parts of the world and advises freelance travel writers to ask permission. "Maybe even tell them that their picture may run in a newspaper and offer some money.

"I judge articles from beginners as I judge them all. Was it an unusual place, or if well-trodden, what have they found about it that is different? Have they taken an everyday experience that anyone might have and made it unusual enough in the retelling to put in the paper?

"That could be a tour bus story, because lots of readers feel comfortable only with a package tour and in a general circulation paper I need to put stories out that will interest everybody. I'm most encouraged when there are pros and cons in the story. I know the armchair travelers are out there who want to read about going to unusual places, but they'll never do anything but book a tour and have a close friend with them the whole time."

Jenkins decides how much to pay based on how much work he has to put into the piece. "I'm not bound to buy bad stuff just to prove I have skills at editing. Here's the lead on one I didn't buy: " 'Most people think of New Brunswick as the pretty wooded province . . .' and this person told me up front that she was a professional freelance writer. Avoid question leads, or generalizations such as 'most people.'

"We don't have readers' time for long, maybe thirty minutes, and there are a couple of hundred headlines in a daily paper, so your writing beneath the headline better be pretty good."

PROTECTING YOUR IDEAS

Over the years, I've spoken with many freelance writers who call with story ideas. I'm not an assignment editor, so I don't buy articles, but part of my job is to route viable stories to the right editorial desk and weed out the obvious duds. When I ask a writer to tell me a little about the idea, to evaluate whether it is appropriate for a newspaper or to determine which section of the paper might be interested in the query, occasionally a writer will demur, suggesting that the paper might use the idea without credit. Some would-be writers even go so far to say "Oh, someone there might steal the idea." Do they really think a publication with staff writers and experienced editors might be so short of ideas that they have to steal from freelancers? Paranoia like this is shooting yourself in the foot; if you can't express the idea, how can an editor respond?

There are times when several people come up with the same idea—the world is full of coincidence. Publications run stories that resemble material that freelancers have submitted months before. Deciding that the idea was "stolen" based on such scanty information is risky, though. Magazines routinely assign stories many months in advance. Your freelance submission may cross the editor's desk after the story was assigned to someone else, but way before the finished manuscript sees print. To you it looks like your idea was taken and assigned to someone else; if you complain to an editor, you could look like a paranoid neophyte who doesn't have a clue about lead times. But if you are certain that a publication used your ideas or written material improperly, strive to negotiate a reasonable resolution.

ENTERING THE GUIDEBOOK MARKET

Writing a guidebook takes more time and effort than travel articles. You could consider the time commitment for a guidebook like producing thirty to fifty travel articles. The rewards are longer life for your work and perhaps a wider audience. If the guidebook endures through several editions, the royalties may build your freelance income. Guidebook writing will not make you rich or famous. The key to a successful travel guidebook is discovering an open niche that you can fill.

Whether you plan to write a regional guidebook about southern country inns that serve tea or beach resorts that accommodate pets, the first step in your project is to establish that your book is needed. Take the time to survey the appropriate categories in the library's on-line or card catalog (Travel, Tourism, Pets, Recreation, etc.) and in bookstores. Check the latest edition of *Books in Print*, available in any library reference section. Are there fifty guidebooks to the region you plan to write about? None that explores your special topic on country inns that serve tea? What other special topics do the existing southern states guidebooks address? For example, do you see titles like Southern States for Wheelchair Users, Free Attractions in Florida, or Vegetarian Restaurants East of the Mississippi? If your topic is already covered, use *Books in Print* for possible ideas to restructure the approach.

If your concept has not been done already, you know it's at least worth your time to pursue the topic to the book proposal stage. There may well be books in the works that resemble your proposed idea. But if there is one book, two on the same topic will find an audience as long as they are promoted effectively. Sometimes publishers follow each other's lead; if one publisher commissions a book on a certain topic, another may consider a similar topic.

As the idea forms in your mind, take the time to brainstorm. Write every aspect of the travel guidebook that is floating around in your mind. Or tape record your thoughts and transcribe them. Remember that nothing will happen until your ideas are on paper and organized in a way that can be understood by others.

Arrange the material in a logical sequence. Construct an outline that includes a table of contents, an orientation or overview, specifics about the place, development of the topic, other aspects of the topic and closure. Rearrange the text you've written thus far so that it is organized with a beginning, middle and end. The draft outline should be three to five pages. If you have more material than that, extract the essence to write the outline and save the explanations by grouping related thoughts under headings, so that you can go back and use or reorganize as needed.

Next, write a statement of purpose. Why is the book needed? Who is the audience? Why should you write it? What special knowledge or experience qualifies you to write the guidebook? Where does the book fit in the travel guidebook market?

When you are satisfied that you have a coherent outline, you'll need to write a plan for your marketing approach. Go back to the library and research prospective travel book publishers. Who will publish this book? What publishing houses are handling travel guidebooks, especially in the region? Why would each be interested (or not) in this guidebook? What audience will buy the book and why? Where could it be sold? What is the competition? Are there multiple markets? For example, a guidebook to southern country inns that serve tea may have several potential audiences— food lovers, regional travelers, Anglophiles.

Call the editors you have targeted through market research. Ask if they would like to see the proposal. Find out what materials the editor or editorial board needs to review in addition to a proposal. Depending on the publisher, you could be asked to send one or more copies of a resume, list of prior publications, samples of your work, a completed chapter or two for the proposed book, a table of contents, book outline and other materials. Package the book proposal neatly typed and double spaced with wide margins. Send to one publisher at a time. If you haven't received a response within a month, call and inquire about the status of your book proposal. Perhaps the first publisher will make a commitment to your project and offer a contract. Perhaps not. Continue sending the proposal package to publishers which you have identified as potentially interested in this travel guidebook topic.

Most general guidebooks are not written by one person. Editors commission several writers to handle different aspects of a place and an in-house or contract editor completes the project to give it a unified tone.

Helpful books about travel have strong potential—how to pack, travel with children or pets, travel options for the visually impaired, shopping for antiques while traveling, how to turn your travel into an import-export business, etc.

Guidebooks age rapidly. Every year or so, a publisher needs a new edition. Generally, the freelance team that produced the last edition will be contracted again. However, if you have developed a travel specialty and notice that the guidebook series omits that special aspect of travel, approach the series editor and discuss the possibility of contributing to the next edition of a particular guidebook about a place you know well. For example, a city guidebook series for a general audience might need information on activities for children in each guide.

Contact the publisher and ask if they would consider adding a chapter on travel with children to the whole guidebook series, or to just one specific guidebook on a trial basis. Explain that you've developed a professional specialty about travel with children, have the published articles to back up your claims, and you know the specifics of this location. Ask if the editor would consider your proposal. If the idea works in one guidebook, the series editor may expand the program to cover other city guidebooks.

CHECKLIST FOR MARKETING

1. You can't write for it if you haven't read it. Go to the local library or newsstand and seek out the publications you are going to sell to. Read several issues.

2. No one starts at the top. Find your own level, work in it, then work up out of it.

3. Start with local newspapers and magazines, small publications, regional travel magazines, and publications with small editorial staffs. Write for your high school or college paper, the alumni magazine, a community newspaper. Use the experience to tackle more complex writing projects for broader publications.

4. Don't give your work away. If the publication doesn't offer a fee, ask for a subscription or free advertising or printing services in exchange for your articles. No matter how small the honorarium or in-kind service, you'll feel better if you receive something for your work and you'll be respected for your professionalism.

EXERCISE 1
Write a short query letter for your travel article. Use the story lead in the first paragraph of the letter.

EXERCISE 2
Write a phone script to query for one of the travel article ideas you wrote down in an exercise for chapter one.

EXERCISE 3

Dream a little. Write three guidebook topics that you would enjoy researching and writing. Analyze why these books should be written. Could you test the merits of these topics by writing travel articles first? Where would you sell the travel articles if you decide to proceed on these ideas?

EXERCISE 4

Assess your personal goals. Write about what is important to you about travel writing—getting your thoughts on paper and writing a story, sharing the stories with friends, writing for a broad audience, the quality of the publication where the articles appear, the pay, a byline, where the publication positions your article, a wide readership, owning reprint rights and selling the article to many publications, or some other aspect of writing or publishing.

EXERCISE 5

Develop a marketing plan. For each of your finished travel articles, identify ten markets that are *not* travel magazines or travel sections in newspapers. Take your list of story ideas and under each, write the names of publications where the finished article would possibly fit.

For example: What publications that are not specifically about travel would be interested in printing stories about:

- a visit to a 1910 carousel with restored painted wooden horses
- an article on finding kinfolks in Germany
- experiences during a two-week painting residency course in the North Carolina mountains
- a fishing tour to a remote Canadian outpost
- an incident in Rome when vagrant children steal a writer's wallet and subsequent interactions with the local police

Chapter Nine

THE PROFESSIONAL TRAVEL WRITER

WHO ARE YOU AND WHAT DO YOU DO?

Like every activity, job, skill or profession, someone who hasn't done it won't have the complete perspective. Often, people have ridiculous ideas about a travel writer's life: "If you travel you must be rich." Some comments are silly and insulting: "Anybody can do that . . . so easy." And a few reactions contain elements of truth. Yes, travel writing can be fun, but good writing is rarely easy and rewarding travel ripe with encounters isn't all that easy to achieve. Experiences worth writing about require a delicate mix of engineering and serendipity.

So what do you tell people who ask what you're up to on those trips? While there is no reward in being completely shy about what you're doing, I've found it helpful to downplay my role. I find myself saying, "Oh, I write the occasional travel article," or "I've sold a few travel articles" or "I like to travel so much that I write about it when I can." That way, privacy and a certain distance is retained which permits your observer and reporter mode to continue unimpeded.

The alternative, if you talk about yourself too much, may lead to time-wasting questions, unsolicited rambling stories and a drain on personal energy and enthusiasm. There is a balance between shutting off bores who consume precious time and missing the special conversation that arises from an expected encounter. You'll have to be the judge.

Keep in mind the joy of travel in travel writing. You are a connecting link in a long line of people who love travel and recognize the magic of a place and its people. You are sharing in a mystery, the secrets of the world, and you are sharing those secrets with other people by writing.

There may be places you won't write about because you want to reserve personal memories. Perhaps you'll recognize that there are places in the world that aren't prepared to handle the impact of mass tourism and you'll refrain from writing about them. There may be places you cannot bring yourself to write about because the aura and the experience will affect you so much and humble you, to a degree that defies the confinement of words. As David Yeadon, an adventure travel writer, said during his lecture at the National Geographic Society on March 22, 1994, "The joy of travel writing is celebrating the richness of the now, but more, all the themes underlying these mysteries. Everything resonates with power and depths you know. The lost worlds, even unlost worlds, are telling you so much, giving so much. Celebration of the un-knowable is the joy of travel."

Are you a travel writer? Here are a few randomly ordered aspects of a travel writer: loves travel; motivated; confident; friendly; curious; professional/serious attitude; has research ability; self-sufficient; organized; has foreign language skills; has knowledge of geography, natural sciences, history and cultures; has writing and photographic ability; has willingness to learn; humble; has stable health and physical stamina; psychologically flexible; and is emotionally balanced. Not every travel writer has all these characteristics; most of us have some of them. Perhaps you need to develop one or more of these traits. Work on what you can change, and strengthen qualities to balance that which you can't change.

Find ways to challenge yourself in daily life so that when adversities happen on the road, you'll have the resources to meet situations without flinching. Pretend you are traveling every day. Use different routes to get to work. Walk two miles in the rain. Eat at ethnic restaurants. Ask directions at a bar instead of a gas station. Vary your mealtimes and other daily routines. Talk to shopkeepers, street musicians, bus drivers. Take notes on what you do each day. Make every transaction or encounter a lesson in thoroughness. Ask the questions you know you'll want answered later. Encourage people to explain things to you. Practice saying, "Can you think of anything else I need to know?"

SURVIVAL ON THE ROAD

Some days just don't go as projected, we all know that. And some days seem stacked against us. We may encounter transportation delays, nonoperational phones, unexpected public holidays, bad weather, closed roads, lost reservations, gasoline shortages, wildcat rail strikes, traffic gridlock, elections, even revolution. If you are going to be out in the world experiencing, then what the world dishes up may not always be tasty.

When the flow of events isn't going your way, it might be best to lose small and head to another locale. On the other hand, if circumstances are ideal, perhaps the best decision is to stay longer than you planned. It is a skill to know whether the judicious course of action is to beat a hasty retreat or to stay on, even though your itinerary says move on. Consider whether you would be happier remaining, even though it might mean passing up another experience. Continue the research you've started, explore a back corner you just learned about, and you just might turn up an unusual story. Sticking with an itinerary worked out in advance would be folly if you miss a superb experience and a great story that you could pursue with a change of plans.

What about those reservations and appointments that will be affected by a change of plans? Well, with a telephone, most dates can be rearranged. If no telephone is available, then delays or postponements are probably expected. In most places, assuming there are sufficient resources, people interpret a visitor's desire to stay longer as flattery.

On prearranged travel writer's junkets, it may be difficult to arrange an impromptu extension. Flexibility usually belongs to those who pay their own way. If an area is particularly attractive, advise people who are arranging your trip well in advance that you might want to stay longer. Whatever the situation, state your needs politely and stay flexible.

Knowing yourself and your personal needs will serve you in every aspect of travel and travel writing. If you've been on the go for weeks and the opportunity arises to relax in solitude, would you turn it down to pursue a prior engagement? The shuffle of reservations and appointments may seem like a burden, but in the long run, your own comfort and energy reserves are at stake. If you luck into a wonderful situation, enjoy it as long as you can.

FINANCING THE FREELANCE LIFE

Yes, there are writers who earn a living freelancing. And you can too. How much you earn depends on the effort you put into marketing yourself and your work. Whether what you earn will support you depends on where you live and how much you spend.

Freelance writers don't have to live in expensive urban centers. While writers may crave the stimulation and networking opportunities of big-city life, settling in a rural area or small town can cut expenses and increase work concentration. A writer's residence doesn't determine skill and a travel writer works in the field anyway. The most important resource is a good library with access to the inter-library loan system and electronic databases. A computer with a modem or fax/modem is a useful tool for the freelance writer who lives in the hinterland.

Figure out what it takes to cover expenses. Find ways to earn that amount with steady contract work or what artists and musicians call the "day job." Eventually, you'll amass clients and can perhaps quit the day job if you want. Don't forget to factor in the subsidized health insurance, pension, paid vacations, access to equipment and other benefits associated with being an employee. If you do keep the day job, the freelance income you earn can be invested in your expanding travel writing business.

Few freelance writers are able to find full-time work in the travel field. Most travel writers I know undertake writing opportunities in several disciplines while maintaining a job, either full-time or part-time. A punishing schedule of full-time work, travel for research purposes and freelance travel writing demands stamina. You'll need an understanding family and a flexible workplace.

Which brings us to negotiating time for travel. Family and work commitments may impinge on a fledgling travel writer's freedom. At the beginning of your career, schedule professional travel writing activities during vacations and weekends. Write about places close to home that don't require extensive travel time.

Extracting yourself from your family commitments requires compromises and communication. During your absences other members of the family may have to shoulder the tasks you normally handle.

On the work front, you'll have to convince the boss that he or she can get along without you for a few days or weeks. I've had administrative positions that can be done by skilled substitutes for a period of time. Your case will sound better if you already have a substitute identified and trained. Whether or not you are paid during your leave depends on company leave policy.

When I started writing travel articles, I would work for six to eighteen months and save enough money so that I could travel for an uninterrupted period of three to six months. This worked quite well while I was a secretary, paralegal and public relations consultant. Those kinds of temporary assignments can be found in most cities. However, once I joined the news staff at *The Washington Post*, arranging for leave became more complex. One of the most difficult issues was to find and train temporary replacement staff who could assume duties so that no disruptions were felt by my colleagues. Then, I had to convince the editor that I needed the time off for legitimate professional development. Fortunately, management attitudes concerning personal and professional development have evolved over the past decade, with employers and supervisors coming to understand that what people do on the job isn't the sum of their lives. Focus the discussion on your professional development and you should get the time you need.

With permission for time off granted, at least in theory, think about finances. Will you be able to afford being away from your job? If the trip is just a few days, perhaps vacation time can be used, but for longer sojourns, you may have to consider leave without pay.

Obviously, we're not automatically entitled to more time off work than the other staff, so even unpaid leave should be treated as a benefit to be cherished. Resentment from co-workers is a possibility, but if it is clear that you are furthering your career rather than just "taking another vacation" perhaps you can win them on your side. Involve your work colleagues with your successes by sharing stories and photos with them.

Find out if your absence impacts other workers adversely. Ask them for suggestions while you are training the person who will replace you and for feedback after you have returned. A company personnel officer may be responsible for identifying the temporary replacement person and supervising the training, but if you can participate in the selection and training of the person who does your work while you are away, there's a better chance of minimizing performance problems or sour interactions with your immediate co-workers.

NETWORKING IN THE TRAVEL INDUSTRY

Gather and nurture the connections that you make as you progress. On press trips, you'll meet travel editors and other writers. All those public relations representatives, hotel publicists, airline executives and tourist board information managers are the players in the travel writer's world. Who you know is as important as what you know, so collect the business cards, develop a firm handshake, a direct smile and a memory for names and affiliations.

Stay abreast of developments in the world of tourism. Subscribing to consumer travel magazines is one way to watch travel trends, but reading industry publications gives you an edge. Check out travel trade publications at the public library or at a nearby university or community college library, especially if the institution offers classes in tourism management or the hospitality industry.

Move even farther back on the food chain of information and you'll put your name on mailing lists of tourist boards, transportation companies, hotels, travel brokers, adventure travel packages and other industry entities. Be careful though, you may be deluged with press releases and E-mail announcing new airline routes or Web sites with discount travel services. What you do with this information is up to you, but a travel writer with marketing ability could figure out interesting angles for articles that transform the travel industry's information into consumer issues.

MAXIMUM MARKETING

You've read the chapter on marketing and editors. Perhaps you've sold several articles. Maybe you are in a slump and think that you aren't getting through to editors. Or, you just want to move ahead faster. Shift your perspective. Broaden your marketing base. Don't just focus on newspaper travel sections or travel magazines. Expand marketing research beyond the travel section in the *Writer's Market* or any other writer's guide.

Tourism is one of the world's greatest economic generators; indeed some countries rely on tourism for the gross national product. Cook up a food angle for your travel article and rewrite it appropriately. Reread your work and figure out a business angle. Recently I read a travel article in a masonry business trade publication. The author had traveled the globe searching for examples of fine buildings made from brick and over the years accumulated material for a book. An engaging travel vignette evolved from one of the author's hunts for brick buildings. Could you develop an article with a travel focus for the business journal of your trade or profession?

Incentive travel, business travel, and the ease of international travel have made the world accessible to a broader range of people. High school and college students have a world of opportunity for foreign study and travel. Older retired people are setting forth on soft adventure tours while single adults are seeking an ever-expanding range of physical challenges in the outdoors. People in wheelchairs travel; children and their grandparents travel. Couples repair frazzled feelings during romantic bed-and-breakfast get-aways while others swim and sail at destination resorts. Families travel, groups travel, high school classes travel. All of these audiences, and many more, want to read travel articles.

To reach all these readers and travelers, study the print media and search the Internet. Consider posting your writing on your own Web site or explore the many on-line sites dedicated to writing.

YOUR RESPONSIBILITIES

Apart from business necessity, traveling is a discretionary purchase. Both time and money are being voluntarily spent and you, the travel writer, influence how people spend that money. This is a responsibility and a challenge.

Another type of responsibility arises from your relationship to the country and the people you visit. Are you telling the truth about the place and its residents? Will your travel article help that small Yukon village prosper or will it pervert their traditional lifestyle? Consider what might happen when a tour operator from Minneapolis decides to organize "Ski and See" tours to the snowbound northern village you visited alone on cross-country skis and wrote about. The tour operator brings busloads of visitors who spend token cash on souvenirs, but the bulk of the fees aren't invested in the village. Tourists overrun the village, drain resources (food, heat, water, electricity, space) all without building sustainable programs. Pay attention to outcomes. Be a travel writer who helps heal the world and her people.

Don't be greedy in your own travel choices. Adhere to a code of ethics for sustainable, responsible travel. Even though you may travel alone or in a small group, be aware of what your presence does to the place you visit. Are water and energy resources adversely affected by the presence of visitors? Select travel options that minimize pollution and wasted resources. Become part of the solution.

THE TOOLS OF YOUR TRADE
Your Morale

You are the most important resource, the most valuable asset, for this trade of travel writing! Learn how to take care of yourself before you travel extensively. How you respond to the act of travel will affect your performance as an observer and writer. Travel can be stressful, which may diminish the immune system. Experiences and situations will unfold depending on your own physical and emotional balance. The way you interact with the world and her people directly relates to how you feel.

Be aware of what you require to sustain health and well being. Know your physical priorities—rest, nourishment, beauty, quiet, cleanliness, companionship. Know what emotional reinforcers you need to support a neutral perspective and cultivate an eager curiosity level. Self-knowledge on a primal level is an extremely important aspect of the travel experience. When you are out of your element, away from home, how do you fare? What kinds of feelings and memories arise when you think of past travel experiences?

Successful traveling is a process. Once you recognize that your personal travel needs are just as important as electricity for the computer, paper and ribbons for the typewriter and fresh rolls of film for the camera, then you will understand how keeping yourself in harmony will make or break the trip. Meet the world you see with a sense of awareness and curiosity and you will have one kind of trip. Meet the world with discontent and obsession and you will have quite another.

Rejection of your work affects morale. It can be discouraging to know that many people without talent get published. But a writer with talent and marketing savvy has an unlimited future as a travel writer.

Setting Up Your Work Space

We discussed the travel journal in chapter three. After you get home and start transcribing your luscious material, you'll need a typewriter or computer and a quiet place to write.

Computers are indispensable for a productive travel writer. Anyone who can type can use a computer for word processing. The time saved in producing stories will pay for the computer within its tax depreciable life. Do we need to mention the advantage a computer gives in the task of reshaping and structuring articles for resale? Or for writing query letters and printing many copies of an article for mass marketing submissions? While many writers swear by hefty full-size desk computers with all the accessories, I prefer a simple portable laptop.

Consider what you are going to do with the computer: massage financial data for corporate annual reports or publish a newsletter or design Web sites or write words? If you plan to use on-line databases, electronic library catalogs, E-mail and the Internet for research, you will need a modem and communications software for your computer, and lots of storage space. Many of these features are standard equipment in desktop and lightweight portable computers. Remember that laptops can be used nearly anywhere.

Adjustable desks and chairs are imperative. Typing for extended periods at a poorly arranged workstation that strains your hands and arms may lead to repetitive stress injury (RSI) in your hands, wrists, elbows, back, neck and shoulders. Consult books on ergonomics to determine the appropriate distances and angles for your chair, keyboard, mouse or trackball, lamp, paper holder and monitor. Rest and exercise your hands, arms and eyes; they are precious tools. Consider using voice recognition software and dictate your writing if you are suffering from repetitive stress injury.

Time Management

Getting to the computer keyboard can be a problem for busy, traveling writers. Finding the time in a busy schedule for extended periods of writing sounds like luxury to me. Most freelancers have learned to carve time out of other commitments. I have learned to write or work on drafts while commuting or tape record while driving. Use the morning hours and write an hour before leaving for work. Stop watching television completely (*yes!*) and you've found, on average, the equivalent of two or three days of writing time per week. Forego gabbing with friends, postpone shopping, hire a teenager to do your chores. A ruthless analysis of how you spend your time will always yield at least an hour a day that could be spent writing. Even parents with small children can find the time, although it might be in fifteen-minute gaps between the demands of that job.

Think about your story when you are driving and idling at stoplights. Even if you can't write down what you think, the exercise of working your brain over the story will help you once you do sit down at the keyboard. The point is to find time for focusing on the writing, not the business of freelancing or research preparations for writing. Get out pen and paper and jostle words around if you can't get to your desk.

The Rolodex

Though some writers prefer to keep a computer based address book, my twin Rolodexes A-K and L-Z are my workday friends. The cards give me access to people and institutions that I've contacted over the years. Smaller and more accessible than a file cabinet, they hold a wealth of information. Develop your own file system for names, addresses and telephone numbers. When you get a new contact name at a magazine, public relations firm or tourist office, make a new index card right away. I staple business cards onto the large size cards. Since I can't always remember the names of individual editors or publicists, I sometimes file cards by locations: country, state or city.

Some cards are grouped by function, such as airlines, railroads, hotels, resorts or travel agents. I have one card for the name of the publication and write down staff names and direct phone or fax lines as I learn them. Once I've worked with an editor, I'll insert a second card under the editor's last name. If I'm searching for a certain hotel in Paris, I'll check the Paris section and if it isn't there, I'll certainly find it behind the H tab filed with Hotels. An airline magazine editor might be listed on the card for the name of the publication or on the card for the name of the airline. Sometimes when I'm stuck for marketing ideas, I'll flip through the Rolodex and chance will guide me to find a wild card. I call those fishing expeditions. My personal information filing system is idiosyncratic and flexible. It has evolved during two decades of work.

In time, you'll construct a system to suit your own needs.

Reference Books

Every writer amasses a personal set of reference books. Consult the Apendix of this book for suggestions. The reference books closest to my desk include the *Oxford English Dictionary*, a word finder to help with spelling, the Bible, a classical dictionary, Eric Partridge's *Usage and Abusage*, Strunk and White's *Elements of Style*, the Prentice Hall *Handbook for Writers*, several language dictionaries (Spanish, German, Italian, French, Russian, Japanese, Latin), a *Dictionary of Literary Terms*, *Larousse Gastronomique*, the *Associated Press Stylebook*, several atlases, the *Columbia Desk Encyclopedia*, *World Book Encyclopedia Dictionary*, a dictionary of English synonyms, *Roget's Thesaurus*, *Bartlett's Quotations*, *Webster's* dictionary, the *Writer's Market*. My library includes hundreds of literary travel books, old guidebooks, recent travel guides, pamphlets on specific historical landmarks, photo books about places and lots of maps. One of these days, I'd like to get a *Gazetteer*, which is a reference book of geographic place names.

Tape Recorder

To capture the sound of church bells or street markets, you'll need a tape recorder. When you are writing, a tape of special music, people talking or the sound of the waves will help you remember and translate the sounds to the article. Simulate your experience and recapture memories by listening to the tape again. A tape recorder is also useful for accurately reporting interviews, note taking and, if it has a playback feature and a headset, you can listen to music tapes while you travel.

Expense Records

Contracts for travel writers sometimes include a clause concerning expenses. A figure may be listed and all expenses up to that amount will be reimbursed. Some publications agree to reimburse "reasonable" expenses related to the writing project. Other publications rely on a verbal agreement to cover mileage and long-distance telephone calls. Before you incur expenses on an assigned writing project, find out what will be reimbursed. If you are writing on spec, ask if the publication repays expenses and to what extent, assuming the article is accepted for publication. Unless you know the editor and the reputation of the publication, try to get this agreement in writing. After you have worked with the editor or the publication, you can be less compulsive about getting agreements in writing.

During the beginning phase of your travel writing career, expenses will probably exceed writing income. Keep a meticulous written log of mileage related to researching and producing articles for sale. Leave the mileage notebook in the car so it is always available to note that brief trip to the post office or the library. Ask for receipts for any expenditure related to travel writing and save these receipts, writing on the back what article it was for or the story source you had coffee with, etc.

Some freelancers carry notebooks devoted entirely to travel writing expenses. They jot down cab fares, telephone calls, magazines bought for research, office supplies, fax charges, express delivery fees, etc. Other writers bundle the receipts in an envelope and attach them to a copy of the final story. To me that seems excessive, but if you are faced with an inquiry from the Internal Revenue Service, evidence that the expenses matched a published article might well be useful.

Here's what I do. During each writing research trip, I save all receipts. On the plane or train home, I sort them and total the categories—transport, hotel, personal meals, entry fees, business meals with contacts and sources, local transportation, etc. The receipts are clipped together and stored in an envelope with the category totals written on the outside. I also keep a mileage logbook in the car and write down mileage for all trips that relate to freelance writing. When April 15 looms and it's time to provide the income and expense numbers to the accountant, I have an easier time of totaling the year's expenses.

What about the expenses of a companion who goes along on your travels? As long as the travel companion has a business purpose—taking pictures, gathering research, translating—then the expenses are part of producing articles for sale. An effective way to handle a companion's expenses is to become a team, sharing the work and a byline.

Each freelance writer's tax situation is different. Before amassing significant expenses related to your travel writing career, read the guidelines that the Internal Revenue Service provides for Schedule C income reporting. Consult a tax advisor about what expenses you can legally deduct and how you should handle freelance income.

FREE TRIPS

As far as free travel goes, be picky. If you decide to take complimentary trips that are offered to you or to seek out free travel when you need it, maintain your perspective and standards. If what you experience and see isn't acceptable, you shouldn't let the absence of a bill shape your opinions. Writers who see no fault, ever, in the places that offer unpaid accommodation, meals or transport have become hired shills.

I've also heard people who earn their living from travel writing brag that they've never paid a cent for travel and have never had to write a negative word about a place. Bombastic talk that perpetuates the public myth that travel writers always travel for free, get the best deals and don't have the same travel experiences as everyone else doesn't enhance the professional image of travel writers. The bottom line is, be aware of biases, influences and other personal slants that color your view of a place or experience.

Accepting junkets and familiarization trips does carry ethical responsibilities. The tourist office or resort or public relations firm that invites you expects that an article will be published. There are times when you have the best intentions, write the article and send it to an interested editor at a publication that has no rules barring articles from press junkets, but for one reason or another the article doesn't get published. You've done your part, but the agency that offered you the trip may not understand why the article wasn't published. They may ask you to try and publish it elsewhere and indeed, since you put so much time and effort into the piece, you'll be eager to market the story elsewhere. Just be aware that if you accept free trips, some publications will not accept any of your work, unless the editor is certain that you only offer stories from trips that you paid for yourself. Don't forget to send thank-you notes to the people who organized the trip or contributed to your travel research. And when the article is published, distribute copies to those who helped make the trip possible.

The free trip issue is really quite simple. Accept invitations for free trips only when there's a certainty you can place a story in a publication. Submit such stories to editors at publications that don't mind subsidized travel. Don't try to fool an editor who has a policy against articles arising from free trips; you will damage your credibility. Don't make promises that you can't deliver to companies or tourist boards that invite you on junkets. Be honest and clear in your research and writing too!

JOINING ORGANIZATIONS

For a novice writer, an organization dedicated to helping writers with their craft can be extraordinarily helpful. A full-time freelance writer may want the professional identification that a writer's organization offers. Some groups provide health insurance, job-finding help, legal assistance and other services needed by freelancers.

There are sound reasons for joining a writer's group. You might need the organization to develop editorial contacts and to move your name and work around the marketplace. For networking purposes, the organization might be a good first stop on the road to successful freelancing. Writer's organizations usually schedule workshops or seminars with editors.

You can expect to meet other writers through a membership organization and they might share tips on which publications are buying material. They might even pass work along to you when they are too busy (a rare situation for a freelancer) and opportunities for collaboration might emerge. Writer's organizations sometimes hold book fairs, marketing seminars or meet-the-agents-and-editors gatherings. Such programs may be open to the general public, so you don't need to be a member to attend.

Before joining an organization find out all the benefits available to members. Each organization has its own focus and resources; benefits vary, but may include a library, a newsletter which accepts articles from members, referrals to literary agents or editors, bookstore discounts, access to computers and desktop publishing software, manuscript reading and analysis.

Most important, though, for writers who are getting started, are the small groups of working writers who provide support for each other when the writing or marketing isn't going well. These focus groups may be under the wing of a larger arts organization, or simply be a group of sympathetic, dedicated writers who meet regularly and discuss their work. If you can't find such a group in your immediate area, inquire at the nearest college English or Journalism department or ask the state or regional arts council for assistance in locating like-minded writers. Internet communicators can access other writers in cyberspace.

Mentioning membership in an organization rarely impresses editors. Fine writing does. Joining an organization with the expectation of improving your publication record is unrealistic. You might meet an editor at a writer's group event, but you'll still have to produce a competently written piece. If you are confident about your writing, then meetings, workshops and other gatherings may enhance your networking opportunities and improve specific skills.

Some travel writer's organizations might introduce you to public relations executives and tourism officials who offer invitations to junkets and familiarization tours for writers. But free or reduced price trips will only be extended to any writer with a solid track record of published work. Membership in a writer's organization does not make you a writer. Writing does. Belonging to a writer's group doesn't make you eligible for free trips. Published articles do.

One way to accumulate published clips is to write for the organization's newsletter. Payment probably isn't an issue with this kind of publication, but you should receive extra copies and a byline. Read the newsletter for two or three months before approaching the editor with your idea. Volunteering to help with production is a way to gain publication experience.

RECYCLING AND RESELLING WORK

After an article has been published, you may have the right to resell it to other publications. Clarify your legal rights before offering any previously published material for sale. If you have written under contract, the terms of sale will be described. Often, a publication will purchase first rights, or exclusive rights for a period of time during which the publication has the right to resell the article. At some point, reprint rights usually revert to the author. If there is no contract between you and the publication, check with your editor. When you sell frequently to one publication, editors may forget to send a contract for each sale unless the terms have changed. You needn't insist on a contract for each sale if you have a trusting editorial relationship, but keep records of what you sell and whether the date of purchase is keyed to acceptance, publication or payment. Then, if you've sold exclusive first rights for six months from the date of publication, you'll know you can resell the piece six months afterwards.

Read the terms of your contract carefully. Before you sign, understand what rights you are selling and for how long. Contracts vary. Sometimes magazines purchase worldwide exclusive rights for a period of time, say three to six months, then the reprint rights revert to the writer. Newspapers may purchase one-time publication rights and electronic reprint rights, which means articles that appear in the paper are stored on a database which the paper leases to customers.

If the original story appeared in a national magazine or newspaper, it's unlikely that a competing publication would purchase the same piece. You can offer travel articles to noncompeting newspapers on a simultaneous basis, selling, for example, the same story to papers in Chicago, New Orleans and Portland.

Advise editors that you are submitting an article that has appeared in print. When sending out the same article to many different papers, write at the top of the first page "Offered for one-time second rights, exclusive in this circulation area or market." Editors then know that you aren't sending the same article to a competing paper in the same or nearby city. These days, however, this is not really a problem; regrettably, because few cities have more than one daily newspaper.

When you are discussing the article you plan to resell, tell the editor the piece has appeared elsewhere. Before reselling your work, make appropriate changes to update the material. When selling your work a second or third time, you may have to make revisions for each sale. Let's say you want to sell the same story to a newspaper in a different city. The "how to" sidebar will have to reflect transportation and hotel costs related to this city. Dates and seasonal activities may need to be updated. In the query letter, state that the story is a second sale, exclusive in that paper's circulation area.

A basic guideline is to seek a resale market where the original piece did not penetrate. If the article appeared in a weekly limited-circulation paper, then step up to a daily newspaper in a different circulation zone. If the piece first appeared in a special interest magazine, try selling it to a news service with national circulation.

Finding your resale path takes time. My formula is to sell to the highest paying, top market publication first, then work down to more obscure publications. Usually, the story changes for each resale so that every article is unique.

Consider selling articles that have appeared in nationally circulated magazines or newspapers to English language papers and magazines in other countries. Or restructure the piece and sell it to a completely different market. For example, after the initial contract expired, I took a brief item about a luxury train in India that I'd sold to *Travel & Leisure* and expanded it for a special interest magazine devoted to railroads.

Reselling Articles as Travel Columns

A nexus of special interest and travel could become the foundation for a regular travel column. Identify an interesting aspect in the story and focus more fully, perhaps using notes that you were unable to fit into the first piece. Determine the special interests in which you have expertise and write three to five sample columns highlighting various aspects of that special interest. Then make a presentation to several newsletter or magazine editors in the special interest field.

For example, if you love trains, you've probably already written several travel pieces about this favorite mode of transportation. Quite likely, those articles could be transformed into a package of sample travel columns. The sample columns might net you a regular space on rail travel in a rail enthusiast's magazine or newsletter. The columns would focus on aspects of railroading—a trip on a narrow gauge railroad, a visit to a railroad museum, a historical account of a famous rail line.

The column format is shorter, more personalized and focuses on a particular incident or subject that has wide appeal. Perhaps you interviewed the conductor of the narrow gauge train but were unable to work all the material into the original travel story. In the column format, reuse some of the travel material within a frame of a brief personal encounter or observation. With a half dozen different columns on various aspects of rail travel, you'll be ready to market them.

Research which magazines and newsletters for railway enthusiasts do not have travel columns. Make phone calls and discuss the possibility of a travel column with the managing editor or publisher. Assess their enthusiasm and send proposal letters with sample columns to the editors who exhibit strong interest. The proposal letter outlines your professional experience, published travel articles, public speaking engagements, etc. Present the column and yourself as a package that will enhance the newsletter or magazine.

In the same way, turn any one of your interests or areas of expertise into regular work. Think in terms of the hobby or recreational activity and write about it with a travel focus. Topics such as medieval music, Civil War history, herb gardening, sulky racing, doll collecting and chocolate all have individual publications. After you've written many columns on a particular special interest topic, consider collecting them in a guidebook.

For example, a series of rail-oriented weekend getaways written in a column format could become the basis of a guidebook about rail travel destinations in the region. The field is wide open for writers with expertise in a subject to make the connection with travel.

SELF-PROMOTION

Are you uncomfortable with promoting yourself? I am. Although you might wonder how I can make that claim while writing a book about my experiences as a travel writer, I have left most of my career path to chance. I have no brochure describing my travel writing workshops, no letterhead, no advertisements. While I can think of dozens of ways that I could be promoting my expertise, thus streamlining my work so that it would be more lucrative, I am loathe to initiate a public relations campaign. The pop-psychology books would suggest I may be afraid of success. I just think that time devoted to promotion doesn't leave much for writing and traveling!

What I have done at various times is send out small packets of my published work with a letter of introduction to editors I'd like to work with in markets that are well within my level of expertise. Some editors have responded; others haven't. When I feel confident, I make "cold calls" to editors and introduce myself, chatting briefly if they have the time. The phone introduction leads to a discussion of what I've written, where it has been published and where I'm planning to travel next. More often than not, the editor asks to see some published clips and agrees to "take a look" at the story I'm offering for sale. An editor who says he'll take a look is not making a commitment to buy the story, but at least the story will be read, and if I'm prompt about sending the packet of clips along with the finished manuscript, there's a chance the conversation will still be in the forefront of the editor's memory.

The goal is to separate yourself from the pack. Distinguish yourself in an editor's mind through your articulate presentation and appropriate story ideas. Then continue the self-promotion effort by sending published examples of your sharpest writing along with a letter that reiterates the story ideas or a completed manuscript in which the editor expressed interest.

Establish yourself as a professional writer by acting like one. Self-promoting editorial conversations lead to assignments when you stay tuned to the process, stay flexible and respond appropriately to each stage of the negotiation. If the editor shows interest, respond immediately with the manuscript. If the editor says your experience level isn't up to the standards of the magazine, ask politely for suggestions where you might meet with success. After you've sent in your work and the editor rejects the story but invites other queries, ask where the editor thinks the rejected article might work. Continue the dialogue by pitching other ideas; don't stay fixed on the last story.

The process by which an idea gets into print can be complex and lengthy; often going a circuitous route that the writer never envisions at the beginning. The manuscript may languish for years in your computer and then be rewritten for immediate publication. Or, it may be rejected by one magazine only to find a more receptive berth at another magazine. For a writer with an emotional investment in the manuscript, this process can be harrowing. Strive for the long view and realize that if you feel emotional dynamite exploding when a story is rejected, you have some growth to work on. Look upon your manuscripts as works in progress and each encounter with an editor as an opportunity to refine and improve both the specific story and your own skills.

Networking and self-promotion are individual efforts. You are always your own best promoter. Don't think you can't do it and don't think someone else would do it better. Any writer is capable of promoting his or her work. In my experience, the primary focus is to remember that you have nothing to lose and everything to gain.

Do wait until you are relaxed and confident before making calls. You wouldn't want to leave the impression that you are insecure, struggling to express yourself or nervous. If your ideas are sound and your product is reliable, editors will want to hear from you.

The most forceful sales point in your writer's quiver is your portfolio of published work. Get a copy of every piece of your writing that is published. That means everything—newsletters, small hometown papers, college newspapers, daily newspapers, letters to the editor, magazines, business writing, etc. When you are written about, make sure you get a copy of the article. Even if you think that the mention that appeared in your employee newsletter isn't important, you can't predict future needs. Store the original clips in acid-free file folders or archival quality plastic pocket holders. Don't paste or tape your clips into scrapbooks. Over time most glue destroys paper. There may come a day when you only have one copy of a favorite article left and you'll need to make a photocopy of that clip. Bear in mind that you may want to have a record of your work to pass on to family members.

Ideally, you'll get two or more original copies of published articles. Most publications send out these contributors' copies or tearsheets shortly after the date of publication. If you don't get yours, inquire immediately. The longer the time lapse between publication date and your request for the issue in which your work appeared, the less likely there will still be back issues available. One original could be placed in a binder for display and reference purposes. The other copies could be used for sending out to editors as examples of your published work or may be retained for making photocopies.

This is my system. I have a large album where one copy of every published work is kept; the "show-and-tell" book. A second copy goes in the file folder I maintain for every publication I write for. Extra copies are filed in a set of folders labeled by year. That way, I can retrieve the article by looking in the folder of the magazine or paper where it appeared or in the yearly folder, depending on which I remember first. I also make photocopies of the best articles and keep them ready in a "Clips to Send Out" file to use when editors ask for samples of my work.

In a three-ring binder filled with plastic sleeves, I store newsletter articles in which I'm mentioned, announcements of readings or workshops and any other material that is related to the publicity of my writing career.

Keep a chronological list of your publications in a standard citation form. Include the title of the article, name of the publication, volume, issue, date and pages. Maintain the list so that if an editor asks for a summary of your publications, you can send a copy of the whole list or extract appropriate titles. The day may come when you apply for writer's residencies, workshops or grants. Almost every application of this type requires a list of published credits. If you develop a proposal for a travel guide or other book, you'll need to include a list of your published credits.

When your level of experience broadens and professional credits accumulate, you'll need a brief biography. In about one hundred carefully chosen words, you should state the facts concerning your education, employment and achievements related to writing and place of residence. Cute descriptions of your pets, spouses, children, hobbies, habits and hopes are best omitted. If an editor asks for a description to put at the end of an article—the ending bio—you could extract a sentence or two from the brief bio. Some publications prefer that the short descriptions be humorous. Read the publication to find out how other writers have described themselves. If you are unsure what the editor expects for the short ending bio, ask for details.

Do you have a writer's resume? Even if you aren't planning to apply for writing jobs, the exercise is worthwhile. Focus on your professional writing experience; jobs where you were hired to write or edit, contract writing work that isn't covered in the list of publications, writing projects you directed, any teaching, writing workshops you attended, prizes, awards, grants, etc. Do your diplomas or academic degrees relate to English or writing? Have you contributed to the community with volunteer work related to writing?

Now, don't forget to leave room for all those contests and awards on your writer's resume. There are only a few writing awards dedicated to travel writing. Some awards require a nomination from the Society of American Travel Writers or similar journalists' organizations. Other awards invite submissions from individual writers. Check a current edition of the *Editor and Publisher's Yearbook* for information on deadlines and categories. The Appendix of this book lists some travel writing awards.

Letterhead and business cards are useful to have, but if you can't afford them, refrain from spending money on business accessories that you can really do without during the early years of your writing career. Business cards are more important than letterhead; when you travel, you may want to give a contact or new friend a card with your name and address. Plain white or cream bond paper is perfectly acceptable for writing business letters.

You will have to decide the comfort level of self-promotion. Spend too much time on self-promotion and I'll bet you don't get much writing done. Ignore the promotion angle and you'll see sources of work dry up. A skilled financial manager strives to augment the capital as well as earn money on the money. In managing your writing capital, you need to expand the places where you can publish even as you continue to write. Think about a spreading pool of water. You don't want to spread yourself so thin that it dries up in places, but you do need to keep pushing your work to new areas.

Self-promotion can be done by networking through friends and business contacts. You needn't boast, but telling people what you are working on, where you are traveling next, where your work has been published recently, keeps you in the habit of communicating. All the people you talk to may mention your successes to their friends and so an informal promotional network begins.

There are writers who send out chatty summaries of their current activities—readings, a book signing, notable publications. An artist friend circulates updated versions of her resume with the current exhibition location and dates. Photocopy news clippings that mention your activities or copy your articles and send to friends who are interested in your successes and will help you in the informal promotional effort.

If you win a writing award, take self-promotion one step further and send out press releases to your alumni magazine, club newsletter, or in-house company newsletter. Should you advise the general media? It's up to you, but only a local paper would really devote space to personal achievements such as prizes and awards. Perhaps your hometown paper would interview you after you won a writing prize and certainly a local paper would announce an upcoming workshop you are leading.

Keep in mind your goal for self-promotion. Are you trying to generate more writing assignments? Attract students to your workshops or classes? Sell more copies of your guidebook?

SUSTAINING RELATIONSHIPS WITH EDITORS

During the time I have been freelancing, many of the editors I have worked with have moved to other publications. I tend to view this as a plus for my marketing plans because it offers me an entree at two points—the magazine where I have already made a successful sale and the magazine where the editor now works.

Keeping track of editors requires some networking. Whenever I talk to other writers, I ask what they are currently working on and which editors they've worked with lately. If I gather information during these conversations, I'll make appropriate changes on my Rolodex cards and possibly follow up with a phone call to the editor to remind him or her of my interest. Another way to gather information about editorial changes is to scan mastheads, or simply call the editorial assistant or telephone receptionist and ask questions.

Many writers make the mistake of thinking that if they don't hear from an editor the editor doesn't want to work with them anymore. Usually, this is not the case. Editors are busy people, focused on the future. A writer's promptness at deadline time is appreciated, but once an article is "dumped" into type, it's out of sight and mind. Alas, the writer is too. Writers grouse that's why we don't get paid promptly; editors have simply forgotten that we exist once the article is off their desk.

So, we writers have to be vigilant about reminding editors who know and like our work about our successes and our sparkling ideas. Do this with a brief phone call. Or send an especially wonderful story of yours that has appeared in print and attach a brief letter. Have a point to your communication; pitch a story idea and ask for an assignment. Mention your other recent significant writing assignments and achievements.

It also never hurts to notice when an editor deserves recognition. When the editor changes jobs, express the appropriate congratulations. Perhaps the magazine has been redesigned or you've read a significant story in its pages; pass on your thoughts to the editor. Editors who've never heard of you might be confused by letters of congratulation. I leave you to determine whether it is appropriate business etiquette to congratulate a complete stranger on a new job or magazine redesign.

When you are planning an important trip, let the editors you've worked with before know your itinerary, because they just might have a story assignment for you. Assuming you've already established your skills and credibility with an editor, offer to scout newly opened hotels or restaurants. This kind of informal networking is almost always done with editors you have already worked with. An exception might be when an editor you've written for suggests that you contact an editor at another publication. In that case, send a letter of introduction explaining your credentials and mentioning the referral from the other editor.

If the networking call with an editor you know is to communicate story ideas, have a few notes ready and a large blank sheet of paper. I can't tell you how many times I've been chatting with editors and the ideas and information are flying as fast as I can jot them down. Then the scrap of paper runs out and I can't read all the one-word ideas afterwards. Here's a tip: Ask editors what they are working on. Many of them are writers too, and, just like you, they enjoy talking about travel. You'll pick up useful information about choice destinations, trends, or changes in the magazine industry. Here's another tip: Be brief, be the first to conclude the conversation, ask intelligent questions, and ask if you can call again with more story ideas. Sometimes the networking call or note is more effective than a formal query letter because the pressure is off, and you aren't selling a story and can talk about your travel plans in a relaxed manner.

DEALING WITH PUBLICATION ERRORS

If you think there has been an error or improper use of your material, approach the publication, find out which editor handled the story in question and gently point out the odd coincidence that material you sent in for consideration has just appeared in print under someone else's name. Review the facts, from your perspective and from the publication's perspective. Keep your tone neutral, your attitude focused on clearing up a misunderstanding. Get the editor on your side.

When it appears that your work was used without credit, or even if you feel nearly certain that a publication used your material improperly, remember that humor and a sense of proportion goes farther than accusations and threats of legal action. What may look like plagiarism or improper use of your writing might simply be another writer covering the same ground. It may be difficult to believe, but the ideas you pitch and the stories you send in may have already been assigned. If you have a good idea, rest assured some other freelancer, staff writer or editor may have had a similar idea. Professionals know this happens fairly often. Similarly, freelancers look through publications for story ideas and often rework stories written by others. Once your work is out in the marketplace, there is nothing to prevent someone else from doing a fresh version of essentially the same story and selling it, perhaps at a higher fee, to a competing publication.

I recall one incident when a freelancer pitched a story idea and included recent clips from a small local paper. The editor didn't react to the story idea and therefore didn't look very closely at the accompanying clips. A few weeks later another freelancer pitched a story that just happened to be based on one of the first writer's accompanying clips. The editor didn't notice the connection and bought the second writer's story. When it was published, the first freelancer thought the editor had purloined her story and slapped someone else's name on it. In fact, the editor was nonplussed when the freelancer threatened legal action. The only error in professionalism was the second freelancer not informing the editor that she had gotten the idea from a previously published story, even though she did her own reporting.

Though you may feel injured, desperation and threats put editors on the defensive. Maybe they did make an error or fail to notice that your story languishing on a desk or in a file was essentially the same as the one some other writer sent in, but pointing out the humor of the situation will go farther for you. Keep the issue in perspective: In the scheme of things, how important is one misappropriated idea stacked up against alienating a publication and editors who might be feeding you work in the future?

The editor's embarrassment may yield you small assignments or at least an adequate hearing when you have story proposals in the future. Threats rarely achieve the effect intended by the angry writer, and unprofessional behavior will nearly guarantee you will not receive assignments in the future.

TANGENTIAL WORK—LECTURES AND WORKSHOPS

Experienced writers know they have to branch out to reach new audiences. Opportunities come through tangential work—teaching, lecturing, readings, guest appearances on discussion panels. You can speed the process through self-promotion. Seek affiliation with a travel agency and host a travel discussion forum. Share your love of travel and your unique experiences and encourage the audience to participate. Find a sponsoring organization for courses in special interest travel; how to travel alone, how to travel happily with children, environmental travel programs, grandparent/grandchildren travel, or tips for handicapped travelers.

Travel is a popular topic for gatherings at community or recreation centers, senior citizen residences and youth centers. Show slides and talk about your travel experiences and build an audience for your writing.

Approach local libraries and bookstores who may want to sponsor an open house or discussion of travel opportunities. Payment for such events may be small or nonexistent. The reason for pursuing these opportunities is to broaden your audience and stay in touch with what the traveling and reading public is doing. It also helps to establish your professional presence in the travel industry.

Publicity for a workshop, class or reading generally is the responsibility of the teacher or speaker—you. Draw up a small public relations campaign plan and write down the interests of the various participants. Enlist the assistance of the organizations you are working with, such as the workshop sponsor or bookstore or travel agency where you are holding your event. Remember that early and often are the watchwords of successful publicity.

Send out your press release to the media and follow up with a phone call. Be sure that you've sent the announcement with sufficient lead time for the publication to list your reading or workshop in the events calendar. For weekly publications, this can mean the announcement has to be received as much as a month in advance; for dailies, up to three weeks in advance. Use radio announcements, flyers and posters. If the organization has a mailing list, send out registration forms or postcards announcing the event. Tell all your friends and colleagues. Be prepared for a full house, but to avoid disappointment, expect a small audience.

Once you have a specialty, or feel that you have developed knowledge and understanding of a particular country or region, you can bill yourself as an expert. Remember though, that even experts don't have all the answers, and if you don't know the answer, say so.

DEVELOPING A SPECIALTY

Set yourself apart from the pack by defining a specialty interest. Project yourself as not just a travel writer, but one specializing in the Caribbean, or outdoor adventure, or children's activities.

Deborah McLaren, a Washington, D.C.-based travel writer, specializes in responsible tourism. She describes herself as an alternative tourism travel writer with a focus on what communities are doing. "Eco-tourism isn't just going to a lodge in the jungle, it is working with communities. I love to travel and it gives me an opportunity to become more involved with the local communities. My travel writing emerged from working in the responsible tourism movement."

Six years ago, as part of a graduate school research project, McLaren traveled to communities in Asia that had rejected the notion of conventional tourism. She thought the information she was gathering would be useful for other low-budget travelers. "I targeted magazines outside of the travel industry—women's magazines, educational magazines—and submitted a list of the alternative tourism projects initiated by villages in Asia." Never having written for publication before, McLaren was surprised at the response; a three-part series in an educational travel magazine and an essay in a national women's magazine.

In addition to travel writing, McLaren works with communities to develop marketable tours that generate involvement, support and funds for preservation. She also lectures, leads workshops and helps colleges plan study travel programs, always with a goal to educate new audiences. "I want to show people a way to make choices about the impact of their travel. The travel industry is still growing and offshoots like eco-tourism, nature tours and adventure travel are really exploding. People are seeking more realistic travel experiences and travel writers have a whole new market to write about. Travel agents need information about community-designed tourism, so write for the travel industry publications."

TEN STEPS TO GET STARTED

Now that you've read this book and sampled the writing exercises, the world is wide open for you to embark on the path of writing about your travels. Perhaps you've even sold an article or two after absorbing the information on marketing and editorial networking. Opportunities abound in the travel industry; right now is the time to make a place for yourself as a travel writer. I wish you every success in creating a rewarding career as a travel writer.

1. WRITE as often as you can, and at least twice a week. The urge to write every day will come in time.

2. READ a variety of strong writers. Seek works by contemporary and classic authors. Explore different styles and subjects—essays, fiction, nonfiction, memoir, humor and, of course, travel writing.

3. RESEARCH travel markets by visiting newsstands and libraries at least once or twice a month. Scrutinize the travel magazines. Check out other magazines and assess whether travel pieces ever appear in them.

4. COLLECT maps, atlases and history books to find interesting landmarks, sites and towns. Start with your home city or state.

5. STUDY the travel sections of large circulation daily newspa-

pers; the *New York Times*, *Los Angeles Times*, *The Washington Post*, *Chicago Times*, *Toronto Star*, *Miami Herald*, *Boston Globe*. Develop a sense of what style and subjects are featured in travel stories that are published.

6. CULTIVATE your senses; try different foods and beverages, scents and music. Note your moods and reactions to adversity, change, transition, solitude and crowds.

7. DEVELOP visual resources; go to art galleries or look at books with reproductions of art, collections of photographs, sculpture and architecture. Look at nature. Think how you would describe what you see.

8. HAVE FUN; break your routines, get lost, encourage an appreciation for the absurd, talk to strangers and ask directions.

9. PREPARE; be ready to write by keeping pens and notepads in your car, briefcase, purse or coat pocket. Pack a small case of travel toiletries and other essentials to simplify packing for a trip. Buy clothes that fold easily. Organize your desk and filing system.

10. TRAVEL; take every journey you can —short, long, near or far. Seek pleasure and personal satisfaction. Be self-oriented and follow your dreams. Your happiness will make others happy wherever you go.

APPENDIX

The Appendix includes useful books about travel writing, suggested reference books and information about periodicals and organizations for travel writers.

This list of resources is not exhaustive and was correct at press time.

BOOKS

A Life in Hand: Creating the Illuminated Journal, by Hannah Hinchman. Peregrine Smith Books, Salt Lake City, UT. 1991. Discussion of the personal journal with a focus on nature. Finding the artist within, exercises to get started, elements of design, developing the individual perspective.

Travel Writing for Profit & Pleasure, by Perry Garfinkel. New American Library, Plume Books. Penguin Books USA Inc. 1633 Broadway, New York, NY 10019. 1989.

A Guide to Travel Writing & Photography, by Ann Frederick Purcell and Carl M. Purcell. Writer's Digest Books, 1507 Dana Ave., Cincinnati, OH 45207. 1991.

The Writer's Lawyer, by Ronald Goldfarb and Gail Ross. Times Books, c/o Random House, 400 Hahn Rd., Westminster, MD 21157, (800) 733-3000. 1989. $19.95.

The Writer's and Photographer's Guide To Global Markets, by Michael Sedge, 292 pages, ISBN: 1-58115-002-4

The Complete Guide to Writers' Groups and Workshops, by Eileen Malone. Citadel Press, 120 Enterprise Ave., Secaucus, NJ 07094, (201) 866-0490. 1995.

PERIODICALS AND NEWSLETTERS

Editor & Publisher, 11 West 19th Street, New York, NY 10011-4234, (212) 675-4380, E-Mail edpub@mediainfo.com. $75/year/52 issues.

Travelwriter Marketletter, % The Waldorf-Astoria, 301 Park Ave., Suite 1850, New York, NY 10022. Editor, Robert Scott Milne. $60/year. Monthly newsletter offering the latest in travel market opportunities, editorial staff changes, new publications and free trips offered by tourism offices, public relations firms and others.

The Writer. 120 Boylston St., Boston, MA 02116. Monthly magazine for writers.

Writer's Digest. 1507 Dana Ave., Cincinnati, OH 45207. Monthly magazine for writers.

Publishers Weekly. The International News Magazine of Book Publishing and Bookselling, 249 West 17th St., New York, NY 10011.

ORGANIZATIONS FOR TRAVEL WRITERS

American Society of Journalists and Authors, 1501 Broadway, Suite 1907, New York, NY 10036.

Garden Writers Association of America, 10210 Leatherleaf Ct., Manassas, VA 20111, (703)257-1032. Membership organization for well-established freelance writers.

International Food, Wine & Travel Writers Association, 5310 Dubois Ave., Woodland Hills, CA 91367, (818) 999-9959, http://www.IFWT WA.org. Ron Hodges, Executive Director. Dues $95 with one-time initiation fee of $50. Includes subscription to *Hospitality World* monthly newsletter. For writers who publish at least ten articles per year relating to food, wine or travel.

Midwest Travel Writer's Association, Beverly Hurley, 12724 Sagamore Rd., Leawood, KS 66209, (913) 451-9023, Fax (913) 451-4866.

North American Snowsports Journalists Association, P.O. Box 74563, 2803 West 4th Ave., Vancouver, B.C. Canada V6K 4P4, http://www.nasja.org/. For NASJA information: stevet@infoserve.n et. For well-established writers.

Outdoor Writers Association of America, 27 Ft. Missoula Rd., Suite 1, Missoula, MT 59804, (406) 728-7434, http://www.owaa.org/owaa .htm. Membership open to freelance magazine writers with twelve published articles on the outdoors.

Society of American Travel Writers, 4101 Lake Boone Trail, Suite 201, Raleigh, NC 27607, (919) 787-5181, http://www.satw.org/,

Chris Adams. Membership limited to salaried travel editors, writers and photographers and freelancers who are recognized for their substantial contributions to the field of travel journalism. Applicants must be sponsored by two members.

Society for American Travel Writing, Dept. of English and Philosophy, Auburn University Montgomery, P.O. Box 244023, Montgomery AL 36124, E-mail jmelton@mickey.aum.edu.

Travel & Tourism Research Association, P.O. Box 8066, Foothill Station, Salt Lake City, UT 84108. *Journal of Travel Research* provides data on tourism to universities and government agencies.

Travel Industry Association of America, 1100 New York Ave., NW, Suite 450, Washington, DC 20005, (202) 408-2137. Fax (202) 408-1255, http://www.tia.org/. Members are hotels and airlines involved in U.S. travel only.

Travel Journalists Guild, P.O. Box 10643, Chicago, IL 60610, (312) 664-9279, Fax (312) 664-9701. Membership organization founded in 1981 for experienced freelance travel journalists. Requirements for membership include sponsorship by two current members, three years professional experience and published clips or photos. Membership is limited to eighty people.

PRIZES AND AWARDS

Travel Industry Association of America, 1100 New York Ave. NW, Suite 450, Washington, D.C. 20005, (202) 408-8422. Business travel writing award to recognize a writer who examines the travel and tourism industry.

Pacific Asia Travel Association, 1 Montgomery St., Telesis Tower, Suite 1000, San Francisco, CA 94104, (415) 986-4646. PATA Travel Story Award. Open competition for travel editors, writers and photographers. Deadline: Feb 1 for articles or photographs published during the previous year.

MARKETING REFERENCE DIRECTORIES

Editor & Publisher International Yearbook. 11 West 19th St., New York, NY 10011, (212) 675-4380. $90. Annual directory of daily and weekly newspapers throughout the world. Lists individual editor names and titles and includes information on syndicates. Listings are by city and state or city and country.

Gale Directory of Publications & Broadcast Media. 835 Penobscot Bldg., Detroit, MI 48226-4094. Annual guide to publications, newspapers, magazines, journals, radio, TV and cable stations organized by state.

Hudson's Subscription Newsletter Directory. The Newsletter Clearinghouse, P.O. Box 311, Rhinebeck, NY 12572, (914) 876-2081. $140. Annual guide to 4,800 newsletters organized in 158 categories and 52 subject headings.

Hudson's Washington News Media Contacts Directory. P.O. Box 311, Rhinebeck, NY 12572, (914) 876-2081. $155.

Literary Market Place, $165. *International Literary Market Place*, $179. R.R. Bowker, 121 Chanlon Rd., New Providence, NJ 07974. Annual directory of the book publishing industry including publishers, agents, editorial services, book manufacturers, associations, awards.

International Directory of Little Magazines and Small Presses. Dustbooks, Paradise, CA 95967 Annual directory of small publishers and limited circulation magazines, most with a literary focus. Check out headings such as Sports/Outdoors/Boating, Transportation/Travel and individual country, state and regional headings. $27.95.

Metro Media. New York Publicity Outlets, Metro California Media, Public Relations Plus, Inc., P.O. Box 1197, New Milford, CT 06776, (800) 999-8448. $149.50 per year. Two issues. Lists circulation and editorial department heads with direct dial numbers and fax numbers. A contacts directory for marketing.

Newsletter Yearbook/Directory. Eds. Brigitte T. Darnay & John Nimchuk, Gale Research Co., Detroit, MI 48226, (914) 876-2081. Descriptive guide to 18,000 newsletters.

News Media Yellow Book. Monitor Leadership Directories, Inc., 104 Fifth Ave., New York, NY 10011, (212) 627-4140. Published quarterly. Lists names, titles, assignments and direct dial phone numbers of news personnel in New York City and Washington, D.C.

The Standard Periodical Directory. Oxbridge Communications, 150 Fifth Ave., New York, NY 10011. Annual. Lists 75,000 periodicals in United States and Canada. Categories include Travel, Skiing, Regional Interest.

Travel Publications Update. Winterbourne Press, 7301 Burnet Rd., Ste. 102-279, Austin, TX 78757, (512) 419-1334, Fax (512) 419-1987. A computer disc containing names, addresses and phone numbers of travel editors at 600 magazines and 200 newspapers. $25.00. Quarterly update service—$75 per year. The list is available on 3.5 or 5.25 size discs, in Mac or IBM, in a variety of word processing formats.

Winterbourne Press also offers a custom mailing label printing service for writers who are mass-marketing travel articles. The basic fee is $5.00, plus ten cents for each name, to select and print mailing labels of your choice. The range of categories is broad, for example: regional publications, in-flight magazines, senior citizen's magazines, publications in a certain state, etc.

Ulrich's International Periodicals Directory. R.R. Bowker, New Providence, NJ 07974. Annual listing of magazines and other periodicals including international publications.

Willings Press Guide. Reed Information Services, West Sussex, UK, 1990. Guide to press in the UK and British Commonwealth.

Working Press of the Nation. Vol 1. Newspaper Directory, Vol. 2 Magazines and Internal Publications Directory, Vol. 3 TV & Radio Directory, Vol. 4 Feature Writers, Photographers & Professional Speakers, National Register Publishing, Reed Publishing, New Providence, NJ 07974. Annual guide to journalists in the United States.

The Writer's Handbook. Published by *The Writer*, Boston. Magazine markets for freelance writers.

Writer's Market. Writer's Digest Books, 1507 Dana Ave., Cincinnati, OH 45207.

WRITING REFERENCE TOOLS

Atlas of the World, National Geographic Society—make sure the atlas is current.

Bartlett's Familiar Quotations—a quote can be an elegant way to open a story.

Webster's Biographical Dictionary—fact checking on famous people associated with the location.

Webster's New World Dictionary of the American Language.

Webster's New Geographical Dictionary.

Museums of the World, K.G. Sauer Verlag KG, Munich.

OTHER USEFUL RESOURCES

American Youth Hostels Handbook. American Youth Hostels, Inc., National Administrative Offices, 733 15th St. NW, Washington, D.C. 20005, (202) 783-6161.

Chamber of Commerce Directory. P.O. Box 1029, Loveland, CO 80539, (303) 663-3231. Published annually in June. $24. Useful for obtaining addresses of chambers of commerce.

Chase's Calendar of Events. Contemporary Books, Tribune News Media Co., 2 Prudential Plaza, Suite 1200, Chicago, IL 60601, (312) 540-4500, Fax (312) 540-4687. Calendar of holidays, special events, anniversaries, etc.

The Ecotourism Society. P.O. Box 755, North Bennington, VT 05257, (802) 447-2121, Fax (802) 447-2122. International nonprofit organization dedicated to implementing the principles of ecotourism worldwide. Sponsors conferences, publishes books and guidelines.

Hotel & Motel Redbook. American Hotel Association Directory Corporation, 888 7th Ave., New York, NY 10019. Published annually. Directory of hotels and motels in the U.S.

Hotel & Travel Index. Reed Travel Group, 500 Plaza Dr., Secaucus, NJ 07096. Quarterly index to the world's hotels. $125/year.

Magellan's. P.O. Box 5485, Santa Barbara, CA 93150-5485, (800) 962-4943. Mail-order catalog of equipment and accessories for travelers.

The Official Travel Industry Directory. Travel Agent Official Travel Industry Directory, 801 2nd Ave., New York, NY 10017, (212) 370-5050. Annual 400-page directory of contacts for travel products, associations and services. $14.95 plus shipping.

Sister Cities International. 120 Payne St., Alexandria, VA 22314, (703) 836-3535.

United States Servas, Inc. 11 John St., Suite 407, New York, NY 10038, (212) 267-0252. Membership organization promoting international hospitality programs in over 130 countries.

U.S. General Services Administration Consumer Information Center. Pueblo, CO 81009. Booklets of interest to travel writers: Discover America—contact list for travel offices in each state and territory of the U.S., National Park System Map and Guide, A Guide to Your National Forests, National Wildlife Refuges, Lesser Known Areas of the National Park System.

GLOSSARY

adventure story—travel story that focuses on physical challenges and outdoor thrills

advertorial—special travel supplement or advertisement section with travel articles paid for by a special interest group such as a national tourist office, a cruise line, airline or destination resort

all rights—writer sells the right to use the material forever; sells the copyright

angle—element of the article which makes it timely or appropriate for a specific publication

assignment—editor commissions a writer to prepare an article for a specified price by a certain date

bimonthly—published every two months

biweekly—published every two weeks

boldface—extra dark typeface useful for titles and subheadings

byline—writer's name, usually printed at the top under the title or at the end for shorter items. Some articles do not carry a byline.

circulation—the printing and distribution of a given publication

clips—your previously published work

column inch—type contained in one inch of a typeset column. Column width varies as does typesize.

contract—a legal document signed by parties to mutually agreeable terms

contributor's copies—copies given to the writer

copy or **hard copy**—manuscript in typewritten form before it is set for printing

copyediting—editing for grammar, punctuation and printing style

copyright—protection of the printed work

correspondent—a writer in the field who regularly provides stories for a publication

cover letter—letter of introduction included with finished manuscript or clips submitted for consideration

dateline—date and place of an article; placed at the start of the first paragraph

destination story—travel article about a specific resort, location or site of interest

domestic—travel within the United States, or, for Canadian tourism within Canada

exclusive market—noncompeting publication in different circulation areas

first-person voice—article written from the author's point of view

first rights—writer sells the publication the right to publish the article the first time; known as first serial rights and first North American serial rights. The exclusive right to publish the material in Canada and the U.S. Copyright reverts to author after publication, unless otherwise specified.

free sample copy— free copy sent by editors if requested. Sometimes there is a charge. Always include an SASE

freelance writer—a writer not affiliated with a publication who has the right to sell articles to any publication that will buy

honorarium—a small payment for writing, speaking, teaching or participating in a panel discussion

hook—element of an article that makes it compelling and timely

justification—spacing type to a specific width so that the right margin is uniform

kill fee—money paid to the writer when the publication cancels the contracted work, usually less than the full fee and rarely paid unless the writer and publication have signed a contract

monthly—publication that is issued once a month

ms.—abbreviation for a manuscript

one-time rights—publication buys the right to print photos or a story once

payment on acceptance—writer is paid when the piece is accepted, before publication

payment on publication—writer is paid after the article is published

peg—aspect of an article that relates it to a date or an event

pen name—use of a name other than legal name. Reputable publications hesitate to use writers who use pen names.

press release—announcements issued by public relations agencies or the communications departments of companies

proof—printed edition of the pages prior to final printing; used for examination and final corrections

quarterly—publication that comes out four times a year

query—letter proposing an article idea to an editor

regional publication—magazine or paper dedicated to a limited area

rejection—letter from the editor stating that a manuscript or a query doesn't suit the publication's needs. Usually a form letter unless you have developed a relationship with the editor or you are well established.

reporting time—length of time it takes an editor to respond to the writer about the query or manuscript

reprint fees—payment to the writer when a magazine or paper selects and uses work that has been printed elsewhere

SASE—self-addressed stamped envelope

second serial rights—a publication purchases the right to print material that has appeared elsewhere

sidebar—small column, box or paragraph with useful information about costs, addresses, weather, etc. A news report that accompanies a longer article with specific information on one aspect of the story.

simultaneous rights—same article being sold at the same time to two or more publications in noncompeting circulation areas

simultaneous submission—manuscript sent to more than one market at a time

slant—writer's approach to the material so that it fits with the editorial needs of a specific magazine or paper

speculation or **on spec**—editor does not commit to buy an article, but agrees to consider it when the writer submits the work

stringer—a writer who has a continuing relationship with a publication and regularly submits articles on a specific area or topic

tear sheet—all the pages from magazine or newspaper which make up an entire article. Like contributor's copies, they are usually sent to the writer shortly after publication.

unsolicited or **"over the transom" manuscript**—article that was not requested by an editor

writer's guidelines—many publications compile guidelines for contributing articles which are available to prospective writers on request

PARIS' LA COUPOLE IS BACK AND BEAUTIFUL

By Peter Mikelbank

Travel & Leisure

There is never any ending to Paris and the memory . . .
    —*Ernest Hemingway*

La Coupole had become Paris' Jazz Age widow. The grand brasserie was settling into decline—a once-celebrated beauty whose increasingly thick lipstick was excused as a dowager's attempt to preserve an impression of youth.

When "Monsieur René" Lafon opened the restaurant-café-dance hall in 1927, its awning was a brash red skirt on a broad terrace at the center of Montparnasse, the lively bohemian district. The newcomer's distinctive neon signature and frosted curls promising "Dancing" and "Bar Américain" attracted the quarter's young moderns. Legends and scandals followed.

Josephine Baker arrived for suppers, setting a pet lion cub on the red velvet banquette beside her. A lovers' quarrel ended in a duel between poets. Picasso and Giacometti argued late into the night. Isadora Duncan, Colette and Papillon passed by the café's Casanovas as they descended to the tango parlor. La Coupole became one with its era—seeming not so much to have customers as to possess habitués. Said one, "The whole world danced at La Coupole."

The appeal was not the simple fare (cassoulet, curry and seafood) but the magic circle, constantly spun wider. Dalí, Man Ray, Chagall and Calder had favorite waiters; other neighborhood artists passed among tables sketching diners. Cubists, surrealists, dadaists and the Lost Generation writers claim corners of the legend. Memories include afternoons on the terrace with Fitzgerald reading the manuscript of *Tender Is the Night*, and Ezra Pound and Gertrude Stein, Saint-Exupéry, Henry Miller, Dos Passos and Beckett inspiring generations of would-be Hemingways. (Arriving directly from the liberation of the Ritz Bar in 1944, Ernest exclaimed, "I'm back!" and swept Lafon into a bear hug.)

Afterward, in the Paris of Art Buchwald, James Jones and Françoise Sagan, France's existentialists gathered at La Coupole—Sartre drinking whiskey and water; De Beauvoir, Coke. Ionesco stops for coffee still. Even Simenon's Inspector Maigret occasionally steps off the trail for the house choucroute.

Resembling a large art deco room on an ocean liner, La Coupole's dining area casually achieved a crossroads-of-the-world reputation. It was an informal late-hours place where actors and kings met Rothschilds and rock stars beneath twenty-four frescoed columns—painted by the likes of Léger and Kisling in lieu of paying their tabs. Lafon's generous patronage and his eye for talent are part of the legend.

In recent years La Coupole's beauty paled in the shadow of high rises, as developers eyeing the site churned neighbors into cinema-office complexes. Whispers grew until, just days after her 60th anniversary, La Coupole closed. By January of 1988, she seemed a dark, lost valentine.

Funeral wreaths turned into bouquets at the reopening a year later. Calling it "the crown jewel of my collection," new owner Jean-Paul Bucher, a former chef at Maxim's, had lavished $3 million on the restoration. The grande dame re-emerged, returning a December beau's flattering attention with her appearance subtly but dramatically changed.

While applying fresh paint and lighting, the makeover artists kept an eye on tradition but added sparkle. Designers banished faded Thirties red for subtler brown and beige tones, replaced age-stained mahogany with lemonwood, and even resurrected the garish deco skirtings around the frescoed columns. The enclosed sidewalk terrace and bars—once lonely, gritty additions—were fully integrated architecturally with the bright 600-seat main room.

Now as then, the food is contemporary French, with cassoulet still the preferred lunch item, and Breton oysters the thing at any hour. Meals pour out of a modern, double-size kitchen. If some people persist in whispers that La Coupole is just not the same, others insist the neighborhood coal yard has been restored to a showplace. Renewing the "see and be scene" tradition, young lively crowds are discovering, as Mehitabel pledged, "there's a dance in the old dame yet."

"It's not the decor or food that makes La Coupole special," says one Parisian, leaning across a table in the revived shirt-sleeves-and-emeralds atmosphere. "It's her conviviality that's unusual."

ISCHIA, ITALY'S SEDUCTIVE ISLE

By L. Peat O'Neil

Special to The Washington Post

From the slopes of Mount Epomeo to the gardens and vineyards at its base to the hot springs along the north coast, the Italian island of Ischia is a testament to the afterlife of a volcano. In the summer, this verdant volcanic island across the bay from Naples swells with exuberant Neapolitans on weekend escapes and other Europeans in search of sun, sand and spa. But the rest of the year, when Ischia turns from frenzied to sedate, it is even more seductive.

Winter was on the cusp of spring when we visited Ischia, and the steady stream of fair-weather visitors had yet to begin. The island was preparing for the solemn services of Holy Week and the celebration of Easter (*Pasqua*), and we found it coming alive with a different kind of fervor: Families were reunited, trips were made to the mainland to visit relatives and friends, churches overflowed with worshipers and splendid food abounded. Easter on Ischia is a season of spiritual renewal and the strengthening of family ties.

We were staying with friends in Ischia Porto, the principal town, when Holy Week began and the extended family started to return to the island. The daughters living in Milan, Modena and Ferrara came to help their mother cook special wheat and ricotta cakes called *pastiera*, a process that consumed the better part of two days. More than 30 cakes were made to give friends and relatives in exchange for their versions of the same traditional Easter cake.

When the cake-making was over, the entire household sat down to celebrate. With the distinctive almond-floral scent of the cakes permeating the kitchen and dining room, we feasted on rabbit in sauce, pork, grilled sardines, *pepperonata* (sautéed green and red peppers), and, of course, pasta. Those who still had an appetite sampled one of the cakes.

On Good Friday, some of Ischia's citizens joined local priests and bishops and sailed to tiny Procida Island, between Ischia and the mainland, where the local people donned Roman-style robes, taking roles to reenact Christ's procession to Calvary. This can be a grueling procession—penitents, transported by the rhythmic dialogue unfolding between the priests' chants and the dramatic prayers and cries of the crowd, sometimes flail themselves with ropes or sticks. (A similar procession takes place in Ischia Porto on March 5, the feast day of St. John Joseph of the Cross, who was born on the island in the 17th century. In fact, his name is popular on Ischia—there are many Giovanni Guiseppes there.)

Easter dawned bright, and on Ischia there was an air of expectation. We gathered with our friend's family and other guests at an aunt's farm for what would become a day-long feast. First came the traditional morning snacks: hard-boiled eggs and cold spiced sausage. But a crisis was brewing.

Though we thought every detail had been attended to during the week of preparations, someone had forgotten the holy water for the blessing of the Easter dinner table by the oldest person in the household. The last Easter Mass was over, and the churches were closing for the day so that the priests could enjoy their Easter meal. Rather than have the family disappointed, my friend secretly filled a couple of bottles with tap water and presented them to her mother.

By 1 P.M., about 15 people had assembled for the table blessing by the granduncle. The meal began with rigatoni and tomato sauce seasoned with home-grown oregano and was followed by three meat courses: a whole kid roasted with rosemary, chicken in a thick tomato sauce and rabbit in gravy.

Toasts were drunk with delicate red and white wines made from grapes grown on family land on Ischia. My friend's father apologized for the wine, saying he was too old to make it properly but that he couldn't find a young person with the interest or ability to take his place—because talented farm children were leaving the island to work in northern Italy.

Ischia Porto (or simply Ischia) is the island's principal town, linked by a modern road to the three main beach resort towns of Casamícciola, Lacco Ameno and Forío. Most of the 14,000 island residents live along the north coast, while the farm land and country villages are concentrated in the southeast.

The island's fertile soil supports family farms as well as small market gardens. Before the early years of this century, when tourists began to include Ischia on the Grand Tour, most Ischians earned their livelihood in the olive trade. But around 1900, many olive growers began to replace their groves with more profitable vineyards.

The volcanic process that gave Ischia such rich soil also left sources of thermal mineral water around the island, which have been developed into spas, particularly in Casamícciola Terme and Lacco Ameno. Some of the spas are open year-round.

Many Ischians, including our friend's family, derive the largest part of their income from the summer rental of their houses to vacationers. In our friend's case, the family retreats to an old family house in a country village on the island.

During the week after Easter we explored some of the sights of Ischia, the most notable of which is Castello d'Aragona. The castle fortress is connected to the small fishing port of Ischia Ponte by a narrow causeway. The Aragona family, once a powerful royal house in Spain, acquired Ischia along with southern Italy late in the 13th century. Fortresses were built at critical defensive outposts along the coasts of Sicily and Calabria and used as way stations during military expeditions.

After paying an entry fee of about $2.50, we followed a winding stone corridor under the walls into the castle keep. The echo of clopping horses hoofs and chattering vassals was not difficult to conjure as we trudged up to the massive interconnected castle, chapels and vaults.

There is a charming little restaurant inside the castle keep, set on a terrace that forms part of the castle walls, where we paused to gaze across the fabulous blue-green depths of the Bay of Naples.

In the village of Lacco Ameno, the Museo Archeologico is another sight worth exploring, with Greek, Egyptian and Syrian artifacts indicating the range of cultures that have influenced the island. And the steep but not difficult trail up the 2,550-foot-high Mount Epomeo, dormant since the 14th century, rewards you with a view that encompasses Capri when the sky is clear.

Our sojourn under the fair skies of Ischia was the perfect remedy for the busy chaos of Naples. When it was over, we stood on the top deck of the ferry chugging eastward to the mainland and looked back at Ischia wrapped in a seafarer's sunset—red sky at night, sailor's delight.

INDEX

More Great Books
for Writers!

The Writer's Survival Guide—Drawing on her own experiences, as well as those of her students and colleagues, Rachel Simon explores the whole writerly journey—offering ways to stay productive on a day-to-day basis, advice for navigating the publishing world, and prescriptions for overall creative happiness.
#48025/$18.99/224 pages

Writing From Personal Experience—There was that moment—a poignant truth, a lesson learned—that turned your life around. Now you can share your story with the help of this inspiring and instructive guide, complete with nuts-and-bolts instruction—from getting your story down on paper to getting it out to editors.
#10510/$16.99/208 pages

Writer's Digest Handbook of Making Money Freelance Writing—Discover promising new income-producing opportunities with this collection of articles by top writers, editors and agents. Over 30 commentaries on business issues, writing opportunities and freelancing will help you make the break to a full-time writing career.
#10501/$19.99/320 pages

1,818 Ways to Write Better & Get Published—If you need to know it, use it, act on it, it's here—in easy-to-search, fast-reference form. Handy checklists detail everything from how to name characters and overcome writer's block to what business contacts can do for writers. *#10508/$12.99/224 pages/paperback*

Writing Personal Essays: How to Shape Your Life Experiences for the Page—Discover how to put your life story on paper. You'll learn how to choose just the right personal-experience topic and how to build a story loaded with emotion and significance. Bender offers inspiration to help you every step of the way.
#10438/$17.99/272 pages

Writing Articles From the Heart: How to Write & Sell Your Life Experiences—Holmes gives you heartfelt advice and inspiration on how to get your personal essay onto the page. You'll discover how to craft a story to meet your needs and those of your readers. *#10352/$16.99/176 pages*

The Writer's Digest Dictionary of Concise Writing—Make your work leaner, crisper and clearer! Under the guidance of professional editor Robert Hartwell Fiske, you'll learn how to rid your work of common say-nothing phrases while making it tighter and easier to read and understand. *#10482/$19.99/352 pages*

How to Write Attention-Grabbing Query & Cover Letters—Use the secrets Wood reveals to write perfectly tailored queries, too good to turn down! In this guidebook, you will discover why boldness beats blandness in queries every time, ten basics you must have in your article queries, ten query blunders that can destroy publication chances and much more. *#10462/$17.99/208 pages*

Leads and Conclusions—Discover how to craft leads that grip readers, use fiction techniques to keep them entranced, write cliff-hangers that keep them hungry for future installments and create closings they will never forget! *#10427/$15.99/176 pages*

2000 Novel & Short Story Writer's Market: 2,000+ Places to Publish Your Fiction—Get the information you need to get your short stories and novels published. You'll discover 2,000+ listings on fiction publishers, plus original articles on fiction writing techniques; detailed subject categories to help you target appropriate publishers; and interviews with writers, publishers and editors! *#10625/$24.99/675 pages/paperback*

The 30-Minute Writer—Write short, snappy articles that make editors sit up and take notice. Full-time freelancer Connie Emerson reveals the many types of quickly written articles you can sell—from miniprofiles and one-pagers to personal essays. You'll also learn how to match your work to the market as you explore methods for expanding from short articles to columns and even books! *#10489/$14.99/256 pages/paperback*

Queries and Submissions—Looking for proven strategies for writing attention-grabbing query letters? This guide has an abundance of ideas, covering topics from formatting and targeting letters to deciding when a query letter is unnecessary. *#10426/$15.99/176 pages*

Writing to Sell, Fourth Edition—You'll discover high-quality writing and marketing counsel in this classic writing guide from well-known agent Scott Meredith. His timeless advice will guide you along the professional writing path as you get help with creating characters, plotting a novel, placing your work, formatting a manuscript, deciphering a publishing contract—even combating a slump! *#10476/$17.99/240 pages*

Writer's Encyclopedia, Third Edition—Rediscover this popular writer's reference—now with information about electronic resources, plus more than 100 new entries. You'll find facts, figures, definitions and examples designed to answer questions about every discipline connected with writing and help you convey a professional image. *#10464/$22.99/560 pages/62 b&w illus.*

Writing and Selling Your Novel—Write publishable fiction from start to finish with expert advice from professional novelist Jack Bickham! You'll learn how to develop effective work habits, refine your fiction writing technique, and revise and tailor your novels for tightly targeted markets. *#10509/$17.99/208 pages*

Writing Life Stories—Author Bill Roorbach explains how to turn life events into vivid personal essays and riveting memoirs. Much more than teaching the rudiments of autobiography, this book will help writers see their own lives more clearly, while learning that real stories are often the best ones. *#48035/$17.99/224 pages*

How To Tell A Story—Gary Provost and Peter Rubie show you how to transform your fiction and nonfiction into captivating tales sure to find an audience in a book packed with proven instruction, advice, writing exercises and examples. Make your narrative gripping from beginning to end. *#10565/$17.99/240 pages*
